Writing

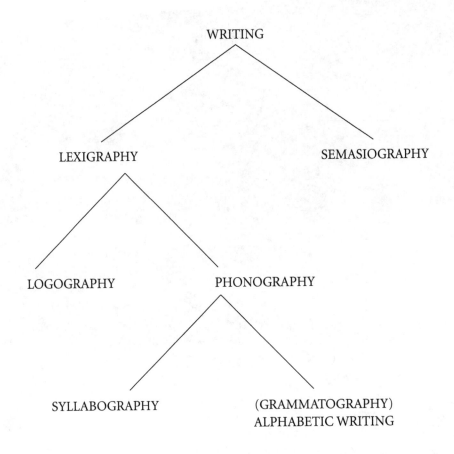

THE CATEGORIES OF WRITING

Writing

*Theory and History of the
Technology of Civilization*

Barry B. Powell

A John Wiley & Sons, Ltd., Publication

This paperback edition first published 2012
© Barry B. Powell

Edition history: Blackwell Publishing Ltd (hardback, 2009)

Blackwell Publishing was acquired by John Wiley & Sons in February 2007. Blackwell's publishing program has been merged with Wiley's global Scientific, Technical, and Medical business to form Wiley-Blackwell.

Registered Office
John Wiley & Sons Ltd, The Atrium, Southern Gate, Chichester, West Sussex, PO19 8SQ, United Kingdom

Editorial Offices
350 Main Street, Malden, MA 02148-5020, USA
9600 Garsington Road, Oxford, OX4 2DQ, UK
The Atrium, Southern Gate, Chichester, West Sussex, PO19 8SQ, UK

For details of our global editorial offices, for customer services, and for information about how to apply for permission to reuse the copyright material in this book please see our website at www.wiley.com/wiley-blackwell.

The right of Barry B. Powell to be identified as the author of this work has been asserted in accordance with the UK Copyright, Designs and Patents Act 1988.

Library of Congress Cataloging-in-Publication Data

Powell, Barry B.
  Writing : theory and history of the technology of civilization / by Barry B. Powell.
    p. cm.
  Includes bibliographical references and index.
  ISBN 978-1-4051-6256-2 (hardcover : alk. paper) ISBN 978-1-118-25532-2 (pbk. : alk. paper)
  1. Writing–History. 2. Writing–Social aspects. [1. Alphabet–History.] I. Title.
  P211.P69 2009
  411.09–dc22

                                                                                    2008046991

A catalogue record for this book is available from the British Library.

Set in 10.5/13pt Minion by Graphicraft Limited, Hong Kong

1 2012

To Emmett L. Bennett, Jr.
colleague, friend, teacher

I'll make you love scribedom more than your mother!
I will place its beauties before you.
It's the greatest of all callings.
There is nothing like it in the land!

from *Satire on the Trades* (or *Instructions
of Dua-Khety*), c.1800 BC

Contents

Contents

Illustrations

Maps

Preface

I hope this book may serve as a brief introduction to an immense, tangled, and obscure topic. Writing can be defined and understood, but only with the help of a careful organization of categories and terms. I know of no other humanistic topic more distorted through the careless use of categories and terms, so that things "everyone knows" are illusions. The professionals, too, offer us neologisms, buzzwords, and terms that attempt a fatal precision. For example, in one of the best books on writing in the last several years (S. D. Houston, ed., *The First Writing: Script Invention as History and Process*, Cambridge, 2004), a series of essays on the origins of writing, the reader will struggle with "glottography," "cipherability," "morphophonic," "alphasyllabaries," "consonantaries," "logophonic," "logophonemic," "logocon-sonantal," "phonological heterography," "taxograms," "semasiologographic," "graphotactical," "numero-ideographic," "phonophoric," "ethnogenetic" – as well as the usual *bête noire* "pictograms" and "ideograms." Is writing really so complex, or esoteric? The study of the history of writing is the study of the explosion of illusions, and such jargon has stood as the greatest obstacle to understanding. Yet we cannot understand the historical past without understanding the technology that made possible our knowledge of it. This book should be of interest to anyone who wishes to come to grips with the question, What happened in the human past?

I have dedicated this book to my friend and colleague Emmett L. Bennett, Jr., but would also like to thank him here for the countless insights into the history of writing he has given me over the years, and the collection of examples that illustrate these insights.

I should also like to thank John Bennet for reading the entire manuscript and saving me from many errors, both of fact and interpretation. I am deeply grateful to him for his help. His hand appears on nearly every page, but I reserve to my own responsibility all remaining failings of both kinds.

To annotate a book such as this properly would require massive documentation that would detract from the synthesis I propose. I have therefore reserved remarks about bibliography to a section in the back.

Photos and translations not otherwise credited are my own. I have included basic maps with many chapters, because where things happened is as important as when. In the text I have highlighted places on the maps by means of small capitals. The reader may find the glossary at the back of the book useful in keeping straight the bewildering terminology of writing.

Chronology

9000 BC

Widespread use of **geometric tokens** throughout Near East, c.8500 BC

Appearance of **complex tokens**, c.4500–3400 BC

4000 BC

Round clay **bullae** that enclose tokens, impressed with cylinder seals, c.3500–3400 BC

Protocuneiform numerical flat clay tablets, sealed or unsealed, with impressions of three-dimensional tokens or imitations of token shapes by means of a stylus, c.3400–3300 BC; first logograms with numbers c.3300 BC

ProtoElamite writing, c.3300(?)–3000 BC

Egyptian hieroglyphic writing, Pharaonic civilization emerges, c.3250 BC

3000 BC *EARLY BRONZE AGE*

Tokens disappear, c.3000 BC

Sumerian cities flourish in Mesopotamia, c.2800–2340 BC

Texts in Sumerian cuneiform that reflect order of words in speech; similar development in Egypt, c.2800–2400 BC

Minoan civilization flourishes in Crete, c.2500–1450 BC

Akkadian Empire in Mesopotamia, c.2334–2220 BC; **Akkadian cuneiform**

Linear Elamite writing, c.2150 BC

Third Dynasty of Ur, c.2120–2000 BC

"Cretan hieroglyphs," c.2100 BC–c.1700 BC

2000 BC *MIDDLE BRONZE AGE*

Arrival of Indo-European Greeks in Balkan Peninsula, c.2000 BC

Babylon's ascendance under Hammurabi, c.1810–1750 BC; **Old**

Babylonian cuneiform
Old Assyrian cuneiform, c.1800 BC
Cretan Linear A, c.1800 BC–1450 BC

1600 BC *LATE BRONZE AGE*

Hittite Empire rules in Anatolia, c.1600–1200 BC; **Hittite cunei-form; "Luvian hieroglyphs"**

1500 BC West Semitic syllabic writing invented, c.1500(?) BC
Destruction of Cretan palaces, c.1450 BC
Destruction of the rebuilt Cnossus, c.1375 BC
Amarna tablets in **Middle Babylonian cuneiform**, c.1350 BC
Trojan War occurs, c.1250(?) BC
Destruction of Ugarit, c.1200 BC
Chinese script first attested in the Shang Dynasty on oracle bones, c.1200 BC

1100 BC *IRON AGE* begins with destruction of Mycenaean cities in Greece and other sites in the Levant
Earliest **Mesoamerican "writing,"** from Olmec territory, c.1140–400 BC

1000 BC Greek colonies are settled in Asia Minor, c.1000 BC
NeoAssyrian cuneiform, c.1000–600 BC
NeoBabylonian cuneiform, c.1000–500 BC

900 BC NeoHittite cities flourish in northern Syria, c.900–700 BC
Earliest "Isthmian" writing, c.900 BC (?)

800 BC *GREEK ARCHAIC PERIOD* begins with invention of the **Greek alphabet**, c.800 BC
Iliad and the *Odyssey*, attributed to Homer, are written down, c.800–775 BC
Greek colonies in southern Italy and Sicily, c.800–600 BC
Olympic Games begin, 776 BC
Hesiod's *Theogony* is written down, c.775–700(?) BC
Rome, allegedly, is founded, 753 BC

600 BC Formation of Hebrew Pentateuch (first "five books" of Bible) during Babylonian Captivity of the Hebrews, 586–538 BC
Cyrus the Great of Persia, c.600–529 BC
"Zapotec" writing from the valley of Oaxaca in Mexico, c.600–400 BC
Expulsion of the Etruscan dynasty at Rome and the foundation of the "Roman Republic," 510 BC

500 BC **Late Babylonian cuneiform**, c.500 BC–AD 75
Behistun inscriptions (**Old Persian cuneiform, Late Babylonian cuneiform, Elamite cuneiform**), c.500 BC
CLASSICAL PERIOD begins with end of Persian Wars, 480 BC
Herodotus, c.484–420 BC
Thucydides, c.470–400 BC
Plato, c.427–347 BC

400 BC
Aristotle, c.384–322 BC
Alexander the Great conquers the Persian Empire, founds Alexandria 336–323 BC
HELLENISTIC PERIOD begins with death of Alexander in 323 BC

300 BC
Earliest Mayan writing, c.250 BC
Mouseion founded by Ptolemy II, ruled 285–246 BC

200 BC
Ptolemy V carves the Rosetta Stone, 196 BC
ROMAN PERIOD begins when Greece becomes Roman province, 146

100 BC
Diodorus of Sicily, c.80–20 BC
Vergil, 70–19 BC
Augustus defeats Antony and Cleopatra at battle of Actium and annexes Egypt, 30 BC
Augustus Caesar reigns, 27 BC–AD 14

Year 0
Last Mesopotamian cuneiform, AD 75

AD 200 Classic Maya Period, c. AD 250 until AD 900
Plotinus, a NeoPlatonist Greek philosopher writes that the hieroglyphs are allegories, c. AD 250
Coptic phase of pharaonic Egyptian recorded in modified Greek alphabet called **Coptic script**, c. third century AD

AD 300
Last hieroglyphs inscribed at Philae near Aswan, AD 396

AD 400 European *MEDIEVAL PERIOD* begins with fall of Rome in AD 476
Hieroglyphics, by Horapollo (?), c. fifth century AD

AD 1500

        Hernán Cortés lands in Mexico, AD 1519

AD 1600   Mesoamerican writing disappears, c. AD 1600

        Travelers' reports bring information about cuneiform to Europe

AD 1700   **MODERN PERIOD**

        Rosetta stone found in Egypt, AD 1799

AD 1800

        Jean François Champollion deciphers Egyptian hieroglyphs, AD 1822

        Henry Rawlinson and others decipher Mesopotamian cuneiform, c. AD 1850

AD 1900

        Michael Ventris deciphers Linear B, AD 1952

        Yuri Knorosov establishes the phonetic basis of some Mayan signs, AD 1952

Introduction: A Difficult Topic, Little Studied, Poorly Understood

It is not hard to see that writing is the single most important technology in human life, yet it is not easy to study or to think about. Nonetheless we use it almost every minute of our lives. Naturally, many handbooks attempt to explain this extraordinary technology, some of good quality, but most suffer from a recurring blindness about what writing is, where it comes from, and how it functions in relationship to speech. All scientific speculation on the history of writing, without exception, is conducted by alphabet-users, including the present study, which gives a bias to our questions and to what we take as answers. Many historians of writing do not read nonalphabetic scripts or have a casual acquaintance with them. The alphabet-using historians of writing make prejudgments that harm our understanding.

In this book I will struggle against such prejudgments by providing a scientific nomenclature for understanding writing built on a coherent model of the different internal structures that govern all writing. I want to explicate this nomenclature and this model (**see diagram facing the title page**) through the study of the history of writing in the ancient Mediterranean, China, and Mesoamerica. This book is not, then, a description of the endless variety of external form in the history of writing, for which good studies exist, but an examination through historical examples of the internal structural principles that govern all writing. By proceeding in this fashion through a dark forest filled with dragons, I hope to slay several and clear away some popular confusions:

- the illusion that the *purpose, origin,* and *function* of writing is to represent speech
- the common supposition that writing comes from pictures
- the misapprehension that writing necessarily evolves toward the goal of finer phonetic representation

A Chaos of Terms

In no sense is the history of writing a discipline with niches in universities filled by experts. Those who write about the history of writing come from different directions and bring with them the expectations of their own disciplines. Linguists occasionally write such books because they feel that "language" is their province and that writing is somehow language. They are unrealistic about the quality of the phonetic information encoded in systems of writing, and their explanations too often ignore the social and historical forces behind change in systems of writing. Archaeologists sometimes work directly with unfamiliar ancient scripts, but they are rarely trained philologists. Perhaps philologists are in the best position to study the history of writing, if they have learned a nonalphabetic script, because they have wrestled most with the problem of deriving meaning from symbols. Thus the Polish-American Assyriologist I. J. Gelb (1907–85), who worked at the University of Chicago and contributed to the decipherment of "Luvian hieroglyphs," wrote the most important analysis of writing in the twentieth century and laid the foundations for the modern scientific study of writing. His famous book *A Study of Writing: The Foundations of Grammatology* appeared first in 1952 (revised in 1963). Gelb was wrong in details, but he understood that the history of writing exists, with discoverable underlying principles, as in all historical study. His outline of those principles stands today, and I refer to them often in this book.

Above all Gelb urged the use of a consistent and rational vocabulary in discussing the history of writing, although few follow his advice. In reading and thinking about writing we struggle with terms that have their origin in the history of study, not in the nature of the subject. For example, we just referred to "Luvian hieroglyphs" to distinguish this writing from "Hittite cuneiform," but there is nothing hieroglyphic about this writing except the casual and entirely superficial resemblance to the historically unrelated Egyptian hieroglyphs. Both scripts are iconic, that is, we can sometimes recognize in the signs objects from the everyday world – for example, a hand, a bird, or an animal – but there is no direct historical connection between the scripts and they work in different ways. Another example is the "Ugaritic cuneiform alphabet," which is unrelated to Mesopotamian cuneiform and is not an alphabet. Unfortunately, such terms have stuck, and we are stuck with them, and we are stuck constantly explaining that this or that term is inappropriate. I will put such casual and inaccurate but common terms in "quotations."

But the misuse of three words more than any others have harmed the study of the history of writing: "pictogram," "ideogram" (or ideograph), and "alphabet." The word "pictogram" means "picture-writing," but carries with it so much imprecision that we must avoid it rigorously. The use of "pictogram" should be the hallmark of the amateur, but careless professionals go on using it. It is always tempting to call any sign that looks like something a "pictogram," implying that the message is communicated through pictures and not through the resources of speech. Underlying the use but usually unspoken is a specious theory that "writing" began as pictures, then somehow became attached to speech, yet still remained pictures. So written characters that resemble something in the world, like Egyptian hieroglyphs, are called pictograms, as if the sign stands for what they picture and not for elements of human speech or sounds of speech. We do find representations of recognizable objects in early writing, but these "pictures" can fulfill a wide range of functions. Even when such designs appear to stand for the object represented, really they stand for the word attached to the object; that is, they refer to elements of speech, and not directly to items found in the world. "Pictures" can fulfill other functions, for example, place the thing described in a category. When wishing to speak of the representational aspects of some writings, we can call these aspects "iconic".

A similar situation pertains to the word "ideogram," often used, for example, of Chinese characters or of a class of signs in Cretan Linear B. *Ideogram* should mean "idea-writing," that is, the graphic symbolization of an "idea," a Platonic, invisible, eternal, unspoken reality. At one time scholars thought that Egyptian hieroglyphs were just that. But Chinese characters never represent eternal, unspoken realities, and neither do Linear B characters. Probably "ideograms" do not exist, so it makes little sense to talk about them.

The deep problems surrounding the word "alphabet" will be the subject of a good part of this book.

Writing, Language, Speech

Writing is old, but writing attached to speech, which I will call *lexigraphic writing*, goes back only to around 3400 BC, as far as we know. That is a rough date, as are all dates in the fourth millennium, but one we can nonetheless work with. Immense changes have taken place in the art of lexigraphic writing since that time, as one will quickly discover if setting out to learn Akkadian cuneiform. Yet such changes rarely result from evolution, except in writing's earliest stages, and were never inevitable. They came about through the accidents of history and the intercession of individual men of genius working across racial and linguistic bounds, when fresh approaches were possible. There is no certain direction that a writing must take. Because writing systems are arbitrary and conventional they do not respond to nature (whose rules of behavior are not arbitrary and not conventional), but to the inventiveness of unknown creators, who had a purpose too often hidden from us.

So improbable is it that anyone should devise a means of encoding elements of speech by means of graphic symbols that in the Old World lexigraphic writing was invented only once, in Mesopotamia, and perhaps a second time, much later, in China. But even in China the idea of "writing" must have come from Mesopotamia over the Gansu corridor north of the Himalayas, where caravan traffic was constant. China was never wholly separated from cultural developments in Mesopotamia. A separate invention did take place in Mesoamerica, providing a test case for principles distilled from the study of Near Eastern writing. We will spend one chapter on writing not attached to speech, which I call *semasiography* (after I. J. Gelb), but most of this book is about lexigraphic writing.

Because such writing is attached to speech, we need a clear description of what we mean by speech. Unfortunately scholars often use "language" when really they mean "speech," as if they were the same thing. "Language" is *a formal system of differences* and by no means restricted to vocal utterances. In the language of speech, the spoken word "water" is not the spoken word "ice" because they have different forms, to which we attach different meanings. In the language of writing, Egyptian 𓏭 is not

𓏤𓏤𓏤, though, both transliterate as *sny*: the one means "two" and the other means "companion." Different meanings accompany different forms. Similarly, in the language of writing [$] means something different from [%] because they have different forms to which we assign different significations. These signs belong to the language of writing, and they refer to words, though they do not have phonetic value.

The broad category of "language" will also include Morse Code, semaphore, and American sign language, which may refer to speech, but can never be confused with it. Such forms of language as Unicode or mathematical notation do not refer to speech at all. In the study of writing we speak of the "underlying language" essential to deciphering an unknown script, so that we easily forget that writing is itself a kind of language. The confusion between "writing" and "language" is profound, ubiquitous, and disruptive, so that in a popular view Chinese "language" is the same as Chinese "writing," a confusion that turns out, oddly, to be true once we understand how little Chinese writing has to do with Chinese speech.

Lexigraphic writing is based in speech, yes, but because we know of ancient speech only through written documents, it is easy to think that we are talking about "language" or "speech" when really we are talking about graphic representations that make use of spoken lexical elements, which may constitute in themselves a kind of language, but by no means intend to preserve actual speech. The intention is to communicate information, and for this purpose a graphic system with systematic phonetic ties to speech is a tool of earth-shaking power. It is not, however, a tool for the preservation of ancient speech.

For this reason the Sumerian speech was of use to nonSumerian Semitic scribes, because the relationships between graphic symbols and symbols originating in speech had been established by ancient usage. Just so, it was logical and practical for medieval Europeans to use Latin as a basic system for understanding across the polyglot confusion of mutually unintelligible local dialects and languages. Sumerian written in cuneiform ("wedge-shaped") writing was a traditional system of signs for communicating information whether you were Sumerian or not, and as such worked well. For the same reason, during the dominance of Assyria over the Near East during the ninth to seventh centuries BC and of Persia in the sixth to fifth centuries BC, the West Semitic Aramaic script encoding lexical forms from the "Aramaic language" was used by nonAramaic-speaking scribes over an area stretching from the Mediterranean to northwest India.

For example, in Figure 0.1, from the palace at Nineveh of Tiglath Pileser III (ruled 745–727 BC), one of the most successful commanders who ever lived, a beardless eunuch on the left calls out a list of booty while the presumably Assyrian-speaking eunuch in the middle records the inventory in the contemporary Assyrian dialect by impressing cuneiform characters with a stylus into a waxed wood tablet. The presumably Assyrian-speaking

Figure 0.1   Relief of bilingual scribes, from the palace of Tiglath Pileser III at Nineveh (in modern Iraq), c.740 BC. (London, British Museum BM118882.)

eunuch scribe on the right makes a duplicate record (to prevent cheating?) by writing on a roll of papyrus or leather, certainly West Semitic Aramaic characters tied to Aramaic speech. The difference in writing medium, part of any writing tradition, accompanies a difference in script and "underlying language."

Lexigraphic writing may refer to elements of speech, but in real speech we find extraordinary local and social differences, so great among English speakers that TV interviews in a regional English are often given subtitles for the greater English-speaking audience; that is, by means of alphabetic writing the speech is reduced to a standard form. Even in the same town speakers may not understand one another across differences in class and social background, although they "speak the same language." In my own experience, once, in Alexandria, Egypt, my middle-class guide was unable to communicate with a street sweeper who may have known the location of our hotel, yet both spoke "Arabic."

Only writing, and especially alphabetic writing supported by political power and social prestige, creates the illusion that a "language" such as English is a single thing, out there, bounded, defined, and capable of discovery. Writing's overarching power stabilizes speech, represses local differences, and fashions standards for thought and expression. Dante's Florentine dialect was one of hundreds of local Italic vernaculars descended from Latin, but his written *Commedia* in a fourteenth-century Florentine dialect created "the Italian language." Many books speak of the Phoenician, Hebrew, Moabite, Aramaic, and Syriac "languages" when, really, they are looking at small variations in the forms of West Semitic *writing* applied over a broad geographical area to a single speech-family that we might loosely call "Semitic," with local differences based on a similar phonology (a selection of voice sounds) and a similar inner structure. For example, in Hebrew the word for son is *bn* and in Aramaic it is *br*, but in Cambridge, Massachusetts, spirits to drink are /lika/ and in Seattle they are /likor/. Still, spoken communication takes place. The imperative "carry!" is *qabur* in the Hebrew "language," *qabor* in Syriac, *'uqbur* in Arabic and *qabar* in Ethiopic, but all are mildly different expressions from a single underlying system. The great family of Semitic languages has very many regional variations, and we are simply never sure when a dialect has slipped over into a new "language," that is, when a speaker within one system can no longer understand a speaker from another system. But twenty years of study of the holy Quran, certainly written in Arabic, will not enable the student to converse, even about simple things, with an inhabitant of Fez, Cairo, or Damascus, where everyone speaks "Arabic."

The confusion is clear in Figure 0.2, a type of chart that appears in many books on writing. The chart catalogues the transformations undergone by the West Semitic signary (in which a hypothetical but wholly unproven priority is given to Phoenician script). Such graphic variations are taken as designating the different languages of "Phoenician," "Moabite," various forms of "Aramaic," and "Hebrew." But such different "languages" are as close to one another as Quranic Arabic is to spoken Arabic in its myriad and often mutually unintelligible varieties. It is true that, schooled in the Phoenician script of 1000 BC, one will have a hard time reading "Palmyrene Aramaic" of the third century AD, the script and language used in the caravan city of Palmyra in the Syrian desert, but these are nonetheless the same script with formal differences growing over more than one thousand years. The underlying "language" has remained the same. Such charts are really a study in handwriting, or paleography, with limited importance for understanding the theory and history of writing, and they do not describe an evolution of "language."

Introduction: A Difficult Topic

	Early Phoenician	Moabite	Hebrew Ostraca (sixth century BC)	Early Aramaic	Late Aramaic Papyri	Palmyrene Aramaic	Monumental Nabataean Aramaic	"Square" Jewish/ Hebrew Printed
ʾ								א
b								ב
g								ג
d								ד
h								ה
w								ו
z								ז
ḥ								ח
ṭ								ט
y								י
k								כ
l								ל
m								מ
n								נ
s								ס
ʿ								ע
p								פ
ṣ								צ
q								ק
r								ר
š								ש
t								ת

Figure 0.2 Various character forms for West Semitic writing, from c.1000 BC to modern times. (After Healey, 1987, fig. 15, p. 223.)

In sum, the ambiguous correspondence of language and speech afflicts all such studies as this one, because speech, sometimes called "spoken language," certainly is a language, but not all language is speech. We will need constantly to speak of the "language" underlying systems of writing, even if we really mean "speech." In this case by "language" we refer to a system of phonic symbols intelligible to speaker and listener, more or less, over a wide range of variation. However, that system of phonic symbols could never itself be the "language" of the lexigraphic writing, because lexigraphic writing is its own language, making use of the resources of speech but never identical with it. "To speak a language" means something – if you speak Greek, you may enter the Mysteries at Eleusis; if you don't, you can't. Nonetheless, language, speech, and lexigraphic writing are all tangled up and, once we acknowledge their boundaries and differences, we must to some extent live with the confusion.

Transliterations

In the case of writing that is related to speech we must constantly deal with reconstructions of the sounds of speech encoded in the writing. In talking about the *forms of characters* and the *sounds of speech* I will follow the conventional practice of using brackets [ ] to enclose a given form or shape, how something looks, how it is written, and slashes / / to indicate the sound.

For example, in Egyptian hieroglyphs the sign [𓅓] represents the sound /m/ (plus an implied vowel). Unfortunately, each discipline has its own system, or more than one, for transcribing sounds, which originated in the history of the discipline. Such systems, internal to a discipline, are not themselves consistent, but may differ in England and Germany and even in the same place. For example, the Egyptian character for /y/ is written sometimes as [i] and sometimes as [j]. The situation is worse between disciplines. The *glottal stop*, when the throat closes as before and between "uh-oh," is represented as ['] in transliterations from West Semitic, but as [ʒ] by Egyptologists, although the sound is the same. Ideally, everyone might use the admirable International Phonetic Alphabet (IPA) as a means to suggest the sound values in systems of writing (see Fig. 14.3), and sometimes you do find this. However, few readers without formal training in linguistics understand the symbols of the IPA, the use of which can become a kind of game of phonetic precision that misrepresents the enormous phonetic ambiguity in all writing systems. Furthermore, the IPA is not easy to learn or to understand.

The problem of consistency in transliteration is not solvable, and in this book I have chosen, as much as possible, to use systems of transliteration traditional within a discipline, explaining myself as I go, but cautioning the reader about the need for flexibility and attention to sometimes subtle distinctions.

1

What Is Writing?

Writing, writing, it is everywhere, yet few have much to say about it, few know about it. Writing is an inherently difficult topic because discussion of it takes place by means of the very medium being discussed. As fish who know nothing of water, scholars who spend their lives studying different traditions of literature, and of writing, rarely reflect on the actual technology that makes their study possible: how it works, where it came from, and what relation it bears to other formal systems of thought.

Writing is magical, mysterious, aggressive, dangerous, not to be trifled with. Although it takes many forms, it is always a technology of explosive force, a cultural artifact based not in nature (whose rules we did not create) but sprung from the human mind. Human groups who possess writing triumph over those who do not, without exception and swiftly. If humans had existed a year, writing was invented not even yesterday, but some time this afternoon, as far as we know. Writing cast a veil across the human past, separating the million human years that came before from the turbulent last five thousand years. In the brief period since the discovery in Sumer around 3400 BC of the phonetic principle in graphic representation – when conventional markings first represented sounds of the human voice – the cultures encoded in this and subsequent related traditions of writing have changed human life forever.

Writing is the most important technology in the history of the human species, except how to make a fire. Writing is the lens through which literate peoples see the world, feel the world, hate the world, love the world, defy the world, and imagine change. What is writing that, like the lens you never see, creates the world? The difficult topic is muddled and mixed up with other things that have their own life – religion, artistic expression, speech, and human thought.

The Magic, Romance, and Danger of Writing

The holy Quran, encoded in the holy, even divine, script that the prophet himself used, is a sacred document that can never be changed or corrected or amended or mutilated or abused or transliterated into Roman characters: That would be an offense to God and punishable by death. Thus a book can be a fetish, as when one swears when placing a hand on a Bible or Quran: If the swearer is foresworn, he will suffer evil consequences. The text of the sacred Quran justifies mass murder, according to some interpretations, but you can never be sure because of the surprising obscurity of the wholly phonetic Arabic script, its distance from speech. What does it really say? The Jewish religion similarly depends on written documents in whose holy, magical, emotive symbols cabbalists discover secrets of the universe. Fortunately, the rabbi ("my master") can explicate textual obscurities to the ignorant, the less learned, as do the wise mullahs to the faithful.

Ancient Egyptian civilization, too, was bound to the forms and expectations of hieroglyphic writing to an extraordinary degree. The conventions of hieroglyphic writing influenced the posture of statues and the shapes and layout of temples, and, in the revelator Akhenaten's sacred city of Akhetaten ("Horizon of the Aten," near the modern village of Amarna), the design of the whole city described the form of the hieroglyph for "horizon," over which the sun god daily rose. Egyptian writing could also make one live forever, a signal advantage.

Mao Zedong (1893–1976), who pretended to hate the past, hoped to replace the obscurantist Chinese system of writing with an alphabet, but even his unlimited power could not accomplish the change. To change the writing would change the sacred ancient culture that the Chinese adore, which the mysterious and beautiful writing encodes. By changing the writing, one loses everything. That was precisely the intention of Kemal Atatürk when, in the 1920s, he outlawed the traditional Arabic script and ordered that Roman script now encode the Turkish language – thus did he break with the corrupt and ruinous past of the Ottoman sultans.

Jesus wrote in the sand (John 8), but in stark wisdom left nothing behind for followers to kill themselves over. They found other reasons. He must have understood how writing, and writings, can lead to fanaticism, social division, oppression, and the tyranny of the mad and the intolerant over the common man. So great is the power of writing.

We would like to know why writing has such exaggerated effects on human life and where it gets its power. The common definition of civilization as "human life in cities in the presence of writing" may be a historical judgment, but it is also a speculation on the superiority of a cultural practice that symbolizes human thought and carries it beyond the place and time of its origin. Writing enjoys intimate affection with the human faculty to create symbols, when one thing stands for another. Without this faculty, we would not be human. The relationship between the sounds of human speech and graphic material symbols that represent such sounds in lexigraphic writing is a central problem.

A Definition of Writing

Writing is hard to see because it governs our thoughts, and hard to talk about because of the lack of consistent names for real categories. We know that writing is there to be read, but are not sure what we mean by "writing," so that it is fashionable in criticism to "read" works of art or to "read" Greek culture or manners of dress or almost anything, as if in understanding a work of art or a building or a social practice we are doing the same thing as when we read a text. Writing has been defined time and again, always in different ways, but let us say that writing is *a system of markings with a conventional reference that communicates information*, like the signs on this page. Where does such a definition take us?

Because writing is made up of markings it is material (not spiritual or emotional or mental). The meaning of such markings, their conventional reference, we might say their intellectual dimension, never comes from nature, as does the human faculty for symbolization and speech, nor from God (as many have believed), but from man. The elements of writing, the markings, are related in an organized way, in a conventional way, in order to tell the reader something, to communicate with the reader. Where there is writing there is a reader who understands the system of conventions, even if the reader is God or a god (as often).

Change and Evolution in Systems of Writing

General principles appear to govern how any writing can work, as they appear to underlie the formation of speech. The possibilities of organization are limited and in some way predetermined. Hence, the history of writing is a history of the discovery of these principles, drawn in intelligible patterns. Because systems of writing are conventional and exist by agreement rather than coming from nature or God, there is no right or wrong to how a system imparts its meanings. Systems of writing serve different purposes for different peoples at different times. It is wrong to imagine that the Bronze Age Mycenaean Greeks would have been better off with the later Greek alphabet or with Chinese writing or anything else. Linear B did what it was called to do, to keep economic accounts in a palace-centered redistributive economy, and no one required more.

Nonetheless, because the history of writing is a history of discovery, we are tempted to compare writing systems as if they were in a competition for greatness and to say, for example, that the Greek alphabet is superior to Japanese writing, so complex that less than a dozen non-Japanese in the United States of America could read it when the Imperial Japanese Navy struck on December 7, 1941. Within the historical competition between human groups and the struggle for political and cultural dominion such comparisons are probably justified and fairly belong to an evaluation of the past. The Greek alphabet in its Roman form has in three thousand years become the dominant writing system by far, whereas Japanese writing remains confined to a small archipelago. Apologists for scripts unrelated to the Greek alphabet like to point out that it was not so much the Roman script as Western political power behind the script that brought the alphabet's hegemony, as if the script did not itself make possible (though not inevitable) such power.

Because among the users of any writing the system will satisfy the needs placed upon it, we cannot expect to find improvement or radical change within a developed lexigraphic writing system except in its earliest stages of formation. Both Sumerian cuneiform and Egyptian hieroglyphs appear to undergo evolution in the several hundred years between the first clear evidence of phoneticization, c.3400–3200 BC, and the creation of texts that reflect grammar and syntax, c.2700 BC; hundreds of years more must pass before we find extended texts. We must, of course, depend on evidence from haphazard finds. In the Eastern civilizations of the ancient world, it was not so much that the scribes who developed the first complex lexigraphic systems served the power elite as that they themselves were that elite; once their systems were in place, they could hardly have imagined, let alone desired, developments that would simplify their systems and undermine their power, or even make them irrelevant in the scheme of things. The Egyptian schoolbook taught that one should

Be a scribe! . . .
You are one who sits grandly in your house;
your servants answer speedily;
beer is poured copiously;
all who see you rejoice in good cheer.
Happy is the heart of him who writes;
he is young each day.
> from Papyrus Lansing, c.1000 BC, a schoolbook
> (Lichtheim 1976: 173–74)

Yes, for

The scribe, whatever his place at the Residence [pharaoh's court],
he cannot be poor in it.
> from *Satire on the Trades* (or *Instructions of Dua-Khety*), c.1800 BC

The scribe is wealthy and content and always in the ancient world male (but some women, especially in Rome, could read and write). Change within developed systems of writing, where it is found, is a kind of tinkering, and then, ordinarily, toward greater complexity and obscurity, more of the scribal art. Egyptian hieroglyphics managed with about 700 signs for most of its history, but, in a quirky development of the self-conscious Ptolemaic period (323–30 BC), increased its repertory to 5,000 signs. Attempts to "improve" a system of writing threaten the conventional basis by which it exists and diminish its intelligibility so that everything worsens.

For example, many have complained about the famously inept – that is, nonphonetic – English or French spellings. The American Philological Association was founded in 1869 to study the world's languages; it boldly encouraged spelling reforms much in the air in the late nineteenth century by publishing its proceedings in a reformed spelling. Today, they can scarcely be read. When Mao Zedong found he could not impose the Roman script, in the interests of the people he simplified the bizarrely intricate Chinese writing by omitting strokes from many characters to improve readability. He thereby rendered Chinese writing unintelligible to Chinese living in Taiwan, San Francisco, and Southeast Asia, whose traditional Chinese characters are now unreadable on the mainland.

Major changes in the structure of writing systems took place when the idea of writing passed from one people to another, always foreign people. Not bound by sacred tradition and the interests of a social class and intellectual elite, illiterate foreigners could make important changes. In the changes made in this way we can speak of the evolution of writing, of a process proceeding from less able to more able systems of writing.

Writing Is Material

Because writing has a material basis it can be created and destroyed, as book-burners throughout history understand. In the ancient Near East the origin of this life-transforming technology seems to be connected in some way with the use of material *objets*, abstract "counters" or tokens made of clay that represented commodities, according to a famous argument by Denise Schmandt-Besserat. One carried such material, tangible things in a pouch or on a string around the neck or dropped them accidentally on the ground or exchanged them during a transaction or wrapped them up in a hollow ball of clay, to preserve details of a commercial transaction. After five thousand years of such token use in the Near East, between c.8000 and c.3000 BC, the abstract shapes of some portable material tokens seem to have become characters in the first lexigraphic writing (see Chapter 3).

Even such obsolete systems of communication based on writing as semaphore require material flags moving in someone's hands. Morse code seems immaterial. Consisting of an ON/OFF digital mode, it is the only digital-modulation mode that humans can understand without a computer. Nonetheless, messages transmitted by Morse code are directly transferred into written documents. As a property protected by law, writing in cyberspace is in an awkward position, because the relationship of cyberspace to the material world is not clear, and we are unsure how laws of copyright apply to a medium you cannot control. The power of hardcopy, whose doom many predicted, remains strong in comparison to electronic documents because the tangible hardcopy is not endlessly permutable and easy to lose. Contracts, wills, and certificates of marriage, anything having to do with money, remain in hardcopy. Even as pixels on a computer screen, even when floating in cyberspace, writing retains its material basis.

Speech and Writing

In seeking a definition of writing, scholars sometimes take account of writing's materiality but nonetheless emphasize writing as a *secondary representation of the primary speech.* The influential L. Bloomfield, in a book called *Language* (1933), wrote that "writing is not language, but merely a way of recording language by means of visible marks" (Bloomfield 1933: 21). By "language" he must mean "speech," which writing obviously is not. But is not writing really a language in its own right?

The distinguished Mayanist Michael Coe, writing on progress in the decipherment of Maya glyphs, notes that "writing is *speech put in visible form* in such a way that any reader instructed in its conventions can reconstruct the vocal message. All linguists are agreed on this, and have been for a long time" (Coe 1992: 13, my italics). Coe agrees with Bloomfield, but sees that language and speech are different things. By having "visible form" writing must be material, but "vocal message" nonetheless lies at the heart of the definition.

A. Parpola, the distinguished scholar of the Indus Valley writing, calls writing "a visual communication system based on the representation of spoken language by conventional marks of some durability" (Parpola 1994: 29). Is Braille a "visible communication system"? Certainly it is writing. Parpola's "durability" implies materiality, but still writing represents "spoken language."

The great Assyriologist and historian of writing I. J. Gelb thought along similar lines, declaring that "writing is *written language* . . . I agree entirely with the linguists who believe that fully developed writing became a device for expressing linguistic elements by means of visible marks" (Gelb 1963: 13). Because in Gelb's view the phonographic element, "a device for expressing linguistic elements," is the essence of "fully developed writing," or "full writing," the Greek alphabet, beyond which the art of writing has not progressed, came at the apex of a long development. The Greek alphabet is even the *telos*, the immanent goal, toward which "writing" has always striven, because in the Greek alphabet the phonographic element is overriding.

P. L. Daniels, in his and P. T. Bright's useful book *The World's Writing Systems*, thinks that "writing is defined as *a system of more or less permanent marks used to represent an utterance in such a way that it can be recovered more or less exactly without the intervention of the utterer*" (Daniels and Bright 1996: 3, original italics). By this definition he agrees that writing is bound up with speech (an utterance) and, in company with other scholars, excludes from "writing" communication by means of symbols or representations not couched in a specific linguistic form. However, in his insistence on recovering an utterance "more or less exactly" Daniels's surprising formulation would exclude all forms of writing up to the Greek alphabet, and even, strictly speaking, the Greek alphabet itself, because no writing before or including it permitted the recovery of an original utterance "more or less exactly." When such recovery took place in actual usage it did so on the basis of a shared language between writer and reader and shared expectations based on the context of the message, not on the basis of the phonetic and semantic information encoded in the script.

Such understandings of writing as being a secondary representation of the primary speech are always re-expressions of F. Saussure's famous dictum: "A language and its written form constitutes two separate systems of signs. The sole reason for the existence of the latter is to represent the former" (Saussure [1922] 1983: 24). Saussure only echoed Aristotle's formulation: "Spoken words are the symbols of mental experience and written words are the symbols of spoken words" (Aristotle, *de Interpretatione* 1.1).

First comes "language," then comes its "written form," which depends on "language." Yet in its dependence on a material basis, writing is fundamentally unlike speech, which is never tangible. The relationship between written form and speech is more complicated than such commentators believe.

Writing is a technology with a material basis, while speech is never a technology and never material but an essentially human aptitude. If dolphins could speak, they would be humans with an odd-shaped nose. In our own definition that writing is *a system of markings with a conventional reference that communicates information,* we do not refer to speech, language, or utterance. In the definitions of commentators quoted above, the words "speech" and "language" are treated interchangeably and in the clumsy way we complained about earlier. How writing functions will depend on the innate faculty of humans to communicate by means of symbols. A *language* is any system of symbols that serves this innate faculty to communicate through symbols: *speech* is one such system of symbols, *writing* is another (**see diagram opposite title page**).

2

Writing with Signs

Such common thoughts about "writing" as those quoted in the last chapter may be more reflections of our own experience with alphabetic writing, tied with unprecedented intimacy to speech, than they are satisfactory descriptions of "writing" itself. For it is easy to see that many kinds of material signs with a conventional reference that communicate information do not refer to human speech at all, even when they appear within a system of lexigraphic writing. Are such signs not writing?

When we see a road sign with the picture of a cow falling from a cliff, we quickly realize how, as drivers, we should beware of cows tumbling down upon our car (Fig. 2.1). The falling cow, the cliff, and the car is a picture designed to communicate information, not to provide aesthetic pleasure (or amusement!). Were the word not ruined by careless use, we might want to call this a *pictogram*, "picture writing," understanding that "writing" does not require the intercession of elements of speech. Instead we will say that the iconic elements in the sign are strong. However, the meaning of the sign also depends on its abstract shape according to a North American convention (different in Europe) that an upended square bordered in black means *This is a warning!* Cows could fall from cliff at any time.

In the same way, by conventional agreement, a circle and slash means

not allowed (see Fig. 2.2). The ubiquitous is understood everywhere

in the world without regard to what language one speaks. We would like to say that here is a "worldwide language," a writing that everyone from everywhere understands – if only all writing worked that way.

Obviously, in such examples *communication* takes place by means of *visible marks with a conventional reference*, but without the intervention of speech. The cow falling from the cliff onto the car, like the dump truck, is

Figure 2.1 Road sign warning of cows falling from cliff
Figure 2.2 A sign prohibiting dumping

a picture of something recognizable, it is iconic. Nonetheless, if you are from Mars, you will be unsure what either sign means because the black-bordered upended square and the circle with a slash have conventional, not natural references.

Gelb's Category "Forerunners of Writing"

The desire to tie "full writing" to speech implies that there are forms of writing that are not tied to speech – "partial writing"? "half writing"? – and we have just seen two examples. Of course, something came before writing, which did not always exist. Gelb categorized representations that precede "full writing" as "forerunners of writing." Let us consider several examples.

Primitive art

We could scarcely say when forerunners of writing began because we find similar kinds of signs all over the world in Paleolithic and later sites. Throughout the world, including America, are found petroglyphs made by pecking with a small stone on a boulder. Seemingly, these signs communicate information, though we are rarely sure what that is. In Figure 2.3,

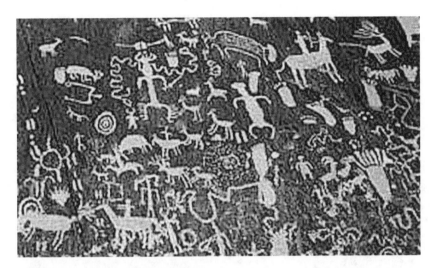

Figure 2.3 Petroglyph from Newspaper Rock State Historic Park, Utah

from a wall in Utah entirely covered with petroglyphs, we recognize in the upper right-hand corner a man on a horse shooting at a deer (this petroglyph was therefore made after the Spanish conquest). In the bottom left is another mounted man, perhaps hunting a mountain goat. We recognize other mounted men, deer, humans, goats, snakes, perhaps a bear print, and such abstract designs as concentric circles. But we can never understand these remnants of the past because we do not know why they were made or what they meant to their maker. Does the man shooting from horseback commemorate a mighty deed, or does the picture magically assist the performance of such a deed? Or does it express an artistic impulse, someone's desire to make a picture of something in his experience? Even so children take up paper and create abstract designs and crude representations for no other reason than the pleasure of doing it. This type of "forerunner of writing" Gelb called *primitive art*. Although sometimes abstract, and perhaps meant to communicate something, there is no writing because there is no conventional system.

Nonetheless, the intimacy between art and writing is initial and strong. Far older representations are found in the celebrated caves at Lascaux, in southern France, c.20,000 BC, perhaps the earliest art ever found and unquestionably "primitive." Contemporary lovers of art nevertheless easily admire the realistic and artistically "modern" horse in one cave, reminiscent

Figure 2.4 The "Chinese Horse," prehistoric cave painting, c.20,000 BC. Lascaux Caves, Perigord, Dordogne, France. (Photograph from Art Resource, NY ART99863.)

of horses in Chinese art from the Tang Dynasty (seventh to tenth centuries AD), and for this reason called the "Chinese Horse" (Fig. 2.4). No one knows the purpose of these paintings found deep in caves, but perhaps a horse drawn on the wall in the womb of the earth makes horses in the plain above more plentiful, more of them to hunt and eat. Perhaps the plantlike objects to the front of the horse and across its white underbelly are arrows or some kind of missile meant to kill the horse: even so may the hunter meet with success in the field. But what is the highly abstract "pitchfork" design made of four lines and a rectangle above the horse? Is this the diagram for a trap, or is it an abstract cue to a ritual, or a name, something to be done or said? Did artist shamans work their magic here, recording their visions on the walls of the caves?

The pitchfork design looks like writing because it is abstract and does not appeal to our pleasure in seeing, but we cannot place it within a conventional system. We will never understand the meaning of the sign. We are never sure what we are dealing with in the illustrations in the Lascaux caves because of our oceanic ignorance of the past, in general, and of what happened then.

The descriptive-representational device

Primitive art has a wide range and maybe does not belong in the category forerunners of writing, but a narrower category is representations called by Gelb the "descriptive-representational device." In a descriptive-representational device the picture tells you something, unlike the pitchfork-like design in the Lascaux cave, which tells you nothing. Descriptive-representational devices can be close to what we think of as simply art because they follow conventions for figurative art, but pictures that are *art* serve to satisfy the aesthetic pleasure of the artist and beholder and not to communicate explicit information. The two goals can combine, as in Chinese and Japanese lexigraphic writing, meant to be beautiful. In early societies artistic pleasure is inseparable from magical power, and Chinese writing and ancient Egyptian writing, were agents of magical practice. Still today we think of strong art as having "magic." (An art dealer described to me that American Indian art is widely collected because it has "magic.") The purpose of the descriptive-representational device, artistic or not, is to communicate information.

A famous example (because Gelb first cited it) appears on a nineteenth-century letter written by a southern Cheyenne Indian called Turtle-Following-His-Wife who lived in Indian Territory (now Oklahoma) to his son Little Man at the Pine Ridge Reservation (now in South Dakota) (Fig. 2.5). The name of each man is written as little pictures above his head, attached by a thread. Lines proceed from the mouth of Turtle-Following-His-Wife then bend back in two forks over a second picture of a small man. Fifty-three circles are drawn between the two men, but closer to Turtle-Following-His-Wife. The meaning is that Turtle-Following-His-Wife had sent $53 to the Pine Ridge Agency to cover Little Man's expenses, a message, confirmed by the Indian agent, that Little Man at once understood.

The descriptive-representational device may be a useful category, but we should not think of it as being a primitive one, something that people did before "full writing" came along. For example, Figure 2.6, printed in 2007, explains how one is to remove the crating from around a refrigerator. In box 1, two schematic men show that this is a two-man job. The men lower the crated refrigerator to the ground on its back, a direction of motion indicated by the arrows. In box 2, the scissors and a now visible cinch around the lower portion of the crating indicate that this cinch is to be cut with scissors. In the remaining boxes the men remove the bottom of

Figure 2.5   Turtle-Following-His-Wife writes to Little Man. (After Mallery, 1893, p. 364.)

Figure 2.6   Instructions for uncrating a refrigerator, 2007

the crate (3), re-erect the refrigerator (4), then remove the top and sides of the crate (5).

In box 1, alphabetic characters, a form of "full writing" closely tied to speech, impart vital information not easily pictured, telling us in four languages which side the DOOR should be on when the refrigerator is lowered, then in English alone where the TOP is. One might think that whoever understood *puerta* would also understand *porte* and *porta*, but a direct appeal to Hispanics, Anglos, French, and Italians reflects the artist/scribe's conviction that with his picture-story he is communicating in a universal European language independent of linguistic forms. Perhaps laziness explains the simple Anglophone TOP, or suggests that in the prejudgment of the artist/scribe mostly Anglos will buy this fridge. The numbers in the boxes are not really needed and do not belong to the category of descriptive-representational device, because they refer to elements of human speech (as we will see), although differing according to the consumer's native language.

In a second example, an international audience learns how to assemble a portable iPod player. The instructions are a descriptive-representational device, and like the instructions for unpacking the refrigerator make use of other kinds of elements: Arabic numerals, the conventional circle-with-a-slash, and a question mark (Fig. 2.7). In (1) we learn to remove from

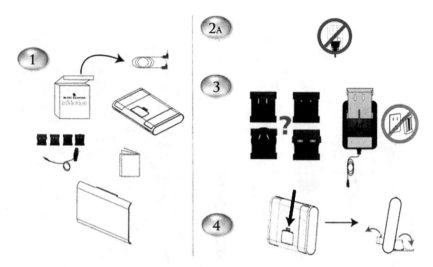

Figure 2.7 Assembling a portable iPod player

the packing five dissimilar objects and four similar objects. In (2A) (but where is 2B? oops!) we learn that we are not to plug in the iPod player as we would plug in an ordinary appliance, following the convention of the circle-with-a-slash indicating prohibition (not a descriptive-representational device). In (3) the question-mark sign (?) (not a descriptive-representational device) in the midst of the four squares we met in (1) seems to explain that we are puzzled about the four similar objects, which turn out to be different kinds of plug, each used in a different country. Also in (3) a new object appears – the artist/scribe omitted to draw it in (1) – of unclear significance; examination of what was really in the packing reveals it to be a plastic holder for whichever plug suits the international purchaser of this portable iPod player. To this holder you must attach the wire with jack pictured beneath the mysterious objects in box 1. For some reason the plug changes color from black to white (the actual plug and holder are white). In (3) we also learn that we are not supposed to do something with the plug, evidently plug it in if it is the wrong plug. Finally, in (4) we learn how to open up little panels that support the speakers.

We never learn the meaning of the cable in the upper right in (1), nor discover what is the little booklet pictured in (1), unless it is these very instructions written in "the universal language of pictures." The object at the bottom of (1) is the cover, but we are not told how to install it.

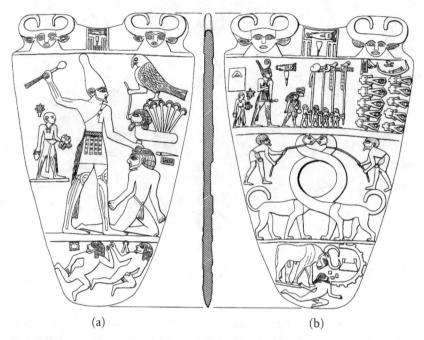

Figure 2.8   Drawing of the Narmer Palette, First Dynasty, c.3100 BC.
(After Quibell, 1898, pls. 12, 13.)

Figure 2.7 well exemplifies the ability of the descriptive-representational
device to communicate complex information, but also the frustration that
comes from inept explication in this form. In fact, the pamphlet cannot
be understood without holding in hand the objects to which it refers, and
even then we are not always sure what is meant.

We might compare such examples with the oldest monument of
pharaoh's power, the Narmer Palette, c.3100 BC, an elaborate stone votive
object made in the form of a practical tool for grinding kohl, a black
eye-makeup (Fig. 2.8). The palette was found in 1898 in a cache near an
early temple at the site of Hierakonpolis ("Hawk City") in southern Egypt,
with which the first pharaohs had a close connection. It is the most
important monument to survive from the beginning of the pharaonic period.
College courses in art history always study the Narmer Palette as an example of early Egyptian art. On the obverse (a), Narmer, wearing the white
crown of Upper Egypt, raises his right hand to execute a subject prisoner.
Others lie dead in the lower register. On the reverse (b), the followers of

Narmer, who now wears the red crown of Lower Egypt, carry standards surmounted by a hawk, another hawk, a standing jackal, and a placenta (?). They oversee a field of 10 dead, whose severed heads lie between their legs. A boat stands nearby. Fantastic beings restrained by bearded men surround a central cup made to imitate a depression for grinding the kohl. In the lower register the pharaoh as bull destroys a town.

This famous monument appears to memorialize an actual battle between north and south Egypt, and many have understood it to memorialize the very battle that resulted in the "union of the two lands," the creation of the Egyptian pharaonic monarchy. To support that interpretation the main figure wears the white crown of Upper Egypt on side (a) and the red crown of Lower Egypt on side (b). In this case the "descriptive-representational device" does not communicate practical information, as does the letter of Turtle-Following-His-Wife, or the instructions how to open a crate or assemble an iPod player; rather, it places in permanent form testimony to one man's achievement. Such use of the descriptive-representational device is found throughout the ancient world and is in common use now.

The creator of the Narmer Palette wishes not only to represent a historical event but to clarify its meaning by marks that refer to elements of human speech, very much as the creators of the fridge and iPod instructions. Some of the very earliest Egyptian hieroglyphs appear on this palette, but we cannot always be sure of their meaning. They appear to encode names and titles. The signs of "city walls" and "special knot"(?) over the heads of

the dead men at the bottom of (a)

may give their names. The "harpoon" and "pool" beside the head of the executed prisoner on (a) should spell his name too, which we can read as *Wesh* according to the classical readings of hieroglyphs

. Within the walls at the bottom of (b)

must be the names of tribes or places. The marks near

the head of the sandal-bearer on (a) and side (b) , a "rosette"

and an "inverted pot" (?), probably refer to words in the Egyptian language that mean "servant of the king." The "skin-float" in the rectangle in the

upper left of side (b) may designate the name of the king's house,

if the rectangle is a palace. The word encoded by "tethering rope" over "bread loaf" above the wigged figure striding in front of pharaoh on side (b)

, with hunting bolas (?) suspended from his neck, may mean "vizier,"

or it may be the man's name *Tchet*. The signs above the decapitated prisoners on (b) – "door," "sparrow," "hawk," "harpoon," "boat" – we cannot interpret with confidence (the boat may not be lexigraphic writing

at all) , perhaps the name of the place

where the victory took place, and the name of the boat.

At least we can easily read "catfish" and "chisel" at the top of both sides

of the palette as *Nermer*, "Striker," that is, Narmer, contained within

a schematic palace-façade design. In later times this design was called a *serekh* and enclosed the first name in a five-fold royal titulary, the name of pharaoh as the incarnation of Horus. A cow-goddess flanks either side. The name, probably an abbreviation for "[Horus] the Striker," is repeated at the top of side (b) and for a third time in front of the king.

A rather different form of communication appears on side (a) of the Narmer Palette. A hawk holds by a nose-rope a human-headed flat oval from which spring six papyrus plants. The descriptive-representational device – white-crowned pharaoh executing a prisoner – tells us that a man from Upper Egypt overcame an enemy force, but now we learn that it was "the man who embodies the power of Hawk [that is, Horus] who overcame the men in the papyrus marshes [that is, the delta]." The design communicates by symbols, then, not by descriptive representation. The hawk symbolizes Horus; the nose-rope symbolizes subjection; the rectangle with papyrus plants symbolizes the delta. In classical Egyptian lexigraphic hieroglyphs the flat oval is a word-sign for "land" or "marsh," and the papyrus plants is a word-sign for "1,000," so there may have been 6,000 men in the delta army, if these signs had the same meaning in the late fourth millennium as they did in the second.

Evidently at the dawn of "full writing," or "true writing," attested by the partly understood hieroglyphs on the Narmer palette, different ways of imparting information are happily rolled into a single document. Today we understand the "message" not through the hieroglyphs, which are opaque, but through the descriptive-representational device: pharaoh executing an enemy (a) and overlooking their decapitated heads (b); and through a form of symbolization: the hawk holding a personalized hieroglyph by means of a nose-rope. In crossing linguistic barriers, as we must do to understand the Narmer Palette, "full writing" brings a loss of intelligibility, not enhancement.

The identifying-mnemonic device

Closely related to the descriptive-representational device is Gelb's third category of the "forerunners of writing," which he called the identifying-mnemonic device. The identifying-mnemonic device makes clear who is meant or what event is meant, by isolating a conspicuous feature of the person or the event. We might include the hawk holding the nose-rope in this category because it reminds the viewer of a specific man who accomplished a specific thing. Such devices were widely used by American Indians; we have already seen examples in the drawing of two turtles and a little man in Figure 2.5, which identify certain individuals. The Winnebago Indians of Wisconsin had a system of written signs to remind them of various songs, if we consider them events, and Indians of the northern plains tracked the passing of years by means of the winter count, whose signs reminded the keeper of a signal event from that year. Good examples of the winter count survive thanks to the efforts of one Garrick Mallery, a Union officer during the American Civil War who lived in the northern plains at the end of the century and wrote numerous books about the "picture-writing" of the American Indians.

Figure 2.9 shows an example drawn by a Lakota Indian whose name meant "Flame." The winter count on muslin is a copy made from the original kept

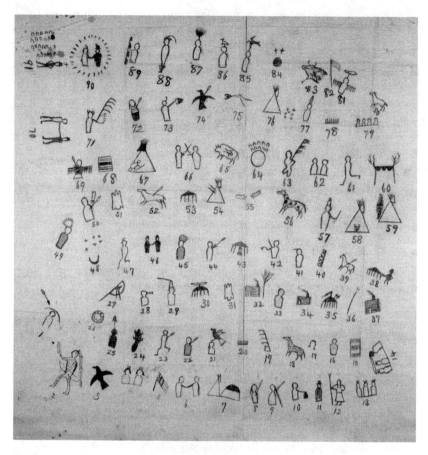

Figure 2.9 Winter count by Flame, a Lakota Indian from the Yanktonai band, a copy on muslin made by Lt. Hugh T. Reed from the original covering the years 1786–1877. 35" × 35½". (National Anthropological Archives, Smithsonian, National Museum of Natural History, Ms. 2372 [08633800].)

by Flame. Arabic numerals have been assigned in the copy. The count begins in the lower-left corner, runs left to right then turns the corner and runs right to left, back and forth in *boustrophedon* style ("as the ox turns," like early Greek writing), covering the years 1786–1877. To each year was assigned an image that, in consultation with tribal elders, embodied a significant event. In this way, the event was itself remembered and a kind of history recorded.

In the northern plains each band had its own keeper of the count who could expound to listeners what happened a long time ago and in what

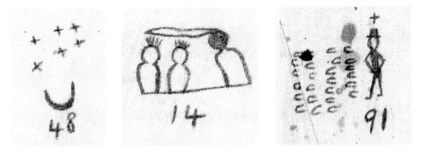

Figure 2.10   Figure number 48 in the winter count of Flame representing the great meteor shower of 1833 by means of stylized stars and a stylized moon

Figure 2.11   Figure 14 from the winter count of Flame showing an Indian from the Hunkpapa band killing two Arikaras

Figure 2.12   Figure from the winter count of Flame for the year 1876 showing an Anglo official wearing a top hat and 25 horse tracks. The cross above the man's head indicates that he is a Christian

order, but of course there was no absolute point of reference. Mallery recognized that counts by keepers from different bands reflected one spectacular event in a similar way, the great meteor shower of 1833, and so was able to assign to individual signs absolute dates in the Western calendar (see Fig. 2.10). Often the years were counted by a martial exploit, for example number 14 (1799–80), the year when "a man from Hunkpapa band killed two Arikaras" (Fig. 2.11). The special hairdo shows the two men on the left to be Arikaras and the bow coming from the Hunkpapa's head indicates that he shot them with arrows. We might imagine that the count for 1876 would refer to the Battle of the Little Big Horn, fought in June of that year, about which more has been written than any battle in history, but instead the count pictures the government capture of some horses (Fig. 2.12).

The winter counts, which do not belong to a conventional system, are mnemonic devices for the keeper of the count, and the form of the counts differs from band to band, although they sometimes share similar images. They are private symbol systems and they do not refer to elements of speech. Among the northern American Indians there never was development of any kind from such pictorial and schematic representations to writing tied to speech, calling into question whether such representations are "forerunners" to anything.

Gelb's category "forerunners of writing" seems in any event an unsatisfactory formulation, because such means of communication are ubiquitous in modern traditions of writing, no matter how developed such traditions might be (compare Figures 2.1, 2.6, 2.7, 2.15, 2.16).

Semasiography

We cannot doubt that the attachment of graphic signs to sounds in human speech was epoch-making in the history of writing, but earlier forms of graphic communication persisted. Rather than omit them from the exclusive club "full writing," where they remain honored guests, we may call all such representations *semasiography*, "writing with signs." The descriptive-representational device and the identifying-mnemonic device and, in some cases, primitive art are kinds of semasiography. Such non-phonetic signs can be abstract, like the circle with a diagonal slash, or the hoofprints in the winter count of Flame, or representational, like the cow falling from the cliff or the Anglo with the top hat, but in semasiography the marks on the material basis always *communicate information without the necessary intercession of forms of speech*. Such signs are a form of writing according to our definition because they communicate information by means of material marks with a conventional reference. However, they represent concepts and meanings directly and may themselves to some extent constitute a language independent of speech, though such signs can sometimes be interpreted in speech.

Musical notation

Once we agree that semasiography is a form of "writing," we realize that we are dealing with an enormous category for study. As always, forms of writing open gates to power and to the refinement of human thought and creative expression. Musical notation provides a good example. Guido d'Arezzo, an Italian Benedictine monk of the eleventh century (AD 995–1050), invented the four-line staff, which he used in combination with a notation earlier developed in the eastern Roman Empire for the recitation of Christian scriptures by means of marks called *neumes* (from Greek *pneuma*, "breath"). The *neumes*, similar to markings in the Quran to assist oral presentation, were written over the text and later used to notate Gregorian chant. They appear to descend in some way from the Greek system of notation whereby different relative pitches were notated by letters of the alphabet (a few examples survive, poorly understood). In the fourteenth century the staff was increased to its present five lines.

The earlier forms of musical notation in Greece, and even ancient Mesopotamia, in India, China, and Japan, did not permit the recreation of the rhythm, pitch, and inflection of a composer, but were an identifying-mnemonic device that reminded a singer of a song whose rhythm, melody, and intonations he learned aurally. Guido d'Arezzo's refinement of these earlier mnemonic devices soon made possible previously unimaginable forms of music and of thinking about the inner laws of musical expression, the technological foundation for academic musicology. His achievements made possible modern "classical music" and the modern notion of "the composer."

For example, in Figure 2.13, from a trumpet concerto by Vivaldi, two trumpets play against each other in elegant counterpoint visible on the page

Figure 2.13 "Trumpet Concerto for Two Trumpets and Orchestra" by Antonio Vivaldi (1680–1743) in modern musical notation

$a = m,$

$b = n(mn+2),$

$c = (n + 1)(mn + m + 2),$

$d = 4(mn + 1)(mn + m + 1)(mn^2 + mn + 2n + 1);$

$ab + 1 = (mn + 1)^2,$

$ac + 1 = (mn + m + 1)^2,$

$ad + 1 = (2m^2n^2 + 2m^2n + 4mn + 2m + 1)^2,$

$bc + 1 = (mn^2 + mn + 2n + 1)^2,$

$bd + 1 = (2m^2n^3 + 2m^2n^2 + 6mn^2 + 4mn + 4n + 1)^2$

Figure 2.14 The mathematical solution to the problem of finding four numbers such that the product of any two of them is one less than a perfect square

as an aesthetically pleasing representation. The mark at the left of each stave 𝄞, called a *clef* ("key"), determines the range of pitches assigned to the five horizontal lines that intersect it, while the shapes of the notes determine their duration. Other marks add information about intonation and phrasing. Here is sound made visible, making possible the creation of patterns never before found in music. Modern musical notation is related to earlier systems of musical notation rather as was the Greek alphabet to Phoenician writing and other earlier traditions.

Mathematical notation

Another form of semasiography familiar to all makes it possible to "find four numbers such that the product of any two of them is one less than a perfect square" (Fig. 2.14). We can couch the problem itself in speech, but the solution, though one might find a verbal equivalent, functions through the symbolic use of alphabetic, numerical, and other signs unattached to speech. It is easy to see that mathematical semasiography is itself a language (but not speech), capable of achieving blinding feats of logic and abstract thought and even describing the governing forces behind appearances in the material world.

Computer icons

The international community of computer-users happily or necessarily tolerates a bewildering plethora of sematograms, the ocean of computer

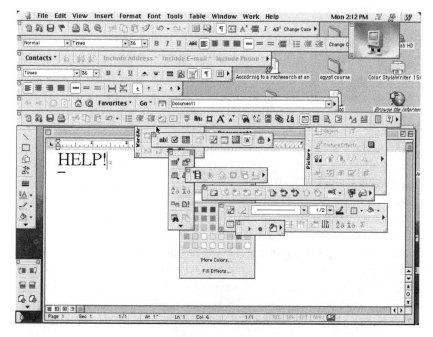

Figure 2.15 Computer semasiography

icons, which proliferate like microbes, most of unknown meaning, though in theory discoverable (Fig. 2.15). For example, in Figure 2.15 one might discover pictures of a lock, a house, and binoculars (and be tempted to call them "pictograms"), then infer that the "lock" locks something up, perhaps that the "house" goes to a general menu (but does it?), and that the "binoculars" bring something up close. The other buttons remain mostly mysterious. Such identifying-mnemonic devices, a kind of semasiography, do not stand for words, but usually for an action: If you press the "lock," the document cannot be opened. Like the identifying-mnemonic devices found in American Indian winter counts, their meaning remains best known to their creators, though their function is different because they enable the user to do something while the counts remind the interpreter of an event. Sometimes we can guess what such icons mean, but most have to be learned one by one, or are never learned.

Observations

Musical and mathematical notation and computer icons are surely writing, markings with a conventional reference that communicate information, but they are semasiographic in nature. Such writing, not tied to speech, works through symbolic means to communicate a variety of kinds of information that can bear great aesthetic, scientific, and social power. Semasiographic systems vary immensely in the sort of information they communicate, from the nature of sounds on the oboe to the relationship between quantities of light and matter, to dance steps on a stage (for which several systems exist). Nonetheless, all such systems are alike in that the information they convey does not make direct use of the resources of speech.

Semasiography preceded lexigraphic writing and is very old, but limitations for the expression of many kinds of information by semasiographic means are enormous. We cannot discuss the origins of the American Civil War or the meaning of life by means of mathematical symbols. The discovery of the phonetic principle in graphic representation in Sumer in the late fourth millennium BC did not, therefore, change writing's fundamental nature as "a system of graphic signs on a material substance with a conventional reference that communicates information," something very unlike speech, but opened to writing the enormous, almost limitless opportunities for precision that symbols originating as speech can offer. It is not surprising that so many scholars have identified the discovery around 3400 BC of the phonetic principle (a way to encode sound in graphic marks) as the moment when "true writing" or "full writing" began, which has led to the common view that writing is not "writing" unless it embodies a reconstructible utterance. "Writing" didn't begin in 3400 BC, but an epoch-making, earth-shattering change in the way writing worked *did* begin then.

The discovery of the phonetic principle in graphic representation made possible a new kind of writing, which I am calling *lexigraphy*, "writing with words," to distinguish it from its older brother *semasiography*, "writing with signs," of which we have considered examples, ancient and modern. Lexigraphic writing is, as a system, always rooted in speech, and no form of it more so than the Greek alphabet. The commentators reviewed in Chapter 1 mistake lexigraphic writing for writing itself, easy to do when one is an alphabet-user and not thinking about writing theoretically or historically. Only an alphabet-user could think that lexigraphic writing "represents language" or "represents speech," but certainly it does refer to elements and features of speech – to nouns, qualifiers, and syntax – in order to present and develop original thought through symbolic means.

In West Semitic writing and in the Greek alphabet most graphemes were in truth phonetic, "with sound value," but in the modern systems descended from the Greek, semasiography has re-

Figure 2.16 Sign in Tokyo airport

emerged as a critical component. The two kinds of writing have nearly a longing to work together and today are found everywhere. For example, a welcome sign for the weary traveler trying to find a toilet in the Tokyo airport contains four strongly iconic sematograms (Fig. 2.16). Schematic representations of a woman and a man at the far left tell you that there are facilities for either sex; the schematic man in a wheelchair reveals that there are toilet stalls with wide doors and adaptations for handicapped users; the figure changing an infant indicates that a changing table is available. We can alphabetize the Japanese lexigraphic writing to the right of the sematograms as *keshoushitsu wa kouhou e,* but should remember that *keshoushitsu* (the first three characters) and *kouhou* (the fifth and sixth characters) are in origin Chinese characters, which do not have phonetic value at all, but here stand for the appropriate Japanese words (the Japanese call the use of Chinese signs with Japanese values *kanji,* "Han [= Chinese] writing"). The remaining signs are phonetic and stand for open syllables (called *hiragana,* "ordinary [because they are not Chinese] writing"). The Japanese phrase translates literally "For the make-up room [go] back," that is "The toilets are back the opposite way." This you will never learn from the iconic sematograms, or from the Japanese lexigraphic writing unless you have mastered *kanji* and *hiragana* scripts. Fortunately the English *lingua franca* explains where to go! Whoever designed this sign believed that one needs both kinds of writing, semasiographic and lexigraphic, and some knowledge of English, to find a toilet in this busy international airport.

3

Categories and Features of Writing

Now that we have begun to face the complexities in the task of understanding the theory and history of writing, it will be useful to organize the categories of writing into a stemma of structural relationships, beginning with the fundamental distinction between semasiography and lexigraphy. In the following chapters we will focus more on several different kinds of lexigraphy.

The **stemma facing the title page of this book** is a chart of structural relationships, not a historical stemma, but let us explore its historical features as well. In the history of writing, earlier forms of symbolization – making one thing stand for another – remain embedded in later forms, precisely what took place in the examples cited in the last chapter of the admixture of semasiographic and lexigraphic writing.

The Rebus

Although we cannot identify the exact moment when the critical shift from semasiographic to lexigraphic writing took place, it appears to have taken place toward the end of the fourth millennium in southern Mesopotamia, probably in the city of Uruk, home of Gilgamesh (the modern name "Iraq" comes from this ancient city). We guess that the shift took place through the working of the *rebus* (= Latin "from the things"). Someone discovered that a graphic mark can encode a sound recognizable in speech by divesting the graphic mark of its "meaning," leaving only the sound. Sometimes this shift is called *phoneticization*. Henceforth, to the shape is attached a certain sound and not a certain meaning. Once organized into a system, different shapes with different attached sounds (or a range of sounds) could be combined to symbolize such elements of human speech as names of people and of places and names of things, useful when a lot of wealth needs to be accounted for. Lexigraphy does not evolve from "pictograms" or "picture-writing," but depends on the discovery of the rebus applied to signs that were sometimes iconic, but just as often abstract and never the picture of anything. Only insofar as we can

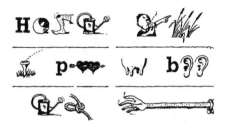

Figure 3.1 Advertisement for Heineken beer as a rebus: HEINIKEN REFRESHES THE PARTS OTHER BEERS CANNOT REACH. (After Harris, 1988, p. 136.)

consider the discovery of the rebus logical can we consider lexigraphic writing to be implicit in semasiography.

Figure 3.1 illustrates in principle how a rebus works, although in this example the rebus-maker three times appeals to alphabetic characters to make his message succeed. Not counting the alphabetic signs, the pictures stand for sounds and are *phonograms*, "sound-writing"; the last sign, however, does not stand for a sound but for the word "reach": It is a *logogram* or word-sign. The sounds attached to the fifth and sixth phonograms, /ref/ and /rushes/ = "refreshes," are not obvious. Fortunately, the slogan is celebrated in the annals of British advertising and once some meaning is recognized, the reader will understand the whole. All writing is rife with similar ambiguities. Of course, the sound values attached to these signs do not belong to a system of writing; they are a game.

The rebus seems to have been discovered three times: in southern Mesopotamia around 3400 BC; in China around 1200 BC in the late Shang Dynasty (c.1600 BC–c.1100 BC, though some Chinese claim much earlier dates); and in Mesoamerica some time before the birth of Christ. In Mesopotamia, the historical inspiration for the discovery of the phonetic principle through the rebus must have taken place through the need to record personal names, place names, and names of commodities in connection with economic transactions. The Mesopotamian tradition is by far the most important because from it descends all modern systems of writing, including the writing on this page. The bizarre Chinese writing and its descendants are confined to a few Asian countries, highly populated, and Mesoamerican writing, which glorified tribal leaders, died with the Spanish conquest.

Logography, the First Division of Lexigraphy

In the earliest lexigraphic systems, in Mesopotamia and Egypt, the phonetic principle was by no means applied to all signs, but only to some. It is practical to divide lexigraphic writing into the two categories shown in the chart facing the title plage, depending on the kind of value assigned to the signs: *logography* and *phonography*. By value I mean the segment of speech to which the sign refers. In logographic writing, such logograms ("word-signs") as the "stretching arm" in the Heineken rebus *do not have phonetic value*, but they *do refer to significant segments of speech*. In phonographic writing, the signs *do have phonetic value*, and they *may or may not refer to significant segments of speech*.

Logograms and words

We ordinarily think of the segments of speech to which logograms refer as words, although in very many cases the notion that such segments of speech are words derives from their association with written signs. Logograms can in exceptional cases also refer to phrases or to portions of words that are independently meaningful (that is, to morphemes, as the syllables in "man-drake"). But in deciding what is a "word," very often the written form comes first; the boundaries of the "word" in speech come second. Literate people cannot easily sort this out, but linguists cannot define a "word" other than the things listed in a dictionary. Words appear not to exist as discrete entities in speech. Rather, in nature they are patterns of sound in a continuous wave (see Fig. 13.4 below), placing us in an awkward position when we want to talk about how "words" are associated with written signs.

We want to believe that words are discrete entities, however, because personal names are surely bounded and discrete, as are the names for the things that surround us in life. Such elements of speech even undergo easy mutation according to circumstance – for example, you may call your wife, whose name is Patricia, "Pattykins." We all read and write and believe that RUN, PERKY, RUN consists of three words. Nonetheless, speakers of languages that have never been written down, or illiterate persons living within a society with a written tradition, do not recognize the category "word" even though they recognize that people have names, as do animals and other objects. In famous studies in the 1930s the classicist Milman Parry showed how when you asked an illiterate Balkan oral singer to sing just one "word," he would sing a whole line, several lines, or even a whole song. Even so we might say, "Do you mind if I have a word with you?"

It may be true that speech is a wave, a stream in which words are not discrete entities, but if you ask a child learning to speak, "What is that?" he will say "ball" or "cat" or "granpa." If as a grownup I want to write down somebody's name, because there is wealth at stake, I have no easy way of symbolizing his name by means of marks. Who is this? Let's say that I've discovered how to make a record of his name through stumbling on the rebus: I am writing phonograms. But what is he herding? That is a "cow." I make a note of it beside the name of the man by drawing a picture of a cow's head with horns: Now I am writing with logograms, a graphic sign that stands for the word "cow," but the sign does not have the sound /cow/ (at least not yet). I have made no attempt to "record speech," but through the rebus have symbolized the man's name and through the resources of sounds in speech have recorded the important information "cow." I have also discovered the concept "word," which writing makes possible, because that is the thing attached to the sign: COW. Now we may expect a number to tell how many cows, recorded in a semasiographic system, strokes or impressions. That is how lexigraphic writing began.

The nonphonetic nature of the logogram, one of the bases for lexigraphic writing, is highly confusing and persistently difficult to grasp. There is *no necessary equivalent in the sounds of speech to a logogram*, although logograms stand for "words," that is, segments of speech with meaning. For example, the logographic Arabic numerals 1, 2, and 3 stand for whole words, in English *One*, *Two*, and *Three* (they do not stand for the "ideas" of unity, duality, and trinity). In German the same signs stand for *Eins, Zwei, Drei*. In Istanbul, they would be *Bir, Iki, Üç*. We might think of logograms as close to sematograms, because no necessary equivalent in sound is attached to either. But logograms represent *significant segments of speech* and sematograms do not – we will continue to call these segments "words" even if philologists cannot agree on what they are. The distinction between logogram and sematogram will be critical to our efforts to understand the theory and history of writing.

To add to the confusion, we can sometimes understand logograms without the intercession of segments of speech, just like sematograms, when the signs represent clearly what an unknown segment of speech might signify. For example, without knowing anything about ancient Egyptian speech it is easy to see that ⊙𓁛 refers to "the sun god," however the Egyptian might have pronounced the name of this god. It is the picture of a sun and the picture of what might be a god. Even if we can understand such signs in this way, they are nonetheless logograms that in history stood for the appropriate segments in the user's language (in this case ancient Egyptian). Sematograms, by contrast, do not stand for significant elements of speech, for "words," but for thoughts that have many possible, and no necessary, equivalent in speech (for example, how to uncrate a refrigerator).

Additional signs

Sometimes logograms are complex, consisting of more than one sign taken together, appearing in a conventional arrangement. Additional signs can add three types of information.

1   They can explain the category of sign. For example, in my own middle initial [B.] the [.] explains that the sign [B], which stands for the word /bē/, is an abbreviation. In the Egyptian writing for "sun" ⊙, the stroke beneath the disk indicates that the disk is a logogram (and not a phonogram).

2   Additional signs may also add phonetic information to the nonphonetic logogram; for example, in English [2nd] the [nd] makes clear that the logogram [2] is to be read not as the cardinal "two," but as the ordinal "second." Notice that the use of such elements, called *phonetic complements*, ties the logogram to a certain language, so that "12mo" instead of "twelve months," or "twelfth month," as an English-speaker might think, must be read as Italian *duodecimo*.

3   Additional signs may place the accompanying signs in a certain category. For example, English [$0.36] is "thirty-six cents" because the [$] tells us that the logogram [36] is to be understood in the category of accounting. In this example, as often, the order of the signs in a complex logogram does not follow the order of words in the corresponding expression.

In the Egyptian complex logogram ⊙𓁛 , the god sign shows that the god Re is meant and not the sun disk itself or something else related to the behavior of the sun disk. Such semasiographic additional signs as [$] or are *semantic complements* or *determinatives*, because they determine the category within which the accompanying signs must be understood. "Semantic complement" is a more scientific term, but "determinative" is long established. In modern European orthographies, capitalization can fulfill the same function as a semantic complement.

Phonography, the Second Division of Lexigraphy

Logograms refer to significant elements of speech, to "words," but in *phonography* ("sound-writing") the signs may refer to significant or non-significant elements of speech. When pronounced in sequence, such sounds provide hints about significant elements of speech, that is, words and phrases. Logographic writing does not require the same linear organization of signs. We would, for example, read the complex logographic

$M6.4

as

"six million four hundred thousand dollars" or "six point four million dollars"

wherein our verbal equivalent to the logograms [$] and [M] and [.] and [6] and [4] by no means follows the same order as the written signs. Nor does it when we render the logographic

♣ QJ82 ♥ A6

as

"queen, jack, eight, and two of clubs, and the ace and six of hearts."

In phonographic writing, by contrast, the *signs follow the same order as the sounds in human speech*, as in "now is the time for all good men to come to the aid of their country."

In history, as we have seen, phonograms ("sound-writings") have at some point acquired phonetic values through the rebus. Phonograms can refer to the smallest elements of speech, to vowels and consonants in alphabetic writing, or to single syllables or to several syllables in syllabic writing; but such phonetic signs are not semantically meaningful in and of themselves, as are the elements in speech to which logograms refer. When pronounced, their sound may refer to something meaningful, as /go/ means "go," but the sign itself does not signify "go," only its sound. In other words, phonograms are not in themselves meaningful: *phonograms have values but no significations*. In an example such as [B 4] = "before" the signs function as phonograms; written as [4 Bs] = "four letter Bs," the signs are logograms (except for the [s] after [B], which is a phonetic complement).

Syllabography and Alphabetic Writing, the Two Categories of Phonography

The two categories *syllabography* and *alphabetic writing* (which Gelb called *grammatography*) are distinguished by the kind of value to which the signs refer. Syllabograms refer to separately utterable but nonmeaningful elements of speech so that a single character may have the value /ba/, /be/, /bi/, /bo/, /bu/, or /ab/, /eb/, or /bab/, /beb/. A repertory of syllabograms is a *syllabary*. In alphabetic writing, by contrast – that is, in the Greek system and its many descendants – there are two categories of signs, one utterable (signs for vowels) and one nonutterable (signs for consonants). Both categories are called *letters*, which exist only in alphabetic writing. Characters in others systems should be called syllabograms or logograms. When combined in sequence, the two categories of letters, vowels and consonants, create graphic images of syllables and words. Letters can be simple, for example *g* or *r*, or by the addition of other letters or diacritic marks they can be complex, for example *th* or *é*. A repertory of alphabetic signs is an *alphabet* or, in historical studies, an *abecedarium*.

Unlike syllabograms, named by their value, letters have names that are different from their values. So [β] is called *beta* and B is called *bee*. In the example [B 4] = "before," the letters function as syllabograms, acquiring their phonetic value by the rebus through the names assigned to the signs.

A common mistake in traditional studies of writing is the belief that the Phoenician writing, which preceded the Greek, worked in the same way as the Greek alphabetic writing, that the Greek writing refined something that the Phoenician writing was already doing in a rather crude way. But the two systems did not work in the same way at all. The Greek letter forms are based on and closely resemble their West Semitic model, yet in structure the Greek alphabet was a radically different kind of writing from the West Semitic family, enabling different mental processes and standing in a different relationship to speech. The casual use of the word "alphabet" to describe both systems of writing disguises the innovation that took place c.800 BC and that has enabled deep change in human culture. One need remember that the Phoenician writing was unpronounceable except by a native speaker, who could only guess at oral equivalents to graphic marks. The Greek writing, by contrast, was pronounceable by someone who did not know the Greek language. By mistaking a historical relationship for identity of function, the word *letter* is casually applied to the signs of Phoenician and its related Aramaic, Hebrew, and other West Semitic scripts, but it should not be.

Auxiliary Signs and Devices

There are, then, three principal categories of lexigraphic signs:

logograms (nonphonetic, words)
syllabograms (syllables)
alphabetic signs (parts of syllables)

However, sematograms are rarely abandoned in systems that use these kinds of signs. Sematograms survive conspicuously in the "determinatives" or "semantic complements" that accompany logograms and syllabograms in ancient Egyptian and Mesopotamian writings, which place the accompanying word in a certain category. For example, as stated on page 42, in the Egyptian ⊙𓏺 𓀭 the bearded man places the word within the category "god."

In phonography we call one kind of auxiliary sign a *diacritical mark*, or *diacritic* (Greek "distinguishing"), something added to a sign to alter its sound. For example, in French *manque* is /mank/ and *manqué* is /mankay/. Such phonetic marks belong to a broader category of *auxiliary signs and devices* that assist the reader's perception of the organization of thought: periods or full-stops indicate the completion of a thought; commas indicate a unit of thought; colons divide a statement from its explanation or elaboration. Such kinds of signs do not constitute a category of writing in themselves but are auxiliary to the principal categories of logography, syllabography, and alphabetic writing.

Here are some examples of auxiliary signs and devices in English from our own experience of writing. In

green   Green

a change in shape of the initial letter changes the meaning from a color to the name of a person. In

hit   "hit"

the first word is a verb or noun and the second word is something to be talked about. In

quit now!   quit *now!*

the odd slant to the letters informs us of meaning through spoken emphasis not contained in the letters themselves. Students are often unsure of the difference between

its   it's

forgetting the meaning of the silent auxiliary mark [']. Through such auxiliary signs we might even distinguish social classes:

lightnin' 'Enry

or through special spelling, nationalities:

grey   gray

Formatting is a similar auxiliary device that aids comprehension. For example, white space between words (which the Greeks never used) indicates conventional word-boundaries, telling you how to look up the word in a dictionary. Indentation indicates a division of thought larger than a sentence. The color of the signs can mean various things. For example, the Egyptian scribe wrote in red and black: red for titles and section breaks, black for the text. The color is semantic, it tells you something.

Spelling Rules

In phonography, both syllabography and alphabetic writing, there are never enough signs for all the possible sounds of human speech, even in the already unwieldy IPA. By nature phonography must make harsh compromise between ideal vision and obdurate reality. For this reason evolve *spelling rules*, which, like auxiliary devices, enable the phonographic system to extend its reach and refine it. Hence in Italian *c* before *i* and *e* is /ch/ as in *ciao*, *civile*, but it is /k/ before *o* and *a*, as in *coca*. For the sound /k/ before *i* or *e* you must write [ch], as in *vecchio*, *che*. In English orthography, the final silent *e* can lengthen a preceding internal vowel:

hid   hide
mat   mate

In phonographic writing, spelling rules are the set of conventions that define the range of sounds that a sign may encode, depending on conditions, as well as the values of certain combinations of signs. In the Cypriote syllabary, used from c.1100 to 200 BC to record Greek solely on the island of Cyprus, there are no signs for sounds represented in the Greek alphabet as consonant clusters. Hence you write the name *Stasikypros* with signs we would transliterate as *sa-ta-si-ku-po-ro-se*, but in other contexts the same signs *sa-ta* could represent alphabetic *santa* and *po-ro-se* could represent alphabetic *poros*. The spelling rules permit this range.

Orthography

If the purpose of writing is to make a visible record of speech, then phonography is better than logography and alphabetic writing is the best of all. A disturbing feature of modern phonographic writing, especially of English and French, is the failure of its signs to reveal the sound of the word written in spite of spelling rules. So English orthography permits

THE BUCK DOES FUNNY THINGS WHEN THE DOES ARE PRESENT

or

THE SOLDIER DECIDED TO DESERT HIS DESSERT IN THE DESERT.

The following list of 13 items contains 15 verbs and 16 nouns:

bow cow dow how jow (to ring a bell) low mow now row sow tow vow wow!

In these cases, the same spelling yields many different pronunciations, hence different meanings, according to context. This is *polyphony*, common in systems of writing.

Just the opposite, words with the same pronunciation but different meaning can be spelled differently:

beau   bow
reed   read
read   red

This is *homophony*, also common in writing systems. In such cases the spelling is semantic, it communicates information: We know what it means not by how it sounds, but by how it is spelled. On this principle, inflated a trillionfold, is based Chinese writing.

Through orthographic convention other words become virtual logograms whose pronunciation, based on the recognition of shape and not on spelling rules, is learned on a case by case basis:

A ROUGH HICCOUGH PLOUGHED THROUGH A DOUGHY COUGH

Even such nonphonetically composed common words as "which," always pronounced as /hwich/, function as virtual logograms. Once I was unable to persuade a copyeditor, after much effort, that not only "which," but "whale" begins with the sound /h/. Such intimate, and in our own world unconscious, relationships between written forms and speech are powerful and explain the conservatism of spoken English since the invention of printing in the mid-fifteenth century and the spread of popular learning that printing made possible.

In many cases historical orthography, always a force in the history of writing, is to blame for the situation in English. We spell *knight* and say /nīt/, but once we said /kniht/. Other causes explain the formation of many English logograms; for example, the influence of intellectuals who inserted the *b* in *doubt* by analogy with Latin *dubitum*. The word has always been pronounced /dout/.

Many of the logograms that pepper English orthography return to the formalization of English orthography in the nineteenth century, especially in America by Noah Webster (1758–1843), who published his first dictionary in 1806, a good example of the influence of a single man on a tradition of writing. During that same year the personal secretary of the president of the United States, the brilliant and driven Meriwether Lewis (1774–1809), wrote on Saturday, February 1, in the journal to his expedition of discovery, according to his own published version:

> we found twenty seven of the best rifle powder, 4 of common rifle, three of glaized and one of the musqut powder in good order, perfectly as dry as when first put in the canesters, altho' the whole of it from various accedents has been for hours under the water. these cannesters contain four lbds. of powder each and 8 of lead.

The orthography is a mixture of logograms (4, lb, 8) and arbitrary alphabetic phoneticization in which nothing is standardized. The entry "lbds" is, first, an abbreviation of the Italian *libra* = [lb], but pronounced as English "pound*s*," as proved by the phonetic complement [ds]. Five generations of Noah Webster's "blue-backed speller" (*The American Spelling Book*, from 1783) put an end to such irregularities as we find in the *Journals* of Lewis and Clark, but froze into American orthography many examples of words whose pronunciation the linear sequence of signs does not reveal, "as everyone knows."

Disturbed by modern English orthographic practices, many have taken seriously the task of reforming the whole system. George Bernard Shaw created his own logical system of phonography, and gave an example of "All human beings are born free and equal in dignity and rights. They are endowed with reason and conscience and should act towards one another in a spirit of brotherhood" (= Article 1 of the Universal Declaration of Human Rights) (Fig. 3.2). Unfortunately such reformist projects ignore the fact that traditional and conventional usage is the essence of a writing system, pre-

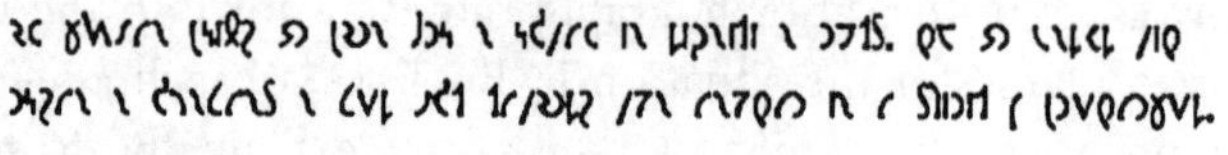

rc ȝʍ/ɾ ꞁɯꞁ? ꞅ ꞁɔʌ ʃʌ ʌ ʀc/ɾc ɾ ꞁꞁꞁʌɾ̃ ʌ ꞊ꞁ7ꞵ́. ꞅrc ꞅ ʌʟ̦ɢ̦ /ꞁꞵ
ᴣ?/ɾ ʌ ꞁꞁ̣ʟ̣/ɾꞨ ʌ ꞓʌʟ̦ ᴣ̣ꞁ ꞁr/ᴣʟ̣Ꞩ /7ʌ ꞁꞁ7ꞵꞁ ɾ ɾ Ꞁ̃ꞁꞁꞁꞁ ꞁ꞊꞊ꞁʌ.

Figure 3.2 Opening portion of Article 1 of the Universal Declaration of Human Rights written in George Bernard Shaw's "Shavian alphabet"

served by a social class or a social system that values a particular system. Orthography is part of traditional usage. To change such usage is to fail to communicate thought and information by graphic means. The trouble with Shaw's alphabet is that no one can read it.

4

Some General Issues in the Study of Writing

It is time to summarize and review the categories of writing and the main features of these categories.

1 *Semasiography*: Writing in which the signs are not attached to necessary forms of speech. *Sematograms*, the elements of semasiography, may be arranged in any conventional way.

2 *Lexigraphy*: Writing in which the signs are attached to necessary forms of speech. They are (usually) arranged in a linear sequence corresponding to sounds in speech. There are two divisions.

   (i) *Logography*: the signs represent words (but not sounds), significant segments of speech. A logography would be a system in which *logograms*, the elements of logography, predominate (sometimes logograms do not follow the same order as words in speech).

   (ii) *Phonography*: the signs represent sounds. Such sounds are ordinarily nonsignificant elements of speech. There are two kinds of phonographic systems.

     • *Syllabography*: the signs represent syllables, the smallest apprehensible elements of speech. A syllabography would be a system in which *syllabograms* predominate.

     • *Alphabetic writing*: the signs represent elements of speech smaller than syllables, although such sounds do not exist in nature as separable elements of speech. In alphabetic writing *letters* predominate.

Although this is a structural description, it is also a rough outline of the history of writing, understood as a technology that underwent broad and radical changes over millennia and came to serve ever more efficient and complex forms of communication and thought. The major changes were three.

First was the discovery of the phonetic principle, the representation of the sounds of speech by graphic means. This discovery appears to have been applied three times in a more or less systematic way: in southern Mesopotamia, in China, and in Mesoamerica. But all these systems are only partly phonetic.

The second major discovery was of a wholly phonetic writing. We cannot date the discovery, but perhaps as early as 1800 BC in the Near East and rather earlier in Crete, c.2100 BC (for the earliest "Cretan hieroglyphs"). While such writings are wholly phonetic, that is, most signs refer to sound and are not meaningful, they still cannot be pronounced except by a native speaker. Wholly phonetic writings made possible an immense constriction in the number of signs over the earlier logosyllabaries (made up of logograms and syllabograms) by focusing on a single semantic aspect of communication, namely sounds of the human voice speaking some "language." This advantageous constriction was gained at the loss of clarity provided by the many semantic nonphonetic elements of the earlier logosyllabaries.

The third major shift was the invention of the Greek alphabet around 800 BC, a system that atomized the sounds of human speech, utilized symbols for these sounds, and made possible the approximate reconstruction of the sound of human speech, even by someone who does not speak the language.

In studying the history of writing we must remember that a continuity of forms can mask an extreme shift in inner structure, while two sets of completely differing forms can function in the same way.

Strategies in the Formation of Lexigraphic Writing Systems

We may regard the tangled course of the history of lexigraphic writing as an ever-living response to the basic problem that speech and writing are different by nature, one invisible and transitory, the other material and lasting. For this reason the two systems can never match one another, but stand in an uncertain relationship. Imagine that one wished to invent a lexigraphic writing (as did the Cherokee Indian Sequoia, and many others). If you make up a different sign for every word, it quickly becomes unmanageable (or like the nightmarish logographic Chinese writing). Much better to assign multiple meanings to a single sign and thus reduce the inventory. You can write

I ♥ NEW YORK

or

MY ♥ LONGS 4 U

or

♥ Q10

in which the single logogram ♥ refers first to a word for a strong emotion, then to a word for the physical organ (though meant as the seat of emotions), then as a category in a game. Something rather like this actually happened in the early systems of writing in Egypt and Mesopotamia, as we will see.

Another way to limit the number of signs is to assign them different functions in accordance with how they are drawn. For example, [2^2] means "two-squared" or "two times two," though we would ordinarily understand its logographic representation directly without the intercession of any forms of speech. We can write [ix] as a logogram for "nine," but by adding the auxiliary sign [.] change the meaning to ordinal "ninth" [.ix]. Thus do auxiliary signs and devices make more flexible a limited repertory of signs and help ease the immense distance between speech and writing.

Another way to extend the range of a repertory of signs which we want to be broad but manageable is to invent the phonetic principle. By discarding the evident meaning of a logogram yet preserving the sound, then arranging the signs in sequential order we can create a material basis for an element in speech; for example,

B 4

or

or

   I M <red>E 2 C U

In using such devices, as do text-messagers the world over today, the writer has ceased to make use of singular logograms *meaningful in themselves*, as ♥ means "love" or "heart" or "the suit of hearts in a pack of cards," to use meaningful combinations of phonetic signs *meaningless by themselves*.

Writing and Play

Because writing is use of conventional signs in a conventional system as instruments in mental processes, writing is a form of thinking. Certain kinds of writing enable certain kinds of thinking. To illustrate the basic disjunction between lexigraphic writing, which appears to imitate speech but which can enable extremely fine forms of thought impossible in speech, and speech itself, governed by its own syntax and rules of expression, we might consider a random passage from *Finnegans Wake*, by the eccentric Irish author James Joyce:

> Of all the stranger things that ever not even in the hundrund and badst pageans of unthowsent and wonst nice or in eddas and oddes bokes of tomb, dyke and hollow to be have happened! (Joyce 1958: 4.15.597)

The alphabetic signs do not represent speech so much as they constitute things in their own right in a system partly self-contained, which means what it means (if it means anything) through hint and innuendo – of course, always in alliance with the resources of speech. When we read "in the hundrund and badst pageans of unthowsent and wonst nice," perhaps we think of "the hundreds and vast pages of the Thousand and One Nights" (of Scheherazade) but *pageans*, "pages," might be also "pageants" or "pagans." Joyce's *hundrund*" looks like German for "dog-round," but why? *badst* "vast" may also be "worst," no doubt to be taken with pagans, and *wonst nice* should be also "once nice," as opposed to *badst*. The *eddas* and *oddes bokes of tombs* are "odds and ends," but also the Norwegian Eddas of Snorri Sturulson (twelfth century AD) . . . and perhaps the medieval Domesday Book, on which a further pun could be Dome = Doom . . .

A less random example makes explicit Joyce's indebtedness to the powers of the alphabet to enable certain forms of thought:

> "(Stoop) if you are abcedminded, to this claybook, what curios of signs (pleasestoop), in this allaphbed! Can you rede (since We and Thou had it out already) its world? It is the same told of all. Many." (Joyce 1958: 1.1.18)

Perhaps he means that if you approach his story as the Greeks taught us, as an orderly narrative ("abcedminded"), with things coming in a row like the ABCs in an abecedarium, you will not fare well with *Finnegans Wake*. So give it up now (*Stoop* = "stop," but also "condescend"), for alphabetic logic won't help because you will have to get down to earth ("this claybook"), off your high horse, and alter your expectations. The Semitic names *alep, beth* are invoked in *allaphbed*, but somebody is in bed too, maybe "reding"? *Rede* is an old word for "advice" . . . one cannot "rede" *Finnegans Wake* from beginning to end because the book is a loop in which the end joins the beginning. You can jump in anywhere, as if you were on the Internet. All possible plots here come together ("the same told of all"), maybe. If you are too logical, you will never understand the stories of man that this book encloses.

The reader has to supply most of the jokes and worry about the allusions and philosophize about what it all might mean, which makes "reding" the book tough going. Many say that *Finnegans Wake* is written in a special or private "language," and one is not sure that *Finnegans Wake* has preserved the common reference we expect from our definition of writing. The close alliance between a late form of the Greek alphabet, our own, and speech makes such jokes and multiple meanings possible, while revealing the arbitrary and conventional nature of alphabetic representation.

Similar exaggerated literary forms appeared in Egypt in the perversely complex, enigmatic hieroglyphic writing of the Ptolemaic Period (where a picture of a "head" could mean the "number seven," because there are seven openings in the head), and in the *technopaignia* of the Greek Hellenistic period, when poets composed poems in the form of pan-pipes or an egg or a pair of wings or an altar. The vocabulary of these poems is obscure in the extreme, as are references to scarcely known facts of myth, and the learned, playful distortion of straightforward expressions. For example, Telemachus becomes "son of No Man," referring to Odysseus's adventure with the cyclops Polyphemus, where he tricks the giant by giving his name as No Man. They are scarcely intelligible as narrative of any kind, but are puzzles, whose solution is in some way encoded in the poems' shapes. Like Joyce, they are games, conundrums, "a playing with poetic skill," as we may translate *technopaignion*.

While such antics as *Finnegans Wake* and the Greek *technopaignia* prove the inadequacy of definitions of writing that view it as a secondary representation of a primary speech, they are also signs of the end of an epoch in the history of written expression. Joyce's punning, allusive, elusive exclamations use the resources of speech and a tradition of writing, but exist in an expressive system parallel to speech. Such has always been true of all forms of writing, including alphabetic writing.

Because greater complexity better expresses the conventional nature of all writing, traditions of writing tend to become more complex over time, as we noted earlier. In the hands of scribes and the intelligentsia, we are given the Egyptian enigmatic hieroglyphs or the Greek *technopaignia* or James Joyce's obsession with puns and his solipsistic indifference to the pleasures of an audience making use of an alphabetic tradition.

"You Have a Lovely Hand": Writing and Beauty

Gelb's three categories of the "forerunners of writing" (pages 20–32) are all, in their way, forms of what we might call art, that is, they are pictures. Gelb thought, as have many, that "writing" began with pictures, although that is not quite what happened. Writing has a reader (information is communicated) while art has an observer (form is enjoyed), so they are different things, but art and writing are close nonetheless. You observe the form of writing too, and art can tell you something. In Egypt, where one of the earliest writings flourished, one can scarcely separate the illustrator from the scribe. For example, a formulaic stela from the Sixth Dynasty, c.2200 BC, shows a table of offerings before a certain nobleman by the name of Sarennewtet (Fig. 4.1; for more on this stele see Chapter 9). The writing above the table explicates the offering. The purpose of the stela is to ensure the feeding of the *ka* of the dead man, his essence, and we can translate the writing as "An offering that the king gives to Osiris [that is, the dead Sarennewtet], lord of Djedu [a place in the delta], the great god, lord of Abydos [center of the god's cult]. May he [the king] grant one thousand of bread (⬭), beer (⬭), beef (⬭), poultry (⬭), alabaster, linen,

Figure 4.1 Stela of Sarennewtet, Sixth Dynasty, c.2200 BC. Carved limestone. (London, British Museum EA 585; drawing after Collier and Manley 1998, p. 48.)

every good thing from which the god [that is, Osiris/Sarennewtet] draws life, the revered one, the grantor of divine offerings of the gods, the counter of the two granaries, the master of the house, Sarennewtet, true of voice [that is, acquitted of wrongdoing in the hall of Osiris], son of Bameket."

The hieroglyphic signs for the staple foods bread $\bigcap$, beer $\ominus$, beef

$\underset{\smile}{\cancel{W}}$, and poultry $\stackrel{\frown}{\supset}$ closely replicate the pictures of produce on and

below the table: loaves of bread (but more elongated in shape), a jug of beer, beef (a leg of beef is on the table too), and fowl. A hieroglyph "seated

man with flail" $\stackrel{\mathbb{R}}{\digamma}$ represents the human figure and the chair in which

he sits in the same posture as Sarennewtet on the stela – his portrait is a kind of character in Egyptian hieroglyphic writing. Egyptian art and the highly iconic Egyptian hieroglyphic writing (but there were other forms:

Figure 4.2 Calligraphic medallion in Santa Sofia, Istanbul, containing a verse from the Quran

see Chapter 9) play back and forth between each other constantly and ingeniously. But the one kind of signs, the hieroglyphs, is lexigraphy, writing associated with elements of speech, and the other is art, with the magical purpose in this case of creating the object represented.

Legion are the apologists for the artistic aspects of systems of writing, but they open themselves to criticism on the grounds that calligraphy works to keep the secrets of writing within a restricted social class, often priestly. For example, Figure 4.2, a nineteenth-century medallion in Santa Sofia, Istanbul, typically encodes a verse from the Quran and possesses magical power for those who think in such terms, but in no sense can or ought one read it, except as a kind of puzzle: Its power lies in the artistic excellence of its curves and twists and flourishes, all that remains for artistic visual expression within the puritanical and iconoclastic Islamic tradition. Even Chairman Mao, who murdered millions, prided himself on the elegant refinements of his beautiful hand.

Art and writing are inextricably entwined, but each has different origins and purpose. The more phonetic a system of writing becomes, the less inclined it is to calligraphic distortions, with the exception of the West Semitic Arabic script within the Islamic context. In the ancient world the other wholly phonetic West Semitic writings (Phoenician, Moabite, Hebrew, Aramaic), then the Greek alphabet showed little susceptibility to exaggerated calligraphic forms.

5

Protocuneiform and Counting Tokens

Good evidence that lexigraphic writing did not "come from pictures" but emerged in the context of a preexistent accounting system comes from clay semasiographic and logographic accounting tablets from late fourth millennium Uruk in what is today southern Iraq (see Map 1 in Chapter 6). The tablets are called "protocuneiform" because the *cuneiform* "wedge-shaped" writing that dominated the Near East for three thousand years grew directly from it. The renowned Gilgamesh was king of Uruk c.2600 BC (as given in surviving king-lists). According to the poem preserved in the library of Assurbanipal at Nineveh, destroyed in 612 BC, the hero

> carved on a stone stela all of his labors,
> and built the walls of Uruk,
> the walls of the sacred Eanna Temple, the holy sanctuary.
>
> *Gilgamesh*, Tablet 1, 8–10

Dates are shaky for the around 5,000 surviving protocuneiform tablets because they were found in a disturbed context, but they belong to c.3500–3100 BC. Their find spot seems to have been within the temple precinct of Eanna dedicated to the sky-god Anu and the fertility goddess Inanna in Uruk, the very temple on which Gilgamesh erected his inscribed stela.

The excavators' strata that contained the protocuneiform tablets are numbered III and IV, stratum IV being the older. The tablets from Uruk IV are unique to Uruk and appear to be close to the time of the invention of the system that was to become cuneiform writing, according to some the oldest lexigraphic writing in the world (but others doubt the ascription of phonetic value to protocuneiform signs). Tablets similar to those in Uruk III are found in several other locations in southern Mesopotamia, and a related writing appears at this time at Susa in Elam in southwestern Iran (the modern Iranian oilfields). In its long run of cultural dominance, cuneiform writing was to encode 15 languages in an immense arc stretching from Anatolia to Iran, from the Black Sea to Arabia. Some of these languages were Indo-European (Old Persian, Hittite), some Semitic (Akkadian, Amorite), and some isolates of unknown affinity (the original Sumerian, Elamite, Hurrian). It was one of the greatest and most successful of all human technologies.

The Protocuneiform Tablets of Uruk III and IV

Figure 5.1 is an example of a protocuneiform tablet from Uruk IV. The marks on the tablet are divided into "cases," rectangular boxes that segregate the groups of signs. In the drawing, the signs on the tablet are transcribed at the sides of the drawings of the tablet. The semicircular impressions within the cases on the obverse 𒁹, made by holding a

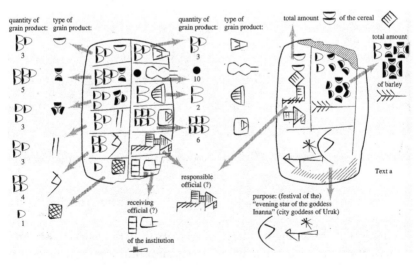

Figure 5.1 Drawing of a protocuneiform tablet from Uruk IV. (After H. J. Nissen, P. Damerow, R. Englund 1993, fig. 32.)

stylus at an angle and impressing its end into the clay, represent single units. The solid circle in the next to upper-right case ●, made by impressing the stylus vertically into the clay, represents 10 units. The other signs in the cases must represent commodities (but are not pictures of them), apparently different kinds of grain products.

The second to last case in the lower right-hand column contains different

kinds of signs , perhaps the name of an official. The name,

if it is a name, makes clear how a phonetic script will support this economy of redistribution, informing us who is involved in the transaction. In the lowest right-hand case, perhaps the first two of the three signs

, one of them a head on its side, refers to the receiving official, and the third, lowest sign may refer to the institution he represents.

The reverse of the tablet appears to give the total of some kind of cereal and of barley needed to produce the products on the other side, though we cannot reconstruct how these sums were reached or, because of the complexity of counting systems in protocuneiform, even what the sums are; for different commodities Sumerian scribes used different systems of

counting. Evidently "10" units of the cereal is meant (but why 2×5

and not ● = 10?) and a quantity of barley .

Again, in the upper left-hand case on the reverse side, are signs for the official and, at the bottom, more or less intelligible, a star ✳ that we understand from later cuneiform as standing for "goddess." Beneath that is the sign for Inanna , the powerful Mesopotamian goddess of

fertility, and finally the sign for "day" , but here referring to the

"evening star" according to a team of scholars in Berlin working on these tablets: Such and such a quantity of barley and some cereal are needed to produce the baked (?) products listed on the other side, in preparation for a festival of the goddess Inanna, who is the Evening Star.

Are these signs semasiographic or lexigraphic? The signs in the cases do not come in a linear order; they can be arranged in almost any order. In lexigraphy we ordinarily expect signs arranged in the same order as the elements of speech to which they correspond. Nonetheless, if the "barley" sign ⟩⟩⟩⟩—— is a logogram for *barley* in some language, as seems probable, it is already lexigraphic writing, because logography is a form of lexigraphy.

The same ambiguity of function attaches to the commodity and other signs. For example, the signs ⊳ = "type of grain product," ⟨⟩ = "day," and "Inanna" ⟨⊤⟨ = "Inanna" could be logograms, standing for words and names. We wish we knew more about how the signs for officials are working, if that is what they are – for example, ⊞ᶮ – but we cannot place them in a system of markings with conventional phonetic value; they are unique. In trying to understand the protocuneiform tablets we seem to stand between semasiographic and lexigraphic writing, with signs that stand for words, a form of lexigraphy, but no clear assignment of phonetic elements in speech to graphic signs.

Context for Protocuneiform Writing

The undoubted economic character of the protocuneiform tablets has colored general histories of writing, suggesting that all writing has appeared in response to economic behavior. In Mesoamerica, however, writing principally celebrated rulers. Early Egyptian writing also typically glorified the king, although recent finds may be economic in nature. In China the earliest lexigraphic writings, from c.1200 BC, are oracular, to reveal the will of the invisible spirits; some Sumerologists have suggested similar motives in the devising of cuneiform by the oracle-obsessed Mesopotamians. Certainly the Greek alphabet did not serve economic needs for three hundred years after its invention, and no evidence survives that the West Semitic writings, including Phoenician, enabled the keeping of economic records. Of course, the Sumerians were writing on imperishable clay,

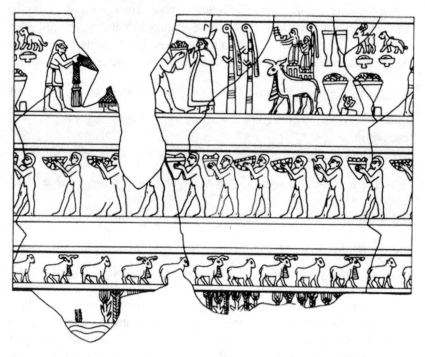

Figure 5.2   Sculpture on a stone vase from Uruk, c.3500–3000 BC. (Drawing after André Parrot, *Sumer*, Paris 1960, fig. 89.)

whereas other traditions preferred a perishable medium, including the West Semitic, so evidence for early economic application of lexigraphic writing may simply be lost.

In any event, in Sumer, where the West began, the scribes worked within an accounting system whose general functioning an extraordinary vase from Uruk nicely illustrates (see Fig. 5.2). This famous vase, one of the earliest relief sculptures in the world, is contemporaneous with the protocuneiform tablets and was found within the same temple precinct. Three feet high and weighing 600 pounds, the large vase was looted during the American/Allied invasion of Iraq in 2003, then returned in the trunk of a car, broken into pieces. From bottom to top appear, in alternating registers, first grain crops, then domestic animals, then naked men carrying baskets of produce, then in the lost portion the king (called the *En*) preceded by a naked priest in the presence of Inanna. This must be her temple, where she is represented by the "ring-post signs," , door posts

for a structure made of reeds with a ring at the top. The ring-post = Inanna

appears on the accounting tablet in a stylized form ⟨⊤⊸. Produce

consisting of livestock and baskets of grains are being brought to the temple, the structure on top of which two votaries stand, and again the ring-post symbol for the goddess. Perhaps the ram, goat, cheetah, and vases behind the standards, but turned toward them, represent produce already within the temple precinct, near where the protocuneiform accounting tablets were found.

Naked votaries bring produce and livestock to the building as if in offering to the goddess, whose province is richness. The men's nakedness may refer to a ritual of sacred marriage, or place the offerings in a context of sexual reproduction. These commodities the authority of the En will redistribute according to service and need in the new redistributive economy of southern Mesopotamia, dependent on sedentary populations, irrigation agriculture, new craft technologies, and a system of written accounting. In this brave new world of wealth and power the tasks imposed on information storage have multiplied a thousandfold. On the one hand is the Uruk vase, which tells a kind of story in pictures, but includes the sign for Inanna, and on the other, contemporary clay tablets present abstract noniconic signs that represent commodities, office, festival, and personal names. They may all be logograms: signs that stand for words in speech. The "star" on

the protocuneiform tablet ✳ (lowest right-hand case of the reverse) seems

to mean "goddess," but is not the picture of a goddess. It may be a sematogram, placing the "ring-post" in a category, that is, a determinative or semantic complement. The ring-post on the tablet derives from a picture of bundled reeds, but it means "Inanna"; the sign must be a logogram. We have pictures of things we recognize that stand for something else (the star, the ring-post), and pictures of things we do not recognize (the commodities, the names, if they are names). Lexigraphic writing has not begun as pictures that somehow became something else, but as a complex system of signs most abstract, some iconic, that refer to elements of speech. These signs relate to each other according to conventional rules in order to communicate information.

Figure 5.3 Plain tokens, found in Tepe Gawra, Iraq, c.4000 BC. The cone, spheres, and disk may stand for various grain measures, and the tetrahedron for a unit of labor, according to D. Schmandt-Besserat. (Courtesy Denise Schmandt-Besserat, The University of Texas at Austin.)

The Tokens of Denise Schmandt-Besserat

The Texas scholar Denise Schmandt-Besserat has offered apparent confirmation of the noniconic origin for signs in the earliest lexigraphic writing. Evidently both the form and meaning of *some* of the protocuneiform signs descend directly from a much older use of geometrically shaped clay tokens found over a large area of the Middle East, including Palestine, Syria, Mesopotamia, Anatolia, Arabia, and eastern Iran (but not Egypt) from as early as 8000 BC (see Fig. 5.3). The tokens are found in ever-increasing numbers down to the time of the protocuneiform tablets, when around 3400 BC they gradually disappear. In the fifth millennium in Uruk (but later, around 3400 BC, in Iran and Syria), in union with an increasing complexity of urban life, originally *plain* tokens became *complex*, with striations and other alterations. Some complex tokens are perforated, as if to be strung on a cord or string (see Fig. 5.4).

Schmandt-Besserat plausibly explains these objects, once ignored or discarded by archaeologists, as representing quantities or commodities in some kind of accounting system, though we can rarely or never be sure which quantities or commodities are meant (but Schmandt-Besserat attempts to explain various forms by referring to later cuneiform usage as standing for sheep, units of oil and grain, units of metal, types of garment, a measure of honey, and other commodities). Critics have disagreed with Schmandt-Besserat's combining token-shapes from different sites and

Figure 5.4 Complex tokens representing (above, from right to left) one sheep, one unit of a particular oil, one ingot of metal, one garment; (below, from right to left) one garment, (?), one honeycomb, according to Denise Schmandt-Besserat, from Susa, Iran, c.3300 BC. (Musée du Louvre, Départment des Antiquités Orientales, Paris; photograph, courtesy of Denise Schmandt-Besserat.)

periods in order to form her categories, but there must have been some way of keeping track of the grain, animals, and cloth deposited in the temple of Inanna and such places, and the tokens may well have represented commodities. What else could these ubiquitous objects be? Of the tokens found in Uruk, 85 percent were found in the temple precinct of Inanna.

Some continuity between this hypothetical system of preliterate accounting and the protocuneiform and later cuneiform tablets appears probable from the practice, beginning around 3500 BC, of enclosing a quantity of plain tokens within a clay ball, or *bulla*, a kind of envelope that prevented the objects from being tampered with. The uniquely Mesopotamian cylinder seal appears around this time, a cylinder made of a usually hard stone with an abstract or figurative design cut in reverse on the outside and a hole down the center so the scribe could carry it on a

Figure 5.5   Envelope showing the imprints of cones and discs, from Susa, Iran, c.3300 BC bearing impressed markings similar to the tokens that were inside. (Musée du Louvre, Départment des Antiquités Orientales, Paris; photograph, courtesy of Denise Schmandt-Besserat.)

string around his neck. Much of what we know about Mesopotamian art and religion comes from designs on these miniature works of art. Rolled across clay bullae, the cylinder seal asserted the identity of the person or office involved or a place of origin. Later, the cylinder seal will often bear the name of the official or place in phonetic characters; possession of a cylinder seal was the privilege of the scribal elite.

In order to record the contents of the bulla without having to break it, the practice appears to have evolved of impressing the actual tokens into the surface of the bulla before sealing it (Fig. 5.5). Such practice allowed for the subsequent abandonment of the envelope and its contents as unnecessary; the shapes of tokens inscribed in clay replaced the tokens themselves. The plain tokens may stand behind characters for quantities on the protocuneiform tablets, for example, the circle for 10 in Figure 5.1, ●, may derive its shape from the base of a common token in the form of a cone. The complex tokens may have become the basis for the proto-cuneiform signs of some commodities. In figure 5.6 token shapes are given in the left-hand column. The middle column gives analogous impressions in clay, and the third column gives meanings established from later traditions. Although we have pictures of things that stand for what they look like – stylized cows and dogs – the purely geometric signs are older. From the use of tokens enclosed in clay bullae appears to descend the use of clay as the medium of writing in Mesopotamia, a substance always abundant on the shores of the Tigris and Euphrates rivers, but never as practical to store and transport as the Egyptian papyrus scrolls.

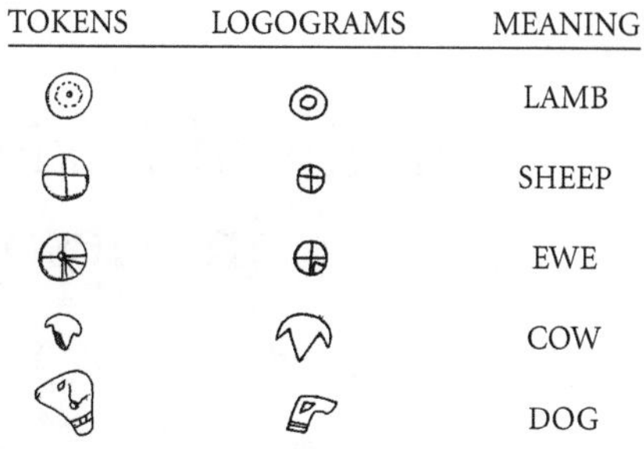

The impressed bullae that contain tokens are critical to testing Schmandt-Besserat's theory that cuneiform lexigraphic writing in some way descended from prehistoric tokens, because they are direct evidence of the translation of a three-dimensional tangible object into a two-dimensional marking.

TOKENS	LOGOGRAMS	MEANING
		LAMB
		SHEEP
		EWE
		COW
		DOG

Figure 5.6 Tokens and protocuneiform signs evidently based on them

However, the unfortunate shortsightedness of museum curators who have been unwilling to break the 80 surviving unopened examples in order to test the theory means her argument rests on only a few sure examples. Only one complex token has ever been found inside a ball. Also open to criticism is Schmandt-Besserat's view that the tokens constituted an internationally recognized Neolithic system of accounting, in which the same shapes had similar values in different regions. Probably they changed over time and were different in different places, making it impossible to draw conclusions based on statistical evidence of numbers of certain kinds of tokens. Certainly it is odd that tokens are not found in Egypt.

Nonetheless, the evidence is strong for continuity between the prehistoric use of tokens and the system of accounting on clay so prominent in Mesopotamia and its cultural admirers. Of course tokens are not writing. What cataclysmic discovery took place to separate their use from the first lexigraphic writing?

6

Origin of Lexigraphic Writing in Mesopotamia

Map 1   Places important in Chapter 6

According to evidence from the protocuneiform tablets, at the moment when marks are about to acquire a conventional reference within human speech, at the moment of the discovery of lexigraphy, signs have different origins (Fig. 6.1). Some (1) are conventionalized sketches of the things they look like, fish, snakes, and oxen; alternatively (2) they symbolize something, as the sign for Inanna; or (3) they depend on a primordial accounting system within which abstract shapes represent commodities: The crossed circle, a common token design, appears to stand for "sheep." We cannot be sure of the nature of these signs, but many appear already to be logograms, referring to the words "fish," "snake," "oxen," "Inanna," and "sheep" in some language. Several early phonetic complements seem to indicate that this underlying language was Sumerian (not all scholars agree).

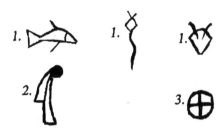

Figure 6.1   Five signs from protocuneiform

Discovery of the Phonetic Principle

Certainly "words" in Sumerian speech were at some time attached to such signs and from these attachments, through the rebus, logographic signs acquired phonetic value to become the world's first syllabograms (Fig. 6.2). For example, the protocuneiform design of a human head may have begun as a logogram for a word meaning "head," then, through the rebus, acquired the sound value /sag/, the Sumerian word for "head." The shift from logogram to syllabogram did not happen by itself but from invention, and over several hundred years, when individual scribes acted on their understanding of the advantages of marks that encode sounds and not number, people, or things. The initial discovery, made once, undoubtedly by one man, probably living in Uruk, enabled the gradual development of a logosyllabic writing in which logograms express nouns, verbs, and adjectives and phonetic signs express affixes, particles, and the spelling of foreign names. As for the form of the characters, we can trace the progressive stylization of protocuneiform characters encouraged by writing with a stylus impressed in clay (Fig. 6.3). Some of the shifts in form are substantial, as in from 2→3 and 3→4 in the evolution of SAG in Figure 6.3 (by convention the scholarly names of cuneiform signs are written in CAPS, as TI.).

We cannot determine precisely when this shift from logogram to syllabogram took place, but a good example of early phoneticization appears on tablets from the strata of URUK III, about 3100–2900 BC: The sign for

arrow △, which in Sumerian is called TI with the value /ti/, is used to

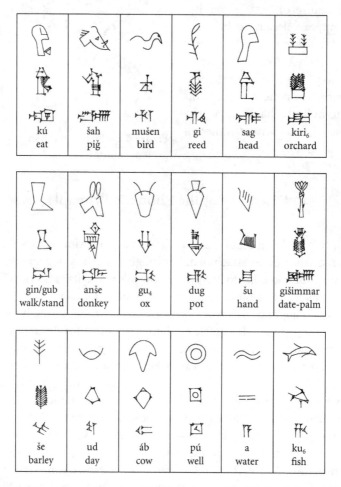

Figure 6.2   Cuneiform signs showing, from top to bottom in each case, first the form in protocuneiform, c.3300 BC; then the form in early cuneiform, c.2400 BC; then the Late Assyrian form, c.650 BC, the signs now turned 90 degrees to the left; then the syllabic value; and finally the meaning. The subscripts (as in *gu₄*) distinguish this sign from other signs that have the same phonetic value (called homophones). (After C.B.F. Walker, 1990, pl. 4, p. 20.)

represent the unrelated but phonetically similar Sumerian word /til/ meaning "life" and /ti/ meaning "rib" through the rebus. What are probably earlier examples of phoneticization come from the deeper Uruk IV layers, where /men/ = Sumerian for "crown" is written with the sign for

Figure 6.3 Seven stages in the evolution of the Sumerian sign SAG = "head," from c.3400 to c.500 BC. (After S. N. Kramer, 1981, p. xxiii.)

crown plus what appears to be a phonetic indicator /en/; or the moon-god Sin is written phonetically as /su/ + /en/. The sign for "reed," GI, is common in archaic texts to express the Sumerian homonym /gi/ = "to render, to deliver." We guess that the dropping of semantic value while preserving the phonetic value of logograms, as in /ti/ = "arrow" used for /til/ = "life," or /gi/ = "reed" for /gi/ = "render," depended on the need in the enlarging economy of fourth-millennium Mesopotamia to record the names of people and places, where the produce was coming from, who was receiving it at the temple and palace, and who was protecting it from theft. Accordingly, early examples of phonetic signs indicating such grammatical relationships as subject and verb by means of affixes are rare. The first full name written phonetically appears to be that of MES-KA-LAM-DUG on a gold bowl from Ur, c.2700 BC: The written name insures the lasting presence of the man. About the same time, four or five hundred years after the invention of protocuneiform, we find an attempt to render grammatical affixes phonetically, hence to fashion a structure of meaning parallel to that in speech. The first clear examples of such expression come from c.2700–2600 BC, inscribed on statues, in the shape of "PROPER NAME, son of PROPER NAME, king of X, gives this statue to SOME GOD for life." Thus will the dedicator live forever in the ambience of the divine power. By c.2400 BC we find longer texts whose signs follow the same sequence as the elements of speech. From this period come the earliest letters and "literary" compositions.

The Discovery and Decipherment of Cuneiform

European travelers even in the seventeenth century reported finds of an unknown script written on stone in impressive ruins in what is now southern Iran, but nobody could make anything of such reports. Then

Figure 6.4   The Behistun inscriptions, western Iran, a drawing by the French traveler and architect Pascal Coste of the pass through the Zagros range and the lengthy Persian proclamation high above it, c.1840

in the nineteenth century a German scholar named Georg Friedrich Grotefend (1775–1853), believing the ruins to be those of PERSEPOLIS, a capital of the Achaemenid Persian Empire (550–330 BC), attempted to find phonetic values for several of the signs by searching for titles like "king of kings," which one might expect to find in an inscription, and for Persian royal names like Hystaspes, Darius, and Xerxes, known from classical writers. Astutely he guessed where these names might appear in the few published inscriptions and discovered the phonetic values of several signs. Because of the paucity of texts he could not carry his discoveries further.

Others refined the work of Grotefend, but it was for a British army major Henry Rawlinson (1810–95) to continue the decipherment of what we now call Old Persian cuneiform. In 1835 he found the BEHISTUN inscriptions high on a commanding rock in the foothills of the ZAGROS range that separates the lowlands of Mesopotamia from the Iranian plateau (see Fig. 6.4).

The immense panels of inscriptions were carved three hundred feet above the road that led down from the plateau to the Great King of Persia's possessions on the plains of Mesopotamia. We are not sure how the inscriptions were carved in this inaccessible position. At great risk to life and limb, Rawlinson scaled the sheer cliff and made paper impressions of a large body of material.

The cuneiform texts were evidently carved in three separate languages, one being the Indo-European Old Persian that Grotefend worked on. There were 15,000 characters in the Old Persian text alone. With the abundant new material, Rawlinson quickly decoded most of the Old Persian text, showing the script to consist of 36 syllabic signs and 7 or 8 logograms. Three of the signs are pure vowels and the others are consonants + /a/ or, for another vowel, sometimes used in combination with one of the three signs for pure vowels. Apparently the inventor is modeling his system on the West Semitic Aramaic writing in which the signs stand for a consonant and an unexpressed vowel (see Chapter 12), although with features borrowed from Mesopotamian cuneiform (the signs for vowels, the logograms). The limited number of signs, most of them phonetic, made the decipherment by sound-substitution possible. In 1846, in the *Journal of the Royal Asiatic Society*, Rawlinson translated the beginning of the text as (š = /sh/, â is a long /a/):

> I am Dârayavauš [Darius] the king, son of Vištâspa [Hystaspes], of the Hakhâmanisiya [Achaemenid] dynasty, king of kings. I am king in Pârsa [Persia]. My father is Vištâspa. Vištâspa's father is Aršâma [Arsames], Aršâma's father was Ariyâramna [Ariaramnes], Ariyâramna's father was Cišpiš [Teispes], and Cišpiš' father was Hakhâmaniš [Achaemenes].

The names corresponded surprisingly closely to those given by the Greek historian Herodotus (fifth century BC) to describe the family of King Darius of Persia (522–486 BC).

The decipherment of cuneiform was the first decipherment of an ancient script without the assistance of a bilingual, but once the meaning of the Old Persian text was known, Rawlinson was able to find the same names in the longer of the two undeciphered texts and gradually to understand its phonology. This writing was a form of "Mesopotamian cuneiform," a general term to refer to a single system with numerous local varieties. A Sumerian scribe such as those who made the protocuneiform tablets invented the system in the late fourth millennium ("Sumerian cuneiform"), then around 2500 BC Semitic speakers applied it to a Semitic dialect spoken in the territory of Akkad somewhere on the mid-Euphrates River ("Akkadian cuneiform"); the site of Akkad is unknown. Later phases of the tradition, each with local variations, were "Assyrian cuneiform" from the courts of the Assyrian kings (second–first millennia) and "Babylonian cuneiform" from the courts of the Babylonian kings (second–first millennia). In this book, "Mesopotamian cuneiform" will include all of these varieties, but not the syllabic Old Persian cuneiform or the similarly unrelated "Ugaritic cuneiform alphabet" (see Chapter 7).

Rawlinson quickly discovered that Mesopotamian cuneiform was a completely different kind of writing from the Old Persian. The script proved to be in a Semitic language and to contain many nonphonetic semasiographic symbols. Evidently the Old Persian syllabic script was a free invention of the Persian court under Darius I (ruled c.520–486 BC), on completely different principles from Mesopotamian cuneiform, but using the ancient Mesopotamian technique of making characters from wedge-shapes like those impressed by a stylus into clay. Few examples of Old Persian survive, and the writing disappeared with Alexander's destruction of the Persian Empire in the fourth century BC. Old Persian cuneiform has no direct connection with the far older Mesopotamian cuneiform.

We do not know Rawlinson's exact sequence of decipherment because he never published it. The decipherment was furthered rapidly by the discovery of the Assyrian capital of NINEVEH on the upper Tigris in 1842. Among its many treasures were the remains of the great royal library of Assurbanipal (c.685–627 BC) containing tens of thousands of baked clay tablets covered with cuneiform inscriptions. In 1857 so much progress had been made in the decipherment that, to test it, Rawlinson and three other scholars submitted to a committee independent translations of a newly discovered inscribed column from Nineveh. The translations were similar.

The third cuneiform text on the Behistun inscription proved to be in Elamite, a language unrelated to any other known language. We can tell what it means from the two accompanying texts, but we cannot read it.

Logosyllabic Cuneiform Writing

Once discovered, the phonetic principle, applied systematically, tied writing to speech in a rough and ready way. Mesopotamian cuneiform writing was conditioned by linguistic features of the Sumerian language. Sumerian is an agglutinative language, like modern Turkish, whereby each fundamental concept, nominal or verbal, is usually expressed by a single unchanging syllable, to which can be added prefixes and suffixes. Sometimes English works that way too, as in our word "man-li-ness," made up of the syllable "man," a thing; "li," a suffix meaning "like"; and a second suffix, "ness," meaning "the quality of."

Because of these features of the Sumerian speech, Sumerian phonographic signs came out mostly as monosyllabic syllabograms with the shape simple V (vowel), CV (consonant + vowel), VC (vowel + consonant), or CVC. Only four vocalic qualities are marked: /a/, /e/, /i/, /u/, but not /o/. Eventually not only names of people, things, and places were written out syllabically, but early syllabograms began to designate grammatical relationships.

We count about 1,200 signs in protocuneiform from around 3400–3200 BC, which may qualify it as a purely logographic system, although many (including I. J. Gelb) have denied that a wholly logographic script ever existed. In fact, rare signs of phoneticization do appear in the earliest texts. If we nonetheless call protocuneiform a logography, we might say that the intellectual world of Sumerian administrators was restricted to around 1,200 items, a significant repertory. By 2800 BC, when the system of syllabograms was well established, the signary was reduced to around 600 signs, a number that remained average for the next 2,500 years in standard cuneiform script (Fig. 6.5).

There was nothing mechanical or inevitable about the discovery of the phonetic principle or its combination with the sematograms and already lexigraphic logograms of protocuneiform in order to create the world's earliest *logosyllabic system* of writing. We must imagine an inventor, someone who first saw how, through the rebus, to tie writing to the sounds of speech; others developed the system over many generations. Logosyllabic writing is a combination of logograms (nonphonetic "word-signs"), syllabograms (the smallest pronounceable elements of speech), and determinatives (or semantic complements, a kind of sematogram). Such semantic classifiers do not have phonetic value and do not stand for words, but place the intended expression in a certain category, as the "star" on the protocuneiform tablet (Fig. 5.1) placed Inanna among the gods. The inventor must consciously have sought out a usable phonetic repertory assisted by the older semasiography and logography. New logograms and determinatives then appeared to accompany an evolving phonetic repertory, many of them iconic

Figure 6.5   Tablet from the most complete version of the Gilgamesh epic in standard Akkadian cuneiform script, found in the library of Assurbanipal in Nineveh, who ruled c.668–630 BC. On this tablet Utnapishtim tells Gilgamesh how he escaped the great Flood. George Smith published the tablet in 1872. (London, British Museum BM K 3375.)

unlike the older abstract commodity signs of the prehistoric tokens. Some shapes from the earlier tokens came into the system. Wet clay, the substance of the prehistoric impressed bullae, remained the material basis. Logograms mixed in with syllabic signs standing for open and closed syllables and for the vowels /a/, /e/, /i/, /u/ were to remain the basic structure of cuneiform writing throughout its thee thousand year history, during which it was applied to the language of the Semitic Akkadians (third millennium), Babylonians (second–first millennium), and Assyrians (second–first millennia); and to the languages of the Bronze-Age Indo-European Hittite and Luvians (in Anatolia); and to the Bronze-Age linguistically isolated languages of the Hurrians (in SYRIA), Elamites (in southwest Iran), and Iron-Age Urartians (in Armenia). Complexity characterized logosyllabic cuneiform from the beginning because of *homophony* in the system of syllabograms, when several different signs have the same sound; and because of its opposite *polyphony*, where a single sign has more than one sound. For example, 14 separate cuneiform signs have the value /gu/ (Fig. 6.6):

gu	*gu₂*	*gu₃*	*gu₄*
FLAX	NECK	VOICE	OX

Figure 6.6   Four of the 14 cuneiform syllabograms with the same value, /gu/. (After http://www.ancientscripts.com/images/su_gu.gif.)

For an example of polyphony, the sign called KA (capitalization means "this is the name of the sign," usually a value in Sumerian) has the initial value of its name /ka/, in origin a head with the mouth shaded in and meaning "mouth." But KA is also used to mean "shout" with the value in Sumerian of /gu/, and can also stand for /zu/ "tooth," /du/ "speak," and /inim/ "word." Although the generous use of determinatives helped understanding, no wonder that the French Assyriologist Jean Bottéro called cuneiform "this hellish script" – but in comparison to what? to Chinese or Mayan writing?

Transliteration Nightmares

Because of the pervasive homophony (many signs with the same sound) and polyphony (one sign has several sounds) the translator's difficult task is, first, to create a theoretical transliteration in which the encoded sounds are appropriate in a given context. On the basis of such a theoretical and often contested reconstruction, the scholar will attempt a translation. Because of homophony and polyphony, transliterations into specific roman characters of cuneiform texts are very different from their highly ambiguous cuneiform originals.

For example, the cuneiform sign called DINGIR ▸▸✝ , so-named after its Sumerian value where /dingir/ = "god," could also stand for the syllable

/an/, because Anu was the great sky god in the Sumerian pantheon. In Akkadian cuneiform, the sign ▶▶┤ can also be a *Sumerogram*, that is, a virtual logogram that has lost its attachment to Sumerian speech and been reassigned a word of comparable meaning in the Akkadian dialect, or a syllabic value based on the rebus. Sumerograms are common in Akkadian cuneiform. The Semitic for god is something like /'lh/ (hence Hebrew Eloah and Arabic Allah; in transliteration from Semitic, ['] stands for a glottal stop, where the throat closes in conjunction with the vibration of the vocal cords). Hence the sign called by the Sumerian word DINGIR ▶▶┤ can take on the syllabic value /il/ in Akkadian texts (different from /'lh/, but close). But the sign DINGIR ▶▶┤ taken with the sign called MU in Sumerian ▶◀◀, which can mean "water" (*mû*) in Akkadian, which is /a/ in Sumerian, that is, ▶▶┤ ▶◀◀, can be read as /ana/; or /ila/; or "god" + /a/ (logogram for "god" in the accusative case); or "god" + "water" = "god of water"; or simply "water," taken to be a divine substance, in which case DINGIR ▶▶┤ functions as a determinative. For ▶▶┤ ▶◀◀ we have, then, three possible transliterations and more than three possible meanings (hyphens separate the signs): *an-a*, *il-a*, DINGIR-*a*. Only context will reveal which is the correct reading and which the correct translation, if you are lucky, because the context can be elusive in the midst of abounding ambiguity.

Changes Across Time and Place

In spite of its desperately complex, illogical, and maddening features Sumerian cuneiform writing became a flexible medium for the expression of phonetic elements in human speech after it was applied to the foreign and wholly unrelated Semitic Akkadian language sometime before the reign of Sargon of Akkad (c.2334–2279 BC). Semitic words have triconsonantal roots, for example *mlk* = "something to do with king," a frame on which the speaker can build verbs and nouns through internal vowel change.

The triconsonantal roots are also combined with prefixes and suffixes. The Sumerian monosyllabic agglutinative language did not work this way at all.

The differences in language structure encouraged the use of ever more phonetic elements. Sumerian logography lost ground enormously to phonography when cuneiform was applied to the foreign Akkadian words. The shift toward phonography did not, however, mean a simplification. In a love of complexity for its own sake common in the history of writing, the learned Semitic Akkadian scribes extended still further the practice of homophony and polyphony, and as an added complication used many Sumerograms, the Sumerian signs referring to Akkadian words. Just so the Japanese writing took over Chinese signs, called Kanji ("Han characters," after the founding racial group of the Chinese Han), but pronounce them as Japanese, a language wholly unrelated to Chinese.

Akkadian was the usual language under the reign of Sargon, called "King of Sumer and Akkad." Under his leadership administration was reformed and the writing standardized, but when his dynasty declined c.2200 BC, remarkably, Sumerian again became the principal language of administrative texts, although the language may no longer have been spoken. An explosion of scribal activity at the city of UR during the twenty-first and twentieth centuries BC, called the Third Dynasty of Ur, has left more cuneiform documents than from all other periods combined. Every collection of tablets has some Ur III documents. Most are in Sumerian, though the rulers of Ur III appear to have been Semitic-speakers, to judge from their names. A kind of Sumeromania gripped the scribal class at this time, a means for scribes to assert their sophistication and to impress their peers through their competence in Sumerian. The use of Latin by European aristocracies until recent times is a good parallel.

After the fall of Ur III in c.2004 BC, Akkadian again became the principal language of Mesopotamian cuneiform. Several cities rose to dominance, but BABYLON's ascendance under Hammurabi c.1763 BC brought with it the phase of the script and language called Old Babylonian, really a form of the earlier Akkadian. Middle Babylonian, c.1600–1000, was the script and language of the famous Amarna tablets found in EGYPT at Akhenaten's capital (c.1352–1336 BC), while NeoBabylonian belongs to c.1000–500 BC. The last phase of the script, c.500–75 BC, is called Late Babylonian, found on the Behistun inscriptions.

A second variety of Akkadian, whose development ran parallel to Babylonian, comprises the Assyrian dialects. Old Assyrian, testified to by a collection of tablets c.1900 BC found at an Assyrian merchant colony at KANESH in central ANATOLIA (near modern Kayseri), parallels the Old Babylonian texts. Middle Assyrian texts come from the time of Assyrian military expansion in the thirteenth century BC. By far most of the Assyrian texts come from the NeoAssyrian period, c.1000–609 BC, from the archives at Nineveh and Kalhu in modern northern Iraq. After the conquests of Alexander the Great (336–323 BC), Aramaic script encoding the Semitic dialect of Damascus (= Aram) rapidly replaced cuneiform. The last known cuneiform text seems to date to AD 75.

Lexigraphic writing had appeared in response to radical changes in human economic life, then in turn caused deep-seated, dramatic changes in the economy and in the whole way of human life. We might wonder why it took human beings one million years, if they are that old, to discover the phonetic principle in graphic representation, but they did eventually discover it.

Summary

Ancient Near Eastern speculations on the origin of writing attributed its invention to a god. For the Egyptians, it was Thoth; for the Sumerians it was Nabu. European scholars before the Enlightenment liked to say that Adam invented the Hebrew writing, or that the angel Raphael revealed it to him, as Hebrew may have been the primordial language. The Greeks knew more about the human origins of their writing than earlier peoples and said either that Kadmos, "the Easterner," brought it from the Levant, or that wily Palamedes, who outsmarted Odysseus and invented numbers and dice, also created the Greek alphabet by adding further signs to a preexisting series.

Such theories imagined that systems of writing come into being all at once, full blown. In this they are closer to modern views than the evolutionary explanation once common, and still found in handbooks and popular descriptions. Once communication took place by means of pictures, according to this view, which became progressively simplified and more abstract, until the pictures began to stand for elements of speech. This evolutionary theory is sometimes called the "pictographic" theory of the origin of writing. But writing is different from pictures, and as a system of marks with a conventional reference, its evolution is never dependent on a picture as ancestor. The highly pictographic semasiography of the North American Indians showed not the slightest inclination to phoneticization.

On first inspection the protocuneiform tablets appear to support evolutionary theories about the origins of writing, because some of the protocuneiform characters resemble things in the real world, for example a fish, a snake, or a cow (Figs 6.1, 6.3). Most protocuneiform signs, however, are abstract and conventional and not iconic, for example, the circle with a cross inside for "sheep" (Fig. 5.6). Lexigraphic writing, an arbitrary and conventional system of signs, came into being when, first, sematograms standing for things, persons, or places became logograms, standing for words, which through the rebus came to stand for sounds. Such a shift in function required arbitrary decisions about how the system is going to work, and only individuals can make such decisions.

Beginning in the 1970s Schmandt-Besserat offered an original and influential recasting of the evolutionary theory by noticing that the forms and markings of tiny clay and stone "tokens" found all over the Near East from the ninth millennium to the time of the protocuneiform tablets, and somewhat beyond, are similar to characters on the protocuneiform tablets. If the tokens symbolized commodities of which the merchant or official wanted to keep track, then the markings on the tablets must have had the same meaning. Whatever the details, there must be continuity in form between this widespread and very old prehistoric accounting system by means of tokens, a sort of three-dimensional semasiography, and the protocuneiform accounting documents.

Yet continuity of form in the history of writing easily disguises radical inner change, a complete inner restructuring. We will find another clear example in the invention of the Greek alphabet on the basis of the preexisting syllabic Phoenician writing. The Greek writing, the first alphabet, rewrote the rules of written expression and changed the world, yet to consider form alone the Greek system appears nearly identical to its model (hence the misnomer "Phoenician alphabet").

Writing is a system with a conventional reference. The tokens, too, may have constituted a system in any one time and place, but we cannot fully understand their reference. Lexigraphic writing, which appears in the fourth millennium, did not *evolve* from a preexisting accounting system, but was an *invention* that took advantage of the resources of preexisting means for keeping track of commodities. Although Schmandt-Besserat's theory explains some things about the character of early Sumerian writing, including the shape of some characters and the use of clay and stylus to keep records, it cannot explain the appearance of writing itself. Some inventor created the system as a coherent structure, using earlier traditions.

In the earliest cuneiform writing there is little variability in the shape of characters and signs, which are laid out in the same way on the same kinds of tablets. Already these signs work together predictably. The conventional system is fully formed as an instrument of abstract thought. Whereas 90 percent of the around 6,000 Uruk tablets are administrative in character, 10 percent are lists – of fish, textiles, vessels, animals, birds – reflecting the need of Sumerian scribes to organize their world into categories and to teach young scribes the contents of these categories. Already lexigraphic writing is enabling abstract thought. All the archaic tablets are administrative or educational – only by a consistent understanding of a consistent repertory could the system be useful. One such list, the Standard List of Professions, first attested c.3000 BC (it has a long life thereafter), seems to set out the social hierarchy within which the scribes lived, the first sociological analysis.

7

Plato's *Ideas* and Champollion's Decipherment of the Egyptian Hieroglyphs

The Roman historian Tacitus (AD 56–125) came close to the truth when he wrote

> It was the Egyptians who first symbolized ideas, and that by the figures of animals. These records, the most ancient of all human history, are still seen engraved on stone. The Egyptians also claim to have invented the alphabet, which the Phoenicians, they say, by means of their superior seamanship, introduced into Greece, and of which they appropriated the glory, giving out that they had discovered what they had really been taught. (*Annales* 11.14)

Egyptian writing is not the oldest writing as Tacitus thought (though recent finds at Abydos are claimed to justify him, see below), but it is from the Egyptian tradition, not the Mesopotamian, that the modern alphabet descends. Furthermore, Egyptian writing held an altogether different place in the imagination of the postclassical Europeans, who scarcely knew that cuneiform writing existed. The history of misunderstanding that characterized European approaches to the hieroglyphs reveals a good deal about how prejudice blinds users of an alphabetic system, ourselves, when attempting to understand a foreign system.

The Allegorical Interpretation of the Hieroglyphs

The last known hieroglyphic inscription was written on the Ptolemaic temple to Isis on the island of Philae near Aswan in AD 396 (the temple was moved to a nearby island after construction of the Aswan High Dam in the 1960s). The Romans had lived in intimate contact with this writing since the death of Cleopatra VII in 30 BC, although no Roman could read hieroglyphs, let alone write them. Classical accounts of hieroglyphs show little understanding of how the script was used. For example, Diodorus of Sicily (c.80–20 BC) writing in Greek in the first century BC, says that

> their writing does not express the intended concept by means of syllables joined to one another, but by means of the significance of the objects that have been copied, and by its figurative meaning that has been impressed upon the memory by practice. For instance they draw the picture of a hawk, a crocodile . . . and the like. Now the hawk signifies to them everything that happens swiftly, because this creature is the swiftest of winged creatures. And the concept portrayed is then applied, by metaphorical transfer, to all swift things and to everything to which swiftness is appropriate . . . And the crocodile is the symbol of all that is evil. (*Bibliotheke historike* 3.4.1–3)

Diodorus describes the real functioning of some Egyptian logograms ("significance of the objects"), and the real functioning of determinatives, signs without phonetic value that place preceding signs in a certain category ("figurative meaning"), but he knows nothing about phonetic aspects of Egyptian writing, or how different signs interact. The influential Greek philosopher Plotinus (AD 204–70), writing in the third century AD, followed a similar thinking, claiming that the signs were nothing less than the Platonic Ideas or Forms (*eidea*) in visual form, "each picture . . . a kind of understanding and wisdom" that could reveal to the initiated true knowledge about the essence of things. Plotinus's complex philosophy, called Neoplatonism, was a late ancient form of Platonic thought. The Egyptian representations were the Ideas or Forms made visible and therefore provided an immediate and direct apprehension of divine knowledge, as opposed to the clouded, partial, and earthbound forms appropriate to natural language.

In this spirit a man named Horapollo ("Horus-Apollo") of unknown date, perhaps an Egyptian grammarian who lived in the fifth century AD, wrote a book on Egyptian writing called *Hieroglyphica*, the only treatise on Egyptian writing to survive from antiquity. Horapollo gathered together the last traces of the Egyptian past and reinterpreted the Egyptian legacy in the light of contemporary Neoplatonism. The two books of the *Hieroglyphica* contain 189 interpretations of hieroglyphs, many demonstrating real knowledge of hieroglyphic writing, but ignorant of the phonetic function of some signs and of their relationship to Egyptian language.

The manuscript of the *Hieroglyphica* was found on the Greek island of Andros in the early fifteenth century and appears to have been the second

Figure 7.1 Hieroglyph of a falcon, from the first illustrated edition of Horapollo, in French, published by Jacques Kerver in 1543

book, after the Bible, to be set in Gutenberg's revolutionary new movable type, for Neoplatonism was the philosophical fashion of the day. The first printed edition appeared in 1505 and went through more than 30 editions and translations during the sixteenth century. Scholars studied the book assiduously, believing it to be a window opening into the secret wisdom of most ancient Egypt. Here is a single entry, on the hieroglyph of a falcon, in which I have highlighted two key words (Fig. 7.1):

What they signify by drawing a falcon. Wishing to signify the **divine**, or sublimity, or humility, or excellence, or **victory**, they draw a falcon. It is divine because it has many children and it lives a long time. Also, it appears to provide an image of the sun more than other birds because it can look at its rays without blinking. For this reason doctors make use of "falcon's grass" to heal diseases of the eyes, and they draw the figure of a falcon to designate the sun as the patron of sight. Of sublimity, because while other creatures, when they wish to fly up, are born at an angle, the falcon flies straight up. Of humility, because other creatures cannot descend in a straight line, but must always fly at an angle; only the falcon can drop down precipitously. Of excellence, because it seems to be superior to all other winged creatures. Of blood, because they say that this creature does not drink water, but blood. Of victory, because this creature overcomes all other winged things. Whenever it is threatened by a stronger bird and fears defeat, it turns on its back in the air with its claws extended, its wings and tail turned downwards, which the bird with which it is struggling cannot do. So easily it puts it to flight and claims the victory. (*Hieroglyphica* I. 6)

In fact the Egyptian sign 🦅 is the logogram for the **divine** Horus, pre-eminent in Egyptian political myth: Pharaoh incarnated him. In Egyptian myth, Horus won a great **victory** over his enemy Seth.

In other typical entries Horapollo records that the picture of a goose means "son" because geese love their children more than any other animal. Or the female vulture represents "mother" because there are no male

vultures. In fact the picture of a goose 🦆 is used *with phonetic value*

to write a word that means "son," and the vulture 🦅 , too, can have the

phonetic value of the Egyptian word for "mother." In allegorizing the signs – goose means "son" because geese love their goslings, not because it stands for the sounds which in Egyptian mean "son" – the *Hieroglyphica* established an illusion that hampered the decipherment and has not disappeared today.

Soon after the *Hieroglyphica* appeared in print it became the fashion among European intellectuals, who had rarely or never seen a real hieroglyph, to compose their own allegorical "hieroglyphs." In 1499 a mysterious book appeared, one of the oddest ever written, perhaps by one Francesco Colonna, called the *Hypnerotomachia Polifili*, "the dream of the battle for love of Poliphilus." The book is a wildly erudite and difficult romance in many languages with woodcut illustrations (possibly by Andrea Mantegna, 1431–1506). Its action is set within a dream, or within a dream within a dream. We learn of the adventures of Poliphilus, "lover of many things" in Greek, who seeks the maiden Polia, "many things," perhaps an allegory for the rediscovery of antiquity. In Poliphilus' quest for Polia, the hero comes across various hieroglyphic inscriptions created according to principles set down in Horapollo. In Figure 7.2, one page from the *Hypnerotomachia*,

Figure 7.2   A page from the *Hypnerotomachia Polifili*, c.1499, containing two original "hieroglyphs"

the Latin caption to the upper example (the main text here is Italian) informs us that "the community of Egyptians" has dedicated this obelisk "to the divine Julius Caesar, the eternal Augustus, ruler of the whole world, on account of his clemency and liberality of spirit. The first sign, an eye, depends on Horapollo's explanation that the Egyptian hieroglyph for eye stood for God, hence the first word in the Latin caption *divo*, "to the divine [Julius Caesar]," but the relation between the other "hieroglyphic" signs and the Latin text can be highly obscure. In the lower example of Figure 7.2, the "hieroglyph," according to its Latin inscription, means "Little things [ants] grow big [elephants] through peace [square knot] and concord [intertwined serpents]; great things [elephants] grow small [ants] through discord [fire burning in pan opposite its destroyer, a pan of water]." No wonder the Egyptians were famous for their wisdom!

In the seventeenth century a leading scholar, the Jesuit Athanasius Kircher (1602–80), compiled the first Coptic grammar and suggested that

Figure 7.3   The obelisk in the Piazza Minerva in Rome some of whose hieroglyphs A. Kircher attempted to translate. The Pharaoh Apries (*Wah-ib-Re*, ruled 589–575 BC) of the Twenty-sixth Dynasty erected it as one of a pair in the city of Sais in the delta

Coptic might be the same language as pharaonic Egyptian. To Kircher goes the credit for realizing this critical fact. Coptic, which appeared in the third century AD written in a modified form of the Greek alphabet, was used almost exclusively for Christian religious texts. It was spoken until the seventeenth century and still today is intoned in the Coptic Church. Kircher also wondered if some hieroglyphs might have phonetic value, but applied the "method" of Horapollo to the cartouche on an obelisk in the Piazza Minerva in Rome (Fig. 7.3). The obelisk, which may have come to Rome in the first century AD, once stood in the Roman temple to Isis. In 1665 Dominican monks discovered it and Pope Alexander VII (ruled 1655–67) re-erected it in front of the Church of Santa Maria Sopra Minerva, mounted on the sculpture of an elephant to imitate another "hiero-glyph" in the *Hypnerotomachia Polifili*. According to the Latin inscription on the base, "he who sees the carved images of the wisdom of Egypt on the obelisk carried by the elephant, the strongest of animals, will realize that it is indeed a robust mind that sustains a solid wisdom."

On the obelisk itself are two cartouches (Fig. 7.4). Kircher translated them as

> The protection of Osiris against the violence of Typho [a Greek chaos god] must be elicited according to the proper rites and ceremonies by sacrifices and by appeal to the tutelary Genii of the triple world, in order to ensure the enjoyment of the prosperity customarily given by the Nile against the violence of the enemy Typho. (Coe 1992: 17)

Figure 7.4 Cartouches of Apries (*Wah-ib-re*, "constant is the heart of Re") on the obelisk in the Piazza Minerva, Rome, c.560 BC

"The sphinx has been killed, her riddle answered," proclaimed Kircher (see Coe 1992). In fact the cartouches give two names of the pharaoh called Apries of the Twenty-sixth Dynasty (ruled c.589–570 BC) and mean "King of the Two Lands, *Haa-ib-Re* ["jubilant is the heart of Ra"]; the Son of Re, *Wah-ib-Re*, ["constant is the heart of Re"].

Background to the Decipherment of the Hieroglyphs

The inspired Champollion himself for long believed that the Egyptian signs were allegorical, except in the writing of names. From early childhood he felt destined to decipher the hieroglyphs and, in preparation for the great day, at an early age became Europe's preeminent expert on the Coptic language. Since the seventeenth century most had agreed that Coptic must be a late form of pharaonic Egyptian. "Coptic" is from Greek *Aiguptios*, our "Egypt," a corruption of an Egyptian phrase "the house of the *ka* of [the god] Ptah," the name of a temple in the Egyptian capital of Memphis. Egypt was Christian by the fifth century AD, evangelized by St Mark according to legend – the grave of his head can today be seen in the basement of the St Mark Coptic Orthodox church in Alexandria. Islam penetrated Egypt in the seventh century AD, but the Copts, or "Egyptians," preserved preIslamic Christianity and the ancient Egyptian language.

We can pronounce Coptic texts because they are composed in a modified Greek alphabet. Coptic texts consist of translations of biblical scripture, liturgies, and rulebooks for monastic behavior: The monastic movement began in Egypt in the fourth century AD and spread from there to Europe. Curiously, Coptic appears to function as an "agglutinative language," where a single sometimes very long word is made up of independent units of meaning (morphemes) strung together (as in Turkish or ancient Sumerian); the language that underlies hieroglyphic, on the other hand, appears to consist of separate morphemes, where word order and context determine meaning (as in English). They are different phases of the same language, yet different systems of writing make this language appear different in structure. Hieroglyphic writing stands at a far remove from human speech, as we will see, as does cuneiform logosyllabic writing.

Knowledge of Coptic was critical because it is impossible to decipher an unknown script without knowing the underlying language. For example, we can pronounce Etruscan texts, written in the Greek alphabet since the seventh century BC and, in many cases, we can guess at the meaning of words from their placement and recurrence in association with objects whose function we otherwise understand. But, because we do not know the underlying language, we cannot read an isolated extensive text written in Etruscan. A second requirement for a successful decipherment is a large quantity of material so that general principles can be discovered in the way the writing functions by statistical comparison of the frequency of signs and a study of the patterning of signs.

Before Napoleon, in his rivalry with Britain, invaded Egypt in 1798 only a tiny amount of Egyptian hieroglyphic writing existed in Europe (as on the obelisks of Rome); some examples were ancient Roman fakes. Before Napoleon, it was not possible to travel to Egypt, which was controlled by the Mamelukes, a warrior caste subordinate, in theory, to the Ottoman Sultan in Istanbul, consisting of slaves captured from nonMuslim families in Europe (thus owing no local allegiance) and Islamicized. In the spirit of the French Enlightenment's rationalism and dedication to science, 165 French savants accompanied Napoleon in order to record all aspects of Egypt's flora, fauna, and history. The results were published between 1809 and 1822 as the 24-volume monumental *Description de l'Égypt*, which made possible the modern science of Egyptology. Without the *Description*, by Champollion's admission, the decipherment would have been impossible.

In July 1799, an officer of the engineers was working in the western delta on defenses at a fort near the small port of El-Rashid, ancient Rosetta, and found reused in a modern wall a basalt block inscribed in three scripts: hieroglyphic; an unfamiliar script (it is demotic); and Greek – the Rosetta Stone. The French surrendered the stone to the British in 1801 after the British fleet under Horatio Nelson, in nominal alliance with the Turks, drove out the French invaders. Removed to the British Museum, the Rosetta Stone is today the most visited object in the museum, and probably the most widely known archaeological object in the world (Fig. 7.5). French officials recognized at once the importance of the stone as a possible key to decipherment, and copies made from direct impressions on the stone soon circulated in Europe. Yet the decipherment of the perplexing and highly difficult script was to take more than 20 years.

The Greek of the stone, easily understood, records a decree of 196 BC establishing a royal cult of Ptolemy V in return for privileges the king has granted to the priests. Because the hieroglyphic portion, of which only 14 lines survive, was taken to be allegorical, scholars focused their attention on the previously unknown demotic script in the middle of the stone. We can assume that the script in some way represents the Egyptian language, whose late form as Coptic in alphabetic script is already well known. Because the demotic text is linear and not pictographic (Fig. 7.6), we can assume that it is not a system of symbolic or allegorical representation, as surely were the hieroglyphs, but in some way a phonetic writing, even an "alphabet" in which single signs represent single sounds. We should be able to begin to unravel the principles of the phonetic structure of this script by finding names in the demotic text that correspond to names in the Greek text, which we read easily. Having achieved some values, we could then begin to unravel other vocabulary known to us from Coptic.

Whereas several names were correctly isolated in just this way, and some phonetic values accurately determined, these values did not yield results when applied to the rest of the text. On close inspection it became clear that there were far more characters in the demotic script than one would expect to find in an "alphabet," where the average is less than 30. Could

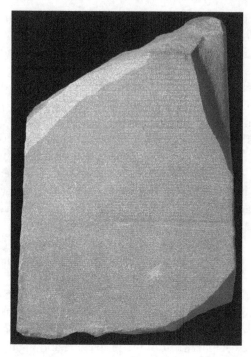

Figure 7.5 The Rosetta Stone, establishing a cult in honor of Ptolemy V in return for privileges granted to the priesthood, 196 BC. (London, British Museum, EA 24.)

Figure 7.6 Demotic, detail from central portion of the Rosetta Stone. (British Museum EA 24.)

the explanation be that single characters had multiple forms, as in Arabic writing today?

In 1814 the British polymath Thomas Young (1773–1829), who made important contributions to the science of optics, noticed that some of the demotic writing appeared to be derived from hieroglyphic forms. If so, the demotic script must be allegorical too, according to the universal prejudice, and not phonetic, as everyone hoped; phonetic signs must be restricted to the rendering of foreign names, as in the writing of "Ptolemy" that appears several times in the Greek text. Young demonstrated that the hieroglyphic forms could not fruitfully be compared to Chinese characters, as some attempted, because there were far fewer hieroglyphic signs than the tens of thousands of Chinese signs. To express complex thought, the hieroglyphic signs must work with each other in combinations. Young correctly identified the name of Ptolemy in the demotic text, and working with other names in the demotic text, which he took to be phonetic representations, he isolated the correct values of several signs. However, he misidentified even more. Young's later unfortunate claim to be the true decipherer of the hieroglyphs spoiled the reputation of his real contribution.

The Decipherment of Jean François Champollion

The precocious man of destiny, Jean François Champollion (1790–1832), grew up in the time of the French Revolution. He learned Greek and Latin at an early age, and at age 16 presented a paper on the Coptic etymology of Egyptian place names in Greek and Latin authors. In Paris he studied Persian and Arabic and when only 19 won a chair at the University of Grenoble – an academic achievement of surpassing brilliance. In addition to his advanced competence in Coptic, he studied the Egyptian monuments in Europe and mastered what classical writers had reported about Egypt. By studying the volumes of *Description de l'Égypt* then appearing, he was first to distinguish clearly between the four categories of Egyptian writing: hieroglyphic, cursive hieroglyphic, hieratic, and demotic (see Chapter 8). He drew up tables of their corresponding signs, later basic to his decipherment. He drew the same conclusion as had Young: because the cursive forms of the demotic text on the Rosetta Stone depended on the hieroglyphic forms, both scripts must work in the same way, that is, be symbolic or allegorical in nature – except for the writing of foreign names,

when the hieroglyphs must carry phonetic information. Therefore the hieroglyphs *themselves* must sometimes carry phonetic information, a step that
Young did not take.

Around 1785 a French classicist and numismatist named Jean-Jacques
Barthélemy had plausibly suggested that the cartouches surrounding some
hieroglyphs, as in the obelisk that Athanasius Kircher studied, contained
divine and royal names. Unfortunately, only a single cartouche survived
on the Rosetta stone. The relative position of the single cartouche agreed,
however, with the relative position of the name of Ptolemy in the Greek
text, confirming Barthelémy's suggestion. Although the hieroglyphic form
of the name of Ptolemy was therefore now known, one would need at least
a pair of names that contain the same sounds in order to establish through
crosschecking the actual phonetic value of any one sign.

At just this time, in 1822, Champollion received the transcript of an obelisk
transported recently to England from the island of Philae near Aswan to
the estate of British aristocrat Ralph Bankes, thus called the Bankes
Obelisk. Ptolemy VIII Euergetes II and his second wife, Cleopatra III (not
the famous Cleopatra VII) had erected it in the second century BC in front
of the first pylon of the temple of Isis on Philae. The shaft of the column
was inscribed in hieroglyphs, but its base was in Greek and contained the
names of both Ptolemy VIII and Cleopatra III.

One of the cartouches on the Bankes Obelisk contained signs similar to
those within the cartouche on the Rosetta Stone (Fig. 7.7). The signs within
the second cartouche on the Bankes Obelisk ended with two signs earlier

suspected of designating a female: $\bigcirc$, "egg," for fecundity, and $\bigtriangleup$, "bread

loaf," which we now know to stand for the sound /t/, a common ending
for feminine nouns in Afro-Asiatic languages (Fig. 7.8). That cartouche,
then, must enclose the name of Cleopatra.

By comparing the spelling of the two names Champollion established
phonetic equivalents for a handful of signs. The /p/ is the first sound in

Ptolemy and the fifth sound in Cleopatra, so that $\square$ "stool" must have

the value /p/. The "lasso" $\leftthreetimes$ that appears as the third sign in Ptolemy's

name, and the fourth in Cleopatra's, must have the value /o/; the "lion"

$\mathrel{\text{🦁}}$, which appears as the fourth sign in Ptolemy and the second in

Cleopatra, should therefore be /l/; the "reed" $\left\lceil\right.$, appearing as a doublet

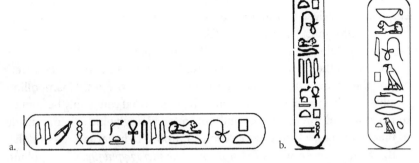

Figure 7.7   The name of Ptolemy (PTOLEMIS) on (a) the Rosetta Stone (reading right to left, top to bottom) and (b) the name of Ptolemy on the Bankes Obelisk (reading right to left, top to bottom). The signs that in each name begin with the *ankh* sign ♀ are royal epithets that did not figure in the decipherment, meaning "living forever, beloved of Ptah," although "beloved" is spelled differently in the two inscriptions

Figure 7.8   The name of Cleopatra (KLEOPATRA) from the base of the Bankes Obelisk, reading left to right, top down

in Ptolemy, but once in Cleopatra, should represent /e/ or something like that; the bread loaf ⌒, which appears at the end of Cleopatra's name as a gender marker, must nonetheless have the value /t/ in Ptolemy. As for the remaining signs, in Ptolemy's name the ⎓ (whatever it is) will have to be /m/ and "folded cloth" ⎮ must be /s/, so that the king's name is spelled PTOLEMIS (for Greek PTOLEMAIOS). The name of Cleopatra yields the values of /r/ for the mouth ⌀ and /a/ for the "vulture" 𓄿 , although in KLEOPA*T*RA the sound for /t/ appears to be represented by "hand" ⎓⎓ whereas in Ptolemy's name /t/ = ⌒. But homophones are common in every system of writing.

Having a group of signs, then, whose phonetic values seemed probable, Champollion turned to the cartouches newly published in *Description de*

l'Égypt, from which he deciphered names well known from the classical period: Alexander (the Great); Berenice (wife of Ptolemy II); the Roman emperors Tiberius, Domitian, Vespasian, Nerva, Hadrian and his wife Sabina, Antoninus, Germanicus, Claudius, and Augustus (in Greek = Sebastos), yielding sounds for around 40 hieroglyphic signs. Still, in a famous paper read to the French Academy in 1822 (*Lettre à M. Dacier*, the secretary of the academy), in which he reports his discoveries, Champollion emphasized that the phonetic system he had unraveled could only be applied to personal and foreign names and not to the hieroglyphic system outside of the cartouches, which Champollion continued to believe were symbolic.

By 1824, however, in his *Précis du système hiéroglyphique*, Champollion at last abandoned his own assumptions by demonstrating that hieroglyphs outside cartouches were also sometimes phonetic. How could they be symbolic, he argued, as everybody believed, when in the Greek text of the Rosetta Stone there are 500 words, while in the corresponding much shorter Egyptian text there are 1,419 hieroglyphic signs? How could one sign stand for one word when there were more than three times as many signs as words? And why did just a handful of signs appear again and again in the hieroglyphic text, he asked, even the phonetic signs that Champollion had earlier deciphered?

From illustrations in *Description de l'Égypt* Champollion now identified the names of numerous Egyptian gods known from Greek and Roman sources. He explained how such names were followed by what he called a "species marker," the picture of a god, a nonphonetic sign that placed the preceding name in a category (what we now call a "determinative" or "semantic complement"). The picture of a man or a woman marked personal names whose phonetic structure he was untangling. Still, so far Champollion had worked exclusively with proper names from the period of the Greek-speaking Ptolemies. Their usage could well have been different from that of the native Egyptians.

One cartouche appeared numerous times in published inscriptions:

Champollion could already read the last two symbols [ⳤⳤ] as /ss/ (seeming doublets for "folded cloth" [⌂] = /s/), and (☉) "sun" must be something like the Coptic /ra/, from which Champollion deduced that [𓄟] must have the value /m/ (in fact [𓄟] = /ms/), perhaps RA-M-SS, surely the famous "Ramses" known from Greek sources. He made a mistake in the value of [𓄟] and did not understand that the first /s/ reinforced the /s/ already in the sign [𓄟] as a phonetic complement, whereas the second /s/ stood for the personal pronoun "him": Ramses (r^c-*ms-s*) means "Ra begot him." Nonetheless this cartouche was the first unassailably Egyptian name ever deciphered, the first time since the closing of the Egyptian temples in the fourth century AD that anyone had read an Egyptian inscription.

The names of other well-known preMacedonian pharaohs followed quickly. Champollion showed how, by assigning discovered phonetic values of the hieroglyphic signs to the text outside the cartouches, sense could be made of the text through Coptic parallels. The system began to unravel, although always with frustrating complexities and maddening obscurities. When, in 1832, Champollion died suddenly at age 41 from a series of strokes, he was reading Egyptian texts with remarkable skill and accuracy. Champollion's accomplishment was one of the great intellectual achievements of the nineteenth century, opening to human understanding a preeminent civilization in human history, its voice silent for one-and-a-half thousand years.

8

Egyptian Writing and
Egyptian Speech

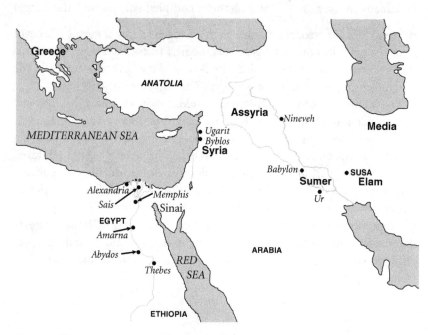

Map 2 Places important in Chapters 8 and 9

Egyptologists now read Egyptian writing fairly well. The extinct language of ancient EGYPT belonged to the large so-called Afro-Asiatic family of languages, which includes such African languages as Berber (spoken in North African countries west of Egypt) and Cushitic (spoken in ETHIOPIA, Somalia, and Kenya), once called "Hamitic" languages after the legendary son of Noah. Afro-Asiatic also includes such Asiatic languages as Akkadian, Babylonian, Arabic, and Hebrew, called "Semitic" languages after the biblical Ham's brother, Shem.

First attested in writing as early as 3200(?) BC, the Egyptian language was spoken until the eleventh century AD, when it died out except for use in ritual in the Coptic Church, the ancient Christian Church of Egypt. The Egyptian speech of the pharaohs therefore has an attested use of over four thousand years, more than any on Earth (Greek is second, first attested c.1400 BC). After Islamic invaders from ARABIA conquered the Nile valley in AD 641, Arabic gradually replaced the native speech. Arabic is the language of Egypt today, written in the Arabic script, a modification of the script of the ancient western Semites, first attested as early as c.1400 BC (see Chapter 9).

The Phases of Egyptian Language/Speech

The confusion between *language* and *speech* is clear in discussions of the phases of "Egyptian language," really the conventions of expression in *written* Egyptian, attached in a rough and ready way to the sounds of actual speech, whose forms, like all speech, were constantly changing. We will speak of the "phases of Egyptian language," remembering that we know nothing about Egyptian speech except indirectly through written forms, which never preserved speech. Egyptian writing was a system of thought with its own internal rules that made use of the resources of speech. Egyptian writing was held uniform by tradition and convention, but changing patterns in speech nonetheless exerted an influence on it, as they do on written expression today. At times such influence imposed real change, but just as often the change took place first in the written form, not the spoken. Scholars follow five broad categories in describing the "phases of Egyptian language":

- *Old Egyptian* is the "language" of the Old Kingdom, the vocabulary, spelling conventions, and grammatical forms used in the first continuous texts from around 2600 BC down to around 2100 BC, the end of the Old Kingdom. There are religious texts (especially the wonderful hymns and spells inscribed in pyramids of the Sixth Dynasty) and private autobiographical texts on tombs, but no literary texts.
- *Middle Egyptian*, sometimes called Classical Egyptian, is closely related to Old Egyptian, and is roughly the "language" of the Middle Kingdom, beginning around 2100 BC, but lasting for two thousand years until the end of pharaonic civilization as a standard learned in schools. The first literary texts and "scientific" texts (on medicine and mathematics)

appear in Middle Egyptian. Modern students of ancient Egyptian writing begin with documents written in Middle Egyptian and can with little additional training learn to read Old Egyptian.

- By 1400 BC, after one-and-a-half thousand years of written expression, the distance between the "written language" and the "spoken language" became so great (though it was never small) that a change took place in the written form of the language, part of the cultural reforms of the wild and radical monotheistic pharaoh Akhenaten in the mid-fourteenth century BC. Akhenaten also sponsored change in the conventions of Egyptian art, with which Egyptian writing was closely bound, turning it to a sometimes startling realism. The changed written language appears to reflect a similar effort to bring written expression into line with experience. Called *Late Egyptian*, this phase was established by 1300 BC and lasted until around 600 BC. The spelling is more complex and seemingly more phonetic and a new syntax, often periphrastic, is in place. Late Egyptian can be quite different from Middle Egyptian and requires special study.

- In the *Demotic* phase of Egyptian "language" appears a difficult linear script based on earlier linear forms of hieroglyphic writing (see below) and confusingly also called *demotic* (Greek for "of the people"; when referring to the script, demotic is not capitalized). The success of Demotic/demotic depended on reform programs encouraged by pharaohs of the Twenty-sixth Dynasty (664–525 BC), called the Saite Dynasty because its capital was in the Delta city of SAIS. At first most Demotic texts were secular, such as business accounts, wills, and letters, but later religious texts and often moralizing literary texts were written in Demotic. As we have seen, the middle portion of the Rosetta Stone is in demotic script. The Saite Dynasty was founded against foreign occupation of the throne and sponsored Egypt's last cultural renaissance. The Demotic phase of ancient Egyptian language lasted for over one thousand years, disappearing in the fifth century AD.

- *Coptic*, the last phase of the ancient Egyptian "language" and essential to the decipherment of hieroglyphs, first appears around AD 200 and, like earlier phases, was to last a thousand years. Closely tied to the Christian Church, it was encoded in a slightly modified Greek alphabet, the script of the gospels, and so, for the first time in the history of Egyptian, writing could be pronounced. As Christianity took hold in Egypt, the older scripts of the hieroglyphic tradition were relegated more and more to the temples until by the fifth century AD they ceased to be understood. Coptic continued in everyday use until the eleventh century

AD when the West Semitic Arabic script, allied with the written Quran, prevailed along with the Arabic language in the valley of the Nile. Although Coptic has not been spoken for hundreds of years, one can still today buy Coptic bibles (with Arabic translation) in the streets of Cairo.

We cannot detect dialectal differences in texts written in the hieroglyphic tradition, though they must have existed in Egyptian speech; the written "language" is distant from speech. Hieroglyphs were a self-contained system for abstract thought intelligible to any scribe regardless of where he lived in Egypt or what local dialect he might have spoken. Coptic script, by contrast, a form of the Greek alphabet, represents the sounds of speech fairly closely so that we recognize five dialects in Coptic and a pronounced difference between the "language" of Upper Egypt (called *Saidic*) and Lower Egypt (called *Bohairic*, the dialect of the Coptic Church).

The Forms of Egyptian Writing

The Greek historian Herodotus, who lived in the fifth century BC, already realized (2.36.4) that the Egyptians had two kinds of writing, which he called *hiera*, the "holy" writing, and *demotica*, the "writing of the people," the origin of our own usage. We now call the whole system hieroglyphic (not "hieroglyphics"), but distinguish three principal types: *hieroglyphic* proper ("sacred carving," a word first found in the Greek historian Diodorus of Sicily, first century AD); *hieratic* (Greek for "priestly"), and *demotic*. In fact the hieroglyphic, hieratic, and demotic scripts are graphic variants of a single system, but such knowledge did not come easily.

The highly iconic hieroglyphic script, which consists mostly of stylized pictures, appears full-blown at the beginning of the pharaonic period, c.3100 BC or somewhat earlier (Fig. 8.1). Hieroglyphic signs were used to write Old and Middle Egyptian phases of the "language"; they were still inscribed in the Middle Egyptian "language" at the end of Egyptian civilization. Ordinarily they are written right to left, but left to right for artistic reasons (as in Figure 8.1, where the serpent faces in the same direction as the hawk). The direction of reading is toward the front of the objects represented in the writing; if the hawk faces to the left, you read towards the right.

In the Old Kingdom, hieroglyphs were written mostly in columns, the signs progressing right to left, up to down (compare Figs 7.7b, 8.3), but in

Figure 8.1   Stele of King Djet, First Dynasty (c.2990–2770 BC). The serpent within the stylized palace design surmounted by a hawk (called a *serekh*, an Egyptian word) is a logogram for the Egyptian word *ḏt* = "serpent," while at the same time being a phonetic sign with the sound transcribed as *ḏ* (= /j/). The sign is logographic and phonographic at the same time. This stele marked Djet's tomb in the early dynastic cemetery at ABYDOS in Middle Egypt. (Art Resource, New York, ART156402; Paris, Louvre.)

the Middle Kingdom they were written on horizontal lines, mostly. The length of the horizontal rows was determined by the amount of papyrus the scribe could hold before him on his lap without unrolling more, the origin of our "page."

Hieroglyphs were written on temples and tombs and such objects as coffins, sarcophagi (stone coffins), and stelae (slabs of stone or wood used for memorial purposes). Hieroglyphs had magical power and so were also used for inscribing the New Kingdom book of spells called the *Book of the Dead*, usually in a slightly cursive form (called cursive hieroglyphs). Short hieroglyphic texts also appear in art as labels or to name figures and, especially in Old Kingdom tomb reliefs, to represent the speech of figures, as in a modern cartoon, sometimes to humorous effect (Fig. 8.2): Long

Figure 8.2   Man roasting a goose over a bowl filled with coals, from a tomb of the Sixth Dynasty, c.2200 BC. The hieroglyphs above him, reading left to right, mean, "I have been roasting since the beginning of time! I have never seen a goose like this one!" The man's gesture reflects his exasperation. (After Collier and Manley 1998, p. 1.)

Figure 8.3   Section from a private letter in the original hieratic script (right-hand columns), with a transliteration into hieroglyphic (left-hand columns). The writing means "With regard to what Hemkanakht says to Merynesu concerning all the water field-plots: I allot them to you as fine plough land. Fight to protect them!" Eleventh Dynasty (2040–1991 BC). (New York, Metropolitan Museum of Art; after Davies 1990, fig. 25.)

hieroglyphic texts are autobiographical (on tombs) or historical (on public monuments) or they present hymns or spells (usually on stelae). The hieroglyphs were treated with careful, sometimes exaggerated attention, even as miniature works of art. Surely, Egyptian hieroglyphic writing was the most lovely ever devised.

Hieratic ("priestly") script, considerably more stylized than cursive hieroglyphs, is related to hieroglyphic script as our longhand is related to a printed text. It is nearly as old or as old as hieroglyphic script. Hieratic was the "fast" hand used when keeping accounts or recording other kinds of information on perishable papyrus, rather as we use longhand when writing a letter (or once did), but formal typeface when printing a book.

Of course, the hieroglyphs came first. A single hieratic sign ordinarily corresponds to a single hieroglyphic sign, although sometimes the signs run together, as in Figure 8.3, which compares hieratic forms in the two right-hand columns, the normal form of Egyptian writing, with their transliteration into hieroglyphic in the two left-hand columns.

Hieratic script was used in the Old, Middle, and Late Egyptian phases of the "language"; almost all Late Egyptian is in the hieratic script. Scribes seem to have learned by beginning with hieratic, not hieroglyphic script, using brush and ink on papyrus; hieroglyphic was a topic of higher education. Hieroglyphic and hieratic were written side by side, by the same scribes, at the same time: hieroglyphic for things meant to last, like public proclamations on expensive stone monuments, and hieratic for things of ephemeral or literary value, on papyrus.

The cursive demotic script, which appeared about 650 BC, was a development of hieratic, but contains many ligatures (two or more signs written as one). As described above, there are changes in the "language" of Demotic. Demotic is a very difficult script and few scholars can read it. The hieroglyphic original underlying the demotic sign has been lost completely. For this reason, specialist Egyptologists called demoticists transliterate demotic signs directly into a system of Roman characters before

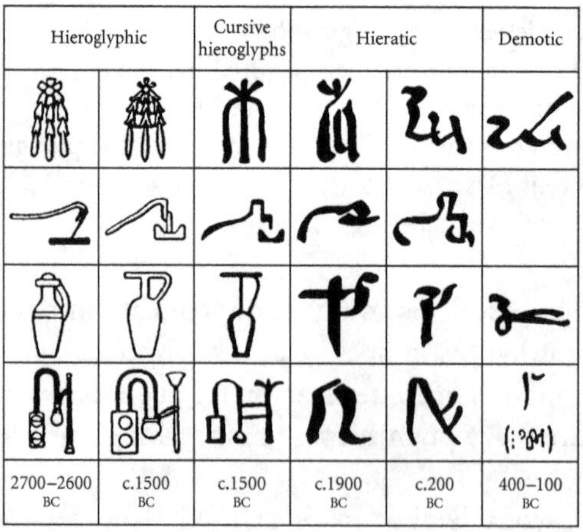

ⲠⲈⲚⲈⲒⲰⲦ	ⲈⲦϨⲚ̄ⲘⲠⲎⲨⲈ
peneiôt	eth'n'mpêue
Our-father	Who-is-in-heaven
ⲘⲀⲢⲈⲠⲈⲔⲢⲀⲚ	ⲞⲨⲞⲠ
marepekran	ouop
may-your-name-be	hallowed

Figure 8.4 The same signs written in hieroglyphic, cursive hieroglyphic, hieratic, and demotic scripts. (After Steindorff and Seele 1942, p. 12.)
Figure 8.5 A sample of Coptic script and language, with transliteration and translation. The ['] in the transliteration is a convention to indicate a "reduced /e/" (represented by a supralinear stroke in the Coptic) and the circumflex over [o] and [e] indicates that the vowels are long. The third sign in the second word (= /h/) is based on a demotic form

wrestling with what they might mean, without going through an intermediary transliteration of the signs first into hieroglyphs, the usual procedure when reading hieratic script. We have seen an example of demotic script as the middle text on the Rosetta Stone from 196 BC (Fig. 7.5), carved in hieroglyphs at the top (the script of the priests, encoding Middle Egyptian), demotic in the middle (the script and language of everyday use), and Greek (the script and language of the Macedonian rulers) at the bottom. Hieratic script continued side by side with demotic script, but in the late period was restricted to religious texts (hence hieratic means "priestly"), while demotic ("of the people") was used for everyday purposes. The last hieratic document comes from the first century AD, the last demotic document from the fourth century AD.

The evolution of four signs from hieroglyphs to demotic is illustrated in Figure 8.4.

The *Coptic* script and the accompanying late stage of the "language" served the interests of Egyptian Christians, who already in the first century AD wanted native-language versions of Christian documents. In order to distinguish themselves from their pagan forebears, whose heritage they rejected, they turned to the Greek alphabetic script of most Christian writings. Like "demotic," "Coptic" refers both to a script and to one stage, the last, of Egyptian "language." Figure 8.5, a sample of Coptic, written left to right, is the opening of the Lord's Prayer with translation into Roman characters (but ordinarily Coptic script did not separate the words).

9

The Origin and Nature of Egyptian Writing

We can never expect to find the very earliest examples of any tradition of writing (although such is sometimes claimed for the protocuneiform tablets of Uruk). Therefore we will not easily establish priority when searching for the earliest lexigraphic writing in the world. The fact remains that at nearly the same time as logosyllabic writing was invented in Mesopotamia in the late fourth millennium, another writing built on similar principles first appears in the southeastern tip of the fertile crescent. In this case, however, there is no prehistory of writing, no evidence for an earlier system for accounting by means of symbols, which began in Mesopotamia around the ninth millennium. The Egyptian writing comes from nowhere, without antecedents. Occam's razor requires that its inventor (whom the Egyptians called Thoth) understood the precedent principles of Mesopotamian logography (not the other way around), though the Egyptian inventor's personal contribution was very great. "Thoth" tied the writing closely to the pictures of things, making the writing potent for magic and beautiful to see, and he eliminated entirely cuneiform's complex efforts at vocalic notation in order to fashion a script in which the reader supplied the vowel sounds himself. In the curious and striking omission of vowel qualities in the phonetic structure of the new system, the Egyptian inventor changed his model's interior design in a way that was to have epoch-making consequences, still felt today.

The differences between logosyllabic Egyptian and logosyllabic Mesopotamian cuneiform are exiguous when compared with truly independent developments in writing in China and Mesoamerica, and we cannot doubt that the two systems are related historically. Clear archaeological and artistic evidence of international trade and commerce between Mesopotamia and EGYPT during the Egyptian predynastic period in the second half of the fourth millennium BC ties the civilizations closely together, though we have never found Mesopotamian tablets in Egypt (whereas in SUSA in Iran tablets clearly related to protocuneiform are found). Evidence of contact between Egypt and Mesopotamia, at opposite ends of the Fertile Crescent, includes a Mesopotamian type of boat represented on an Egyptian knife handle, the ubiquitous Mesopotamian palace-façade design in Egyptian architecture, long-necked animal Mesopotamian biforms on Egyptian votive tablets, and the Mesopotamian cylinder-seal, mark of the scribe, as an Egyptian hieroglyph. In the fourth millennium Mesopotamians are evidently living in Egypt. We should dismiss the notion, sometimes heard, that writing might have appeared independently in Egypt and in Mesopotamia at the end of the fourth millennium in the world's two earliest riverine redistributive economies. It is not hard to see how someone who understood the Mesopotamian invention reinvented it for conditions in Egypt.

Strikingly, the principal purpose of Egyptian writing during its first six hundred years of existence appears to be to promulgate and make eternal the name and being of pharaoh, not to manage a complex economy. We are, of course, dependent on the finds, and the Egyptians were using fragile papyrus from the beginning. There is some evidence from commodity labels, recently discovered, of early writing in Egypt used for economic purposes, but the evidence is hard to interpret (see below). In any event, in the hieroglyphic tradition Egyptians approached writing in a different spirit from their Mesopotamian forebears. Hieroglyphic writing was indivisible and indissoluble from Egyptian art. Not only do hieroglyphs and human figures in art exhibit the same conventions of representation, but Egyptian paintings and statuary and decoration are normally accompanied by some kind of hieroglyphic writing.

The Earliest Egyptian Writing

In sum: Both cuneiform and Egyptian writing consist of nonphonetic *logograms*, phonetic *syllabograms*, and nonphonetic semantic classifiers or *determinatives*. Both traditions are *logosyllabic*, each with about the same number of signs (around 600–700) working in similar ways, except that the Egyptian phonetic signs omit information about vibration of the vocal cords: They represent syllables, but only a native can pronounce them, through his knowledge of Egyptian speech. Cuneiform writing presented

Figure 9.1   Non-legible ivory and bone labels from Dynasty Zero, c.3300–3200 BC. (After V. Davies and R. Friedman, *Egypt Uncovered*, New York, 1998, p. 37.)

similar ambiguities, because the vowel sounds attached to syllabic signs needed constantly to be manipulated in accordance with spoken forms; cuneiform writing, although it had signs for pure vowels and although its other syllabic signs "encoded the vowels," was no more pronounceable than was Egyptian. Omission of vocalic qualities was an inspired simplification, avoiding the many confusions created by cuneiform's system of syllabification, and we might regard it as a refinement and improvement on the cuneiform system.

When did this writing first appear in Egypt? The earliest examples may be on ivory and bone labels that a German excavation discovered in 1991 in Upper Egypt in a tomb belonging to a mysterious King Scorpion of a so-called Dynasty Zero (not the famous King Scorpion of the First Dynasty), carbon–dated to around 3300–3200 BC (some scholars doubt the accuracy of this dating). Most of the labels cannot be read (Fig. 9.1). We recognize (left to right) a shrine (?); an ibis (?), an elephant; a sheaf of wheat (?), a jackal; a crested ibis; a bird with a long neck, a fetish on a stand (?); a shirt; a swallow (?) on a papyrus umbel (?); a goose, a flail (?). We cannot explain these signs but two types of label appear to make sense according to later conventions of hieroglyphic writing (Fig. 9.2). The circles in the upper right of each label are the holes used to suspend the labels from some commodity. In the upper label, the serpent

(serpent glyph) in later Egyptian writing

represents a single consonant *d̲* (something like /j/), as on the stele of King Djet (Fig. 8.1). The mountains *(mountains glyph)* = *d̲w*, beneath the serpent, represent two consonants, one already expressed by

the *(serpent glyph)*, which is therefore a

phonetic complement; the sounds *d̲w* means "mountains" (but *(mountains glyph)* could be a nonphonetic logogram: As often in logosyllabic writing, we cannot tell). The sky glyph on the left, from which is suspended a kind of magic wand

called a *was* scepter *(scepter glyph)*, in

classical Egyptian has the value *grḥ*, all consonants (the *ḥ* is an emphatic aspirate): *grḥ* means "night" in classical Egyptian. These signs might therefore mean "mountains of the night" in classical Egyptian.

The crested ibis *(ibis glyph)* on the

lower label in classical Egyptian has the value *3ḫ*, which means

Figure 9.2 Two legible (?) bone labels from tomb U-J at, from Dynasty Zero, c.3300–3200 BC. (After Günter Dreyer et al., *Umm el-Qaab I: Das Prädynastische Königsgrab U-J und seine frühen Schriftzeugnisse.* Deutsche Archäologische Institut, Abteilung Kairo. Archäologische Veröffentlichungen 86, Mainz 1998, pp. 134, 143.)

"shining" ([3] is an Egyptological convention for representing the glottal stop, which Semitists represent as [']; *ḫ* = /kh/). Again taken with *d̲w* for "mountains," the lower label may therefore mean "mountains of day." Do the two labels indicate the eastern and western banks of the Nile where the over which the sun rises, over which the sun sets, the mountains of day and the mountains of night? Are these places of origin for commodities to which these labels, found in a tomb, once were attached? "East" and "west" banks of the Nile seem vague to designate a commodity's origin. Similar labels survive from the First and Second Dynasties to identify commodities, but usually with a pharaoh's name inscribed on them. If the explanation of these two inscriptions is correct, we might wonder why the other labels do not in a similar way reveal their mysteries (Fig. 9.1). Perhaps the labels from Dynasty Zero do not in fact constitute lexigraphic writing, but contain elements of an early symbolic system later adapted in the hieroglyphic writing. Such a conservative development from a sema-siographic system used for accounting might help explain the radically different outward appearance between the inwardly related Egyptian and Mesopotamian lexigraphic writings.

In any event, simple names, such as might appear on these labels and certainly do appear on the somewhat later Narmer Palette (see Chapter 2), are all that survive of Egyptian writing for six hundred years until the Third Dynasty of King Djoser (c.2650 BC), when we first find sentences. Again, unlike the Mesopotamians who wrote on durable clay, the Egyptians wrote on papyrus, and it is hard to be sure what stands behind the tiny fragments that have survived.

Different Kinds of Signs in Egyptian Writing

There is more than one kind of sign in Egyptian writing, and a review of the different kinds is an excellent way to understand the orthography of a logosyllabic writing. Failure to grasp that signs work in different ways frustrated early attempts at decipherment and baffles students still. Scholars kept thinking that the hieroglyphic signs were all one thing, symbols, or all another thing, phonograms, "sound signs," as in an alphabet. Different theories still compete for our understanding of Egyptian writing and grammar, and there is no consistent terminology, but all agree that, as in logosyllabic Mesopotamian cuneiform, there are three principal categories (see Chapter 3):

- *phonograms*: "sound signs," where the signs have phonetic value:
  are two phonograms that spell the name of r^c = Re, the sun god. Phonograms often repeat phonetic information already encoded in other signs, when they function as phonetic complements, as in the

spelling of $\underline{d}w$ as ⟨glyph⟩ where the serpent ⟨glyph⟩ = $\underline{d}$ repeats the $\underline{d}$ in ⟨glyph⟩ = $\underline{d}w$.

- *logograms*: "word signs," where the nonphonetic signs represent whole words: ⟨glyph⟩ stands for the sun god, whose name is Re, and not for the sounds /r‹/.
- *semantic complements*, or *determinatives*: nonphonetic signs that add meaning to the phonetic hints in earlier signs, usually by placing the word within a category. For example ⟨glyph⟩ follows the names of gods and kings to indicate that the preceding phonetic or logographic information is the name of a god or king.

Exasperatingly, as in Mesopotamian cuneiform, the same sign can serve two or even three of these functions, and we are not always sure which function operates at any one time. For example, the diagram of a house ⟨glyph⟩, written with a diacritic stroke beneath it to indicate that the sign is a logogram, means "house," which in Egyptian speech has the two consonants *pr*. In writing ⟨glyph⟩ = *pr*, however, the "house" sign has through the rebus become a phonogram, a two-sound sign, with the value *pr*, now meaning to "go out," because this verb in Egyptian had the same two consonants as the noun "house." The "mouth" ⟨glyph⟩ = *r* repeats the *r* in the two-sound sign that precedes it, a phonetic complement, so the correct transliteration of ⟨glyph⟩ is *pr*, not *prr*. The "walking legs" is a semantic complement informing the reader that in this case "go out" is meant, not "house."

Types of Phonograms

The Egyptians did not themselves distinguish between different kinds of phonograms, but for purposes of learning and study scholars divide Egyptian sound signs into three classes, according to whether they designate one, two, or three sounds (a feature in Egyptian writing Champollion did not understand).

One-sound signs (uniliterals)

Around 25 signs designate a single consonant plus an unspecified vowel, sometimes called "uniliterals"; really, they are syllabograms in which the reader, a native speaker, must supply the correct vowel. Some of these consonants will not be familiar to speakers of modern European languages. Table 1 presents the 25 or so "uniliteral" hieroglyphic signs in a modern conventional order, together with names for the objects pictured by the signs; a conventional transliteration into Roman characters; the sound of the sign; and finally the "name" of the sign, how we refer to it. These uniliteral signs appear in most Egyptian words, as Champollion already noticed about the Rosetta Stone, but the consonants assigned to these signs are theoretical reconstructions and by no means an accurate guide to how they actually sounded, and, of course, they were accompanied by an unknown vowel in most cases. The conventional order of these signs given in the table is a modern construction followed in hieroglyphic dictionaries and depends on the linguistic affinity of the sounds of the signs (for example, the dentals, pronounced behind the teeth, are grouped at the end of the series). Here I adopt the European (not American) conventions for transliteration; by SOUND I mean how an Egyptologist will conventionally pronounce the sign, saying, for example, /a/ instead of attempting to reconstruct the ancient Egyptian glottal stop accompanied by an unknown vowel. In this book, when referring to Egyptian words, I have been using this system of transliteration, evolved within the discipline of Egyptology and modeled on a system for the transliteration of some Semitic languages.

Table 2 is an aid to understanding the unusual sounds and signs in Table 1, often referred to in the following chapters.

This "system" of one-sound signs within Egyptian writing is sometimes called an "alphabet" (see Fig. 13.1), a phonetic notation that might in theory have described all the basic sounds of ancient Egyptian speech (except for the vowels!). But the Egyptians did not think of their writing in this fashion, as a system of purely phonetic encoding, and they never distinguished as a group the one-consonant signs (uniliterals) from the two-consonant (biliterals) and three-consonant signs (triliterals). In no sense did the 25 uniliterals constitute an "alphabet" or function as a separate system within hieroglyphic writing.

Table 1   Twenty-five uniliteral signs

Sign	Object	Transliteration	Sound	Name
	"vulture"	ꜣ	a	aleph (**al**-ef)
	"reed"	j	i/a	j
or	"double reed"	y	y	y
	"arm"	ꜥ	a	ain (**eye**-in)
	"chick"	w	w/u	w
	"lower leg"	b	b	b
	"stool"	p	p	p
	"viper"	f	f	f
	"owl"	m	m	m
	"water"	n	n	n
	"mouth"	r	r	r
	"reed shelter"	h	h	h
	"twisted flax"	ḥ	h	dotted h
	"placenta"(?)	ḫ	kh	third h

Table 1   (*cont'd*)

Sign	Object	Transliteration	Sound	Name
	"animal belly with tail"	$\underline{h}$	kh	fourth h
	"garden pool"	*š*	sh	shin (sheen)
	"door bolt" **or**			
	"folded cloth"	*s*	z	s
	"slope of hill"	*ḳ*	q	q
	"basket with handle"	*k*	k	k
	"jar-stand"	*g*	g	g
	"loaf of bread"	*t*	t	t
	"tether"	*ṯ*	tj	second t
	"hand"	*d*	d	d
	"serpent"	*ḏ*	j	second d

Table 2   Some unusual sounds in transliteration from Egyptian

	Sign	Sound
ꜣ =	"vulture" called *aleph* (= Semitic "bull") after the Hebrew name	a "glottal stop," like the sound before the two vowels in "uh-oh"
ꜥ =	"arm" called *ain* (= Semitic for "eye"), after the name of the Hebrew character that encodes the same sound	like trying to say "ah" while clenching the muscles of the throat (this sound, a pharyngeal consonant, is common in modern spoken Arabic)
ḥ =	"twisted flax"	"emphatic" *h*, pronounced in the throat
ḫ =	"placenta"(?)	as in Scottish "lo**ch**" (back in the throat)
ẖ =	"animal belly with tail"	as in German "I**ch**" (front of the throat)
š =	"garden pool"	as in "**sh**ip"
ḳ =	"slope of hill"	back *k* (further back in the mouth)
ṯ =	"tether"	perhaps as in "**ch**oose"
ḏ =	"serpent"	as in "**j**udge"

Nonetheless, sometimes the Egyptians used just one-sound signs in spelling out words, as the name of the famous Khufu of the Fourth Dynasty (c.2575–2465 BC), builder of the great pyramid at Giza:

ḫwfw
Khufu

Two-sound signs (biliterals) and three-sound signs (triliterals)

There are about 80 biliteral or two-sound signs, sometimes hard to distinguish from logograms. Often these signs spell out (or as logograms represent) whole words. Unlike the uniliterals, they do not have "names," which for the uniliterals are really their alphabetic equivalents. Instead in Table 3 I give the sign's meaning; the biliterals, which are often logograms, can be independently meaningful.

Table 3   Some Egyptian biliterals

Sign	Object	Transliteration	Sound	Meaning
	"wooden column"	ꜥ3	aa	great
	"swallow"	wr	wer	great
	"basket"	nb	neb	lord; all

In still another class, about 30 signs appear to stand for three consonants. They always designate full words, however, and often really are logograms. Table 4 shows some common examples.

Table 4   Some Egyptian triliterals

Sign	Object	Transliteration	Sound	Meaning
	"sky and *was* scepter"	grḥ	gereh	night
	"sandal strap"(?) "female symbol"(?)	ꜥnḫ	ankh	life
	"heart and windpipe"	nfr	nefer	beautiful
	"loaf on mat"	ḥtp	hetep	be content
	"statue plinth"	m3ꜥ	maa	justified
	"dung beetle"	ḫpr	kheper	become

Nonphonetic Signs: Logograms and Semantic Complements/Determinatives

As we have seen, sometimes the signs have no phonetic value but are logograms, "word signs," standing for a word without telling the reader how that word will sound. Of the other nonphonetic signs, Table 5 lists a few common semantic complements/determinatives (which Champollion called *species*).

Table 5   Some common semantic complements/determinatives

Sign	Category
	man and his occupations
	god, king
	sun, light, time
	motion
	small bird used for weak, bad, or little things
	town, village

10

"The House of Life": Scribes and Writing in Ancient Egypt

Writing is a technology, based in the material world and intimately related to the substance that supports it. The Mesopotamians used clay, but the Egyptians made a great technological advance in their invention of papyrus, a flexible, tough, durable, inexpensive, reusable basis for preserving and transmitting written information. The papyrus-using cultures of Egypt, Greece, Rome, and Palestine were set against the older clay-tablet using cultures of Mesopotamia, Anatolia (central Turkey), and Crete, and the triumph of a light flexible medium for written expression is today universal. Probably the most common medium for writing in the East was, however, except in Egypt, the wooden folding tablet, or diptych, coated with wax and impressed with a stylus. The perishable diptych was common in Anatolia, Palestine, Syria, and Mesopotamia, and a few examples survive (Homer refers to a diptych in the story of Bellerophon in *Iliad* 6.155–203 as containing "baleful signs"). The wax-coated diptych was suited to cuneiform writing, but also the West Semitic Aramaic. In Egypt wood covered with gypsum replaced the diptych as an exercise and composition board, and, again, some examples survive.

The Tools of the Egyptian Scribe

Our "paper," which replaced papyrus, is a Chinese invention of the first century AD brought to Muslim Spain in the eighth century AD by Arab conquerors, who seem to have learned of it from Chinese prisoners. The etymology of "papyrus," a word not found in Egyptian, is unclear, but may derive from a late Egyptian phrase *p3 pr ˤ3*, "the [thing] of the Great

House," as if papyrus production and distribution was a royal monopoly. The early Greek word for papyrus is *byblos*, from the port on the eastern Mediterranean coast whence the Greeks no doubt obtained papyrus in the late Iron Age.

Papyrus is made from a tall marsh plant growing to 10 feet, triangular in shape, with a tough external rind. At the top it spreads into an umbel of stalks at the ends of which small flowers appear. The papyrus umbel was prominent in Egyptian art and was worn as a good luck charm. Papyrus was extinct in northern Egypt when Napoleon invaded in 1798, but grows today in the southern Sudan, in other equatorial African countries, in Jordan (perhaps imported in ancient times), and for some reason in Sicily in the marshes around Syracuse.

Paper is made by breaking up cloth or wood products into small fibers, mixing the fibers with water to form a pulp, then spreading the pulp over a screen and pressing out the water so that the fibers bond together. Papyrus, by contrast, was made by removing the rough rind, then cutting, or peeling, the moist and soft interior pith into strips. The strips are then cut to around one foot in length and laid side by side. Long strips are placed at right angles over the short strips. The two layers are pounded together so that the upper layer of long strips, whose grain runs horizontal, adheres to the lower layer of short strips, whose grain runs vertical. In this way a single sheet is formed. Sheets are attached to each other by overlapping them at the edges and pounding again. In this way a roll is formed, made up usually of about 20 sheets. Each roll contained as much information as seven or ten pages of this book. This luminous invention, the papyrus roll, in Latin *volumen*, was the material basis for the transmission of Mediterranean intellectual culture for perhaps four thousand years.

When rolled, the scroll was tied with a string, then a lump of clay was pressed on the knot and a seal impressed into the clay to identify the owner or preparer of the roll. Such seals were kept on strings worn around the neck, or around the finger, one origin of the modern finger ring. The hieroglyph of a tied roll with clay seal is a determinative for anything abstract, such as "plan" or "thought," evidently because the written content of scrolls could be abstract. Impressed clay sealings that were once attached to papyrus and other objects are found in the tens of thousands in the excavation of ancient sites all over the Mediterranean.

Figure 10.1   Old Kingdom limestone statue of a noble named Kai, from his tomb at Saqqara, c.2450 BC. He holds the fresh papyrus roll with his left hand, while his right hand holds a stylus (missing), inscribing the page before him. (Art Resource, New York, ART332685; Paris, Louvre.)

There were no desks in the ancient world. To write, the scribe squatted on the ground cross-legged, drawing his linen skirt taut, like a mini desk. Holding the scroll in his left hand, he unrolled it with his right. He inscribed as much text as the surface allowed, then unrolled the next section. The written portion of the papyrus fell off to the right, or was rolled up as the scribe continued his work (Fig. 10.1).

Egyptian papyri were inscribed in black ink made from carbon, and red ink made from a natural iron oxide. Mostly the text was black, but headings and important words were in red. The red headings allowed the scribe to find and keep his place as he made his way through the logosyllabic forest, reading aloud as he went. Written documents, though they are unpronounceable as such, were always meant to support speech.

Hieroglyphic documents also kept their close association with magical power. For example, as the ill-omened color of the dangerous desert, red ink was changed to black in an otherwise red section to write the names of gods or kings (who might be harmed by the color). In pyramid texts such dangerous signs as crocodiles, snakes, and ducks (!) were truncated, cut, and stabbed to destroy their power.

In the Old Kingdom the scribe's equipment consisted of a tube to hold a selection of styluses, two mixing pans, and a sack for pigments of ink: the hieroglyphic logogram for scribe . The stylus was a reed whose end the scribe has chewed to make a kind of brush. Writing on papyrus is similar to painting. A wooden relief of an official named Hesire (he-si-re, "praised by Re") from the Third Dynasty (c.2650–2575 BC) shows him standing, in his right hand the *sekhem* "power" staff , really a three-dimensional logogram and a staff of authority, and in his left hand other staves of power and the scribal equipment. Hesire's titles include "foremost of dentists and doctors," "known to the king" (his relative?), "governor of Buto" (a town in the Delta), and "chief of the scribes of the king, greatest of Upper Egypt" (Fig. 10.2).

After the Middle Kingdom (c.2100–1750 BC) a different style of writing apparatus became common, an elongated hollow box to hold the reeds and two blocks of ink. A luxurious example from the tomb of

Figure 10.2 The name and titles of the nobleman Hesire, from a wooden panel from his tomb at Saqqara, c.2575 BC

Tutankhamen appears actually to have been used by the king. The king, too, could read and write.

The Role of Scribes

The title *sš* "scribe," written logographically ⬚ , is an important title that often appears with the names of such powerful men as Hesire, who controlled knowledge and governed the state. An official rank was that of "lector priest," as we translate *ḥry ḥb* (⬚ , the first two signs inverted for aesthetic reasons). The phrase really means "bearer of the ritual [book]."

The thousands of prayers, hymns, and other texts that cover the walls of Egyptian temples often begin with "words to be spoken by . . ."

(⬚ *ḏd ḥmw jn*), usually by a god, but the lector-priest's ability to actually create effective speech from written signs gave him his power within the offices of state and temple (Fig. 10.3). Literate Egyptians were not a body of functionaries of modest social status who served the economic, legal, and religious needs of the state – a "scribal class." Rather, the tiny number who could read and write (with few exceptions) *were* the elite, those who controlled state power, such men as Hesire. There was no illiterate nobility in ancient Egypt, as was true, for example, in Europe during the medieval period. Those very few who understood Egyptian writing were the same men who commanded the army, performed temple ritual, and imposed civil control on the population. They shared a common culture based in a common religion.

When we try to estimate how many Egyptians were literate, we really estimate the size of the ruling elite. Guesses, based on no statistical evidence, range from 0.3 to 5 percent. When we study "the Egyptians," really we study the thought, religion, achievements, and aspirations of this tiny elite. About the thoughts of those who worked the fields from birth to death, then were buried in unmarked graves at the edge of the desert or thrown into the Nile, we have no information. Writing preserves only the thought of literate peoples.

Figure 10.3   The lector-priest, dressed in a long linen gown with a linen apron, holds a papyrus roll at left. He reads aloud the ritual of "opening the mouth" to revivify the mummy. From the Papyrus of Ani, Nineteenth Dynasty, c.1200 BC. (London, British Museum EA 10470/3.)

An Example of Egyptian Writing

Let us consider an actual example of the scribe's power as keeper of the secrets of eternal life. One of the most common spells, called the offering formula, is found in wide variety on thousands of steles over most of Egyptian history. In it we can observe the many orthographic complexities of Egyptian logosyllabic writing, similar to those found in cuneiform. The spell was meant through magic to guarantee eternal sustenance for the *ka*, the essence of the deceased. Earlier we examined the close affinity between artistic representation and Egyptian hieroglyphs on the stele of one Sarennewtet from the Old Kingdom (c.2200 BC) (Chapter 4); let us now consider the first 11 lexigraphic signs on this same stele written from right to left and top to bottom (Fig. 10.4): A standard transliteration into Roman characters of the first 11 signs reads (< > means that the enclosed character is not written in the Egyptian)

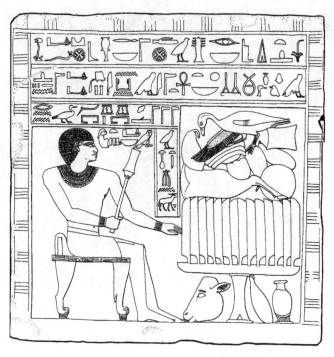

Figure 10.4 Stele with offering formula, Sixth Dynasty (c.2200 BC). Carved limestone. (London, British Museum, EA 585; drawing after Collier and Manley 1998, p. 48.)

ḥtp dj nsw <n> ꜣsr nb ḏdw

meaning

"An offering that the king gives to Osiris, lord of Djedu . . ."

The first sign ⸙ "sedge plant" = *nsw* "king" functions as a triliteral, but is out of place, transposed to the beginning of the sentence in order to honor the king (called "honorific transposition").

The second sign ⌒ "bread loaf" = *t* functions as a phonetic complement to the third sign, the triliteral "offering mat" ⬭ = *ḥtp*, placed beneath "bread loaf" for aesthetic reasons: note how the Egyptian signs are grouped into quadrants – invisible boxes – and are not written in a line ⬭ ⌒ .

The fourth sign ⩘ "offering loaf" is a biliteral with the value *dj* = "give,"

but here (for complex reasons) with the meaning "that [the king] gives."

The inscription omits the preposition *n* = "to," that is, "to Osiris," because the phrase is so common the preposition is not felt to be necessary.

The fifth and sixth signs, ⎕ "throne" = *ȝs* and ⬯ "eye" = *jr*,

together form a phonetic spelling for Osiris, either *ȝsr* or *ȝsjr*, but are written together so often that the two signs taken together have become a virtual logogram for the god's name. From this spelling Horapollo was able

to claim that the ⬯ meant "divine" or god (compare Fig. 7.2), the

Masonic origin of the eye over the pyramid on the American dollar bill where the eye (= "God") is the grammatical subject of *annuit coeptis*, "favored the undertaking" (that is, the foundation of the American republic). This conceit goes back to Horapollo.

The seventh sign ⬭ "basket" = *nb*, "lord" is grouped in a quadrant with the "eye" according to Egyptian preference for arranging characters.

The biliteral eighth sign ⧦ "djed pillar" (a fetish sacred to Osiris) is to

be read *ḏd* along with the ninth sign, the uniliteral phonetic complement "hand" ⬭ = *d* (this sign appeared on the Bankes Obelix in the name

of Cleopatra). The tenth sign "chick" 𓅱 adds the value *w* to spell *ḏdw*,

the name of a town in the Delta where Osiris was important. The "chick" precedes "hand," although the sound comes afterwards, in order to form a pleasing arrangement of the signs within the quadrant.

The eleventh sign is a "city-diagram" ⊗ , a determinative classifying

Djedu as a town.

In only 11 signs, therefore, we find uniliterals, biliterals, triliterals, a kind of logogram, and a determinative. It is easy to see why hieroglyphs were not understood by most Egyptians, and why the scribes' knowledge of this system of thought ensured their power within the state.

11

Syllabic Scripts of the Aegean

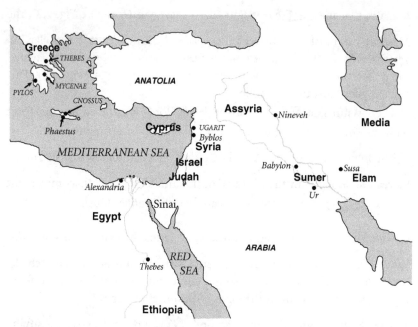

Map 3   Places important in Chapter 11

The extraordinary civilization that sprang up on Crete in the Bronze Age, claimed by the British Arthur Evans as the "earliest European civilization" two years after Crete broke from the Ottoman Empire in 1905, did not come from a vacuum; it emerged under the influence of Mesopotamian and sometimes Egyptian traditions. The structuring of the economy and society around a central palace that controlled agricultural production and the distribution of commodities and the assignment of personnel closely parallels Mesopotamian and Egyptian models, as does the use of writing to serve this economic structure. Mesopotamian influence is conspicuous in Cretan writing on clay tablets, but, just as in Mesopotamia, they must also have written on leather and wood. Unlike in Mesopotamia, they may have written on papyrus too, acquired from Egypt, with which they had close contact from an early time.

Of course the Cretans were not Mesopotamians, and their distance in culture and space from Mesopotamia and Egypt allowed them to break from older traditions of writing, to discard the heavy apparatus of logograms and determinatives and reduce their writing to phonetic elements. The notion of a writing that consists solely of phonetic signs may be an Aegean invention, but we cannot think that the Cretans sought consciously to improve the technology of civilization. Seventy percent of words on surviving Linear B documents are names of people and places. Cretan innovation toward a phonetic system was a response to the needs placed on that system. Cretan administration must have depended on a social network. Personal names were a system for social control. Unlike that of Mesopotamia, Cretan writing scarcely went beyond accounting, though Linear A signs on libation tables and jewelry occur in a noneconomic context. As far as we know, Aegean syllabic scripts were never used in the Bronze Age for literary, ritual, commemorative, or scientific purposes, although they lasted for hundreds of years.

"Cretan hieroglyphs"

Around the beginning of the second millennium BC, during the Egyptian Middle Kingdom (c.2100–1750 BC), two writings appeared at about the same time on Crete. One of them Arthur Evans, the excavator of CNOSSUS, called "hieroglyphic" because of a supposed resemblance to Egyptian writing; the other he called Linear A. Many take the undeciphered Linear A, first attested c.1800 BC, as somehow a development from the undeciphered "Cretan hieroglyphs," which are first attested c.2100 BC; on formal grounds such a development is not obvious. "Cretan hieroglyphs" and Linear A are used side by side for generations in the early second millennium BC, but Linear A is almost never found on seals. Yet if each writing system consists of phonetic signs that encode syllables with few logograms or determinatives, as seems probable from the number of signs in either case (around 100), "Cretan hieroglyphs" and Linear A must be closely related.

Figure 11.1　"Cretan hieroglyphs," c.1700 BC inscribed on four sides of a rectangular sealstone found at Lyttos, in east central Crete. The signs are artistically arranged and include filler decoration. We do not know in what direction to read them. (Heraklion, Crete, National Archaeological Museum; after Chadwick 1987, fig. 25.)

Perhaps different languages underlie the two systems, but we cannot know because we know nothing about the languages of Crete before Greek is attested around 1400 BC.

"Cretan hieroglyphs" is a misnomer because the shapes of the signs have nothing to do with Egyptian signs. They must be free inventions made in Crete. About 1,700 inscribed signs survive on all objects: The complete corpus of "Cretan hieroglyphs" amounts to 30 lines of text in this book, too little material to allow for a decipherment. (Michael Ventris had 30,000 inscribed signs to work with in deciphering Linear B in 1952.) About half of extant "Cretan hieroglyphs" are found on seals made of stone, ivory, and metal, and on the impressions in clay made by these seals (Fig. 11.1). The other half of the corpus are often linear characters in archives inscribed on tablets of unbaked clay from the same period as the seals. These accounting documents have the same general layout current five hundred years later on the Linear B tablets. We wish we knew to what the clay sealings were attached, perhaps to rolls of papyrus as in Egypt and the Levant, and to commodities as a sign of ownership or responsibility. Vigorous trade between Crete, Cyprus, Syria, and Egypt exposed Cretans to older Eastern traditions and inspired such use of seals.

Figure 11.2   The Phaestus disk, c.1850–1600 BC. (After A. J. Evans, *Scripta Minoa*, Vol. 1, Oxford 1909, pl. 12.)

Impenetrable, and thoroughly puzzling, without comparative evidence, is the celebrated Phaestus disk, found in 1908 at the palace of PHAESTUS in southern Crete. Dated to 1850–1600 BC, its signs are different from Cretan hieroglyphs and represent objects and humans not easily paralleled in Cretan art (Fig. 11.2). The inscription runs in a spiral made up of 30 compartments on one side, 31 on the other. Each compartment contains a group of from two to seven signs. Some groups are repeated, suggesting that they represent words. Forty-five separate signs, most pictorial, are uniquely impressed in the clay by means of stamps, the earliest "printing" on earth.

Nothing like the Phaestus disk has ever been found since. Because no signs resemble those found in the hieroglyphic Cretan script or elsewhere, many wonder if the object is from Crete at all. If the stamps are lexigraphic writing, it must be a syllabary, because there are too few signs for a logo-syllabic system. The disk was deliberately fired, unlike the accounting tablets, which were fired accidentally. Some have thought the mysterious disk to be a game, similar to a spiral-shaped game played in Egypt. In spite of many fanciful attempts, we lack the three things that make a decipherment possible: abundant comparative material; a bilingual inscription one of whose languages is known; knowledge of the underlying language.

Linear A

"Cretan hieroglyphs" are confined to central and eastern Crete, but Linear A is found throughout the island and on several other islands. "Cretan hieroglyphs" fall into disuse around 1650 BC at the end of the so-called First Palace Period (no doubt a connection), whereas Linear A continues until the cataclysm of c.1450 BC. Around this time, under obscure conditions, Linear B appears, now deciphered as representing Greek. Arthur Evans found a large cache of Linear B tablets at Cnossus shortly after he began excavation in 1900, and other tablets have been found in Chania in northwest Crete. Linear B tablets also turn up on the mainland at MYCENAE, TIRYNS, PYLOS, and THEBES, with scattered finds of Linear B elsewhere (mostly inscribed on "stirrup jars," large amphoras for storing produce), and persist until c.1200 BC near the end of the Bronze Age. The writing disappeared with the collapse of Mycenaean Greek civilization and the centralized palace redistributive economies that the writing supported. Only on the island of Cyprus did the Aegean tradition of syllabic writing survive, first in the undeciphered "Cypro-Minoan" script (related to Linear A) found after c.1500 BC on Cyprus (and some finds at UGARIT on the Syrian coast), then in the "Cypriote syllabary," clearly attested between the eighth and second centuries BC (but certainly older) and used side by side with the Greek alphabet.

The undeciphered Linear A script survives in about 1,500 separate inscriptions, many on small, neatly inscribed clay tablets from central and eastern Crete, many of these from the important southern center of Ayia Triada (near Phaestus). Greater in number are single-sign inscriptions on clay sealings. Signs also appear on clay pots and engraved on metal and stone objects, in some cases apparently the names of people and commodities, but in other cases they are too long to be just names. "Cretan hieroglyphs" and Linear A share about 20 of their approximately 100 signs and use the same simple decimal system for records.

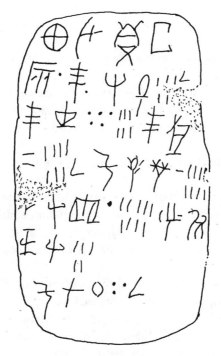

Figure 11.3 Linear A tablet from Ayia Triada, c.1500 BC. (After Chadwick 1987, fig. 26.)

About 7,500 inscribed signs survive in the entire corpus of Linear A, four times as many as hieroglyphic signs, about five pages of text in a book this size. Working backward from our knowledge about Linear B, we can draw some conclusions about Linear A documents. In Figure 11.3, an accounting tablet, the vertical strokes represent "ones" and the dots represent "tens." The "check-mark" ∠ at the bottom means "one-half" and the circle ◯ to its left means "one hundred." The signs read from left to right. The top four signs may designate a place name. The first sign of the second row designates "wine" in Linear B, which presumably took over this sign and its meaning from Linear A. The second sign in the row is preceded and followed by a dot ⚹ , perhaps meaning "paid out" or the like, because now follow six groups of signs, each followed by a numeral. The groups of signs must be names, of persons or places, and the numbers indicate the quantities of wine (?). The writer is happy to break a name at the edge of the tablet (as in line 5) and run it on to the next line; this rarely happens in Linear B. At the end of the tablet, the first two

signs ⚹ must mean "total" because the number "130 1/2," a circle,

three dots, and a check mark, is the correct total for the above tallies.

In this way we can offer a plausible interpretation of this unusually well-preserved tablet, but we cannot decipher it. Most Linear A material is of just such a restricted nature, lists of names and commodities and perhaps places.

Around 50 Linear A signs are taken up, often in modified form, in the later Linear B script (see below). Now that we know the phonetic values of the deciphered Linear B signs, we can try to plug these values into Linear A documents and so "read" them. In this way, Michael Ventris was able to transfer the sound values of about 10 signs from the later, related "Cypriote syllabary" (see below) into the Linear B system, as his decipherment of Linear B took shape. Often signs change value when a preexisting system is applied to a new language, yet some values may stay the same. On general principles, Linear A signs are likely to represent both pure vowels and open syllables like *pa*, as in Linear B. We assume the same about the structure of the "Cretan hieroglyphic" script, because in the same tradition you will expect the same underlying structure. Unfortunately, giving Linear B values to Linear A signs has yielded poor results. All we seem to learn about the underlying language is that it is not Greek. In the Linear

B tablets a totaling formula parallel to the Linear A ⚹ appears with

the phonetic values *to-so*, familiar from the classical Greek form *tosos* = "so much." Here in Linear A, using known values taken from the Linear

B signs, we should therefore read ⚹ as *ku-ro*, which cannot be

explained as a word in Greek or in any other known language. The signs

꒕ 十 must mean "total," but in what language? And what is their real phonetic value?

Linear B

Whereas relationships between "Cretan hieroglyphs" and Linear A are unclear, we have more confidence about the origin of Linear B. Around 1450 BC palaces all over Crete were destroyed, whether by earthquake or foreign invasion or both. Only Cnossus was rebuilt, then destroyed again c.1375 BC, again by unknown agency. We would welcome a historical connection between the invention of the Linear B script, which encodes Greek, and Greek presence in Cnossus around 1450 BC, and for many years such a date seemed plausible. However, recent study of the irresolvably tangled stratigraphy of the tablet-finds at Cnossus may point to the later date of c.1350 for the accidental firing of the tablets in a palace conflagration. A third destruction may have taken place at Cnossus c.1250 some think. Do the tablets belong to the third destruction level, or are they mixed in with earlier destruction levels? We cannot securely date the Cnossus tablets except to say c.1400–1250 BC.

Not only the presence of tablets encoding Greek, but changes in ceramics and styles of building similar to those on the mainland in the mid-second millennium prove that a new people was living in the land. Whether the Greeks occupied a land already ruined by natural disaster or were themselves the agents of that ruin cannot be known. The correlation between the Greek occupation of Cnossus c.1450 and the invention of the script by Greek invaders at about the same time remains plausible. The Greek occupiers of Cretan lands and property used the script to conduct an economy similar in basic features to that of the Minoans whose world they had usurped.

Evidently one man has created the Linear B script by modifying, often in an arbitrary way, the earlier Linear A script, the writing of the nonGreek Minoans. He must have been a Greek speaker, bilingual, working with Minoan scribes; or a Minoan who learned Greek, probably in Cnossus itself. Linear B retained about 50 of the Linear A signs, modified another 10, discarded the rest, and invented 17 new signs to make a total of around 87 phonetic signs. A second category made up of logograms stands outside the system of phonograms: commodity signs that establish a context for the transaction recorded by means of phonograms.

About 5,000 tablets with Linear B writing on them survive. From Cnossus alone come around 3,400. We detect the hands of 100 scribes from Cnossus. From Pylos on the mainland come more than 1,100 tablets by 32 scribes, securely dated to c.1200 BC. The other finds are small but always associated with a Bronze Age palace, the centers of power in Greek myth: at Thebes, Orchomenus, Mycenae, Tiryns, and a few other sites. According to a common view, some Greek myths go back to the Bronze Age. We find in the tablets the names of Neleus and Hector, evidently common names in the Bronze Age. We also find the names of some Olympian deities, but not all.

The tablets survived in every case because they were burned in a deliberate destruction, direct testimony to the end of the Bronze Age in the Aegean. In everyday life, unlike in Mesopotamia, the tablets were sun dried, remoistened, erased, and reused. They are temporary records, notations meant to be summarized and catalogued some place else, perhaps on papyrus (Linear B signs are hard to draw in clay). The deposits from Cnossus and the deposits from Pylos come from a single year, as if once a year the old records were discarded and accounts began anew.

In contrast to Linear A, few examples of Linear B writing survive on surfaces other than clay tablets. Only three Linear B inscriptions, on drinking vessels, are private inscriptions. Inscribed seals exist but are rare. Linear B seems to have been used by a special group of men whose task it was to keep track of economic data in a primitive but highly bureaucratized state. Linear A writing was more widespread, perhaps on the model of Egyptian practice, in which "literacy" was a prerogative of all the ruling elite. No doubt Mycenaean scribes were an elite in their own right. Because we recognize so many hands in the tablets at Cnossus – a large office even in modern times – and in the tablets from Pylos, the economic reach of the palace must have been considerable, or enormous.

The Decipherment of Linear B

In 1952 the remarkable British architect Michael Ventris (1922–56) deciphered Linear B, one of the finest intellectual achievements of the twentieth century. Like Champollion, he was short-lived; he died at age 34 in an automobile accident. By proving against his own assumptions (like Champollion) that the underlying language of Linear B was Greek, Ventris pushed back historical knowledge of the Greeks by four or five hundred years into the Bronze Age, meaning that it is the longest recorded language on earth of any still spoken today. The consequences of his decipherment have deeply enriched our understanding of the history of the Greek language and Greek culture and our understanding of the Bronze Age, and of the seminal poet Homer, whose poetry seems somehow to have roots in the Bronze Age.

There are no bilingual texts for Linear B and the underlying language was unknown – Ventris thought it might be Etruscan – but there was an abundance of comparative material. A rigorous and scientific analysis of statistical patterns in this material allowed Ventris to discover the phonetic values attached to some signs.

Arthur Evans, to his discredit, kept the tablets from Cnossus to himself until his death 40 years later, always thinking he would decipher them. He published some tablets in archaeological reports and in his *Scripta Minoa I* of 1909, but the majority were not published until 1952, 10 years after he died, and then only partly. Although Evans found his tablets in 1900 no one knew even what the repertory of signs was, not easy to say when the same sign may be written differently by different hands. In 1951 the American Emmett L. Bennett Jr. (b. 1918) at last established the repertory of signs by examining the tablets found at Pylos in 1939 just before the outbreak of war, which prevented further exploration.

Most tablets contained numerical tallies, and earlier Bennett had deciphered the numerical system as consisting of vertical strokes for units, horizontal strokes for tens, circles for hundreds, and a rayed circle for one thousand (similar to the numerical system in Linear A). Hence

$$\bigcirc\,\substack{\bigcirc\bigcirc\\\bigcirc}\,\substack{=\,=\\=}\,\substack{||||\\|||} = 1,000 + 300 + 50 + 7 = 1,357.$$ Such tabulations

repeatedly came at the right end of lines on the tablets, preceded by a recurring symbol. The tablets must read from left to right and the recurring symbols followed by vertical strokes, a number tally, must represent a commodity (Fig. 11.4). Undoubtedly accounting documents, but of what?

Evidently there were two kinds of signs, because one kind was never mixed with the other. Presumably one kind of sign was phonetic, the group with around 90 signs, and the other logographic or semasiographic commodity signs, of which there were over 100 (professional Mycenologists may call these signs "ideograms"). The more than 100 commodity signs

Figure 11.4 Linear B tablet, c.1200 BC, from the palace archive at Pylos listing contributions of some kind of bronze ⊟ from all over the kingdom, perhaps to meet the needs of a military crisis. Sixteen places are named. Note the numbers in the middle and at the right ends of each line, denoting quantities of bronze. ⊞ means "× 4," ⌇ means "× 30." (Pylos tablet Jn 829, after Chadwick, 1987, fig. 17.)

are stylized pictures of recognizable objects (Fig. 11.5). About 40 of the 60 logographic signs in Linear A also turn up among the logographic signs in Linear B.

Bennett counted 86 nonlogographic signs, that is, phonograms, in his decisive publication of 1951 (present research recognizes 87). The system was presumably syllabic, because one expects around 70 to 90 signs in a syllabary that encodes vocalic qualities. A logosyllabary, by contrast, will have several hundred, as did Egyptian hieroglyphic and Mesopotamian cuneiform. Chinese is a kind of logography, with 50,000 signs in its full

Figure 11.5 Some Linear B logographic (nonphonetic) signs designating commodities, with the meanings we now attribute to them. (After http://www.omniglot.com/writing/linearb.htm.)

range. In any event, without knowing the underlying language, there was no obvious way to discover phonetic values assigned to the Linear B signs. The sometimes similar and certainly related Cypriote syllabary (Fig. 11.11), deciphered in the nineteenth century, suggested values for some of the Linear B signs, but substitution of their values did not solve the puzzle (in fact some are the same). Without a bilingual it was not clear how a decipherment could proceed.

In larger rectangular tablets, ruled lines divide each line of writing, unlike in Linear A, which did not rule the lines (see Fig. 11.4). Words were separated in the Linear B tablets by a space or a change in the size of the characters, or separated by short vertical strokes. The American classical scholar Alice Kober (1906–50, who died at a young age of lung cancer before Ventris's decipherment, to which she contributed), made lists of such word groupings and noticed that in some cases the first signs of a grouping would be constant, while the ending sign or signs would change. Such behavior looked like the inflection we find in *amo, amas, amat,* the way that Greek and Latin work when the endings change but the root is fixed. If one could control statistically the kind of variations found at the end, or beginnings, of word groupings that shared a common core, it might be possible to guess about their actual phonetic values. Following such reasoning, Kober took a first step toward the decipherment.

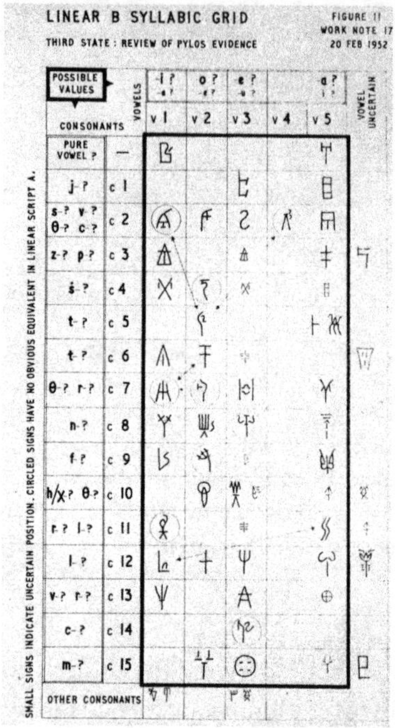

Figure 11.6 A grid by Michael Ventris with the columns representing vowels and the rows representing consonants. (After Pope 1999, fig. 114.)

Michael Ventris, like Champollion, took a keen interest in his topic as a boy, when he met Arthur Evans and learned of the mysterious script that Evans found at Cnossus. Ventris did not pursue an academic career but trained and practiced as an architect. He worked on Linear B as a hobby.

Obviously the system was a syllabary, probably of open CV (consonant/vowel) signs, to guess from the number of signs. One might be able to construct a grid with vowels across the top and consonants down the side, creating slots for the 86 or 87 characters, Ventris reasoned (Fig. 11.6). If one knew the underlying language, one might find values for the signs that would produce appropriate words when these values were plugged in. However, in the 1950s the scholarly world lay under the influence of Arthur Evans's theory that the certainly nonGreek "Minoans" had controlled a great thalassocracy, a sea-empire that included the southern mainland of the Balkan peninsula. For this reason, Evans thought, the tablets found at Pylos just before the Second World War indicated a Minoan outpost on the mainland. The underlying language would be the unknown "Cretan," and certainly not Greek.

In an unusual spirit of scholarly collaboration, Ventris made up a series of these grids and circulated them among a small group of dedicated scholars as the decipherment went forward. He began to deduce the phonetic values of the signs in the following way, making use of Alice Kober's approach. The combination 𐀵 𐀰 appears often before a tally, with a logogram designating a male; whereas the combination 𐀵 𐀱 appears with logograms designating females. Probably the second signs in the combination, 𐀰 and 𐀱 share a consonant, but have different vowels, masculine and feminine. Therefore these two signs must fall some place in the same "consonant" column of his grid.

Astutely guessing that certain place names were the same in the classical period as in the Bronze Age, Ventris began to suggest actual phonetic values for several signs. From the Cnossus tablets he isolated sign groups explicable as *ko-no-so*, that is *Knossos*, and *am-ni-so*, or *Amnisos*, a Cretan harbor mentioned by Homer. By the same token, the combination 𐀢𐀫 appears repeatedly, sometimes in very large characters, on tablets from Pylos. Hence 𐀢 may stand for *pu* and 𐀫 for *lo*, that is, a liquid plus the vowel /o/ (in fact Mycenologists transcribe 𐀫 as *ro*, a convention for a *liquid* + /o/).

On the basis of phonetic probabilities determined in this fashion, the tally signs 𐀵 𐀰 would appear to yield the value *to-so*, which is classical Greek *tosos*, "so much," masculine gender, and 𐀵 𐀱 would yield the value *to-sa*, "how much," the feminine form in classical Greek. Evidently Linear B writing was attached to a form of the Greek language, to the great surprise of Ventris and everyone else. If so, to the ground fell Evans's theory of a Minoan thalassocracy with outposts on the mainland and all that implied for understanding the Mediterranean Bronze Age. Other Greek words and forms emerged in the writing. There could be no doubt that Greek speakers were living in Cnossus in the fourteenth century BC, somehow, and they were using Linear B as an administrative tool.

Figure 11.7 The values of the Linear B syllabic signs. The vowel sounds are given at the top of the columns, and the consonantal values at the left-hand side. (After http://www.ancientscripts.com/linearb.html.)

How Linear B Works

We can now read Linear B writing almost with facility. There are around 87 purely phonetic syllabic signs. 5 are pure vowels and 82 stand for consonant–vowel combinations. Some signs are doublets or their value is unclear or unknown, but the basic system is given in the 60 signs shown in Figure 11.7.

Transliterations of Linear B signs into Roman alphabetic characters, as in Figure 11.7, are conventional, however, and do not represent the real sounds such signs might have borne in ancient times. Complex spelling rules allow a limited number of signs to cover a wide range of phonetic expression. Hence no distinction is made between /p/, /ph/, and /b/, or between /k/, /kh/, and /g/, or between /t/ and /th/. The only consonants

sign sequence	transliteration	Mycenaean Greek	classic Greek	meaning/ derivations
𐀓𐀈𐀜	ku-mi-no	•kuminon	kuminon	cumin
𐀓𐀙𐀊	ku-na-ja	•gunaia	gune	woman (*gynecology*)
𐀓𐀬𐀰	ku-ru-so	•khrusos	khrusos	gold (*chrysanthemun*)
𐀞𐀳	pa-te	•pater	pater	father
𐀞𐀔𐀒	pa-ma-ko	•pharmakon	pharmakon	medicine (*pharmacy*)
𐀵𐀰	to-so	•toso	tosos	so many
𐀵𐀨𐀐	to-ra-ke	•thorakes	thorax	thorax
𐀤𐀄	qo-u-	•gwou-	bou-	cow
𐀂𐀦	i-qo	•hikkwoi	hippos	horse (*hippopotamus*)
𐀩𐀄𐀏	re-u-ka	•leuka	leukos	white (*leukemia*)
𐀩𐀀	re-a	•rea	rhis, rhino-	nose (*rhinoplasty*)

Figure 11.8   Chart of transliterations of various words in Linear B.
The asterisk* designates a reconstructed and hypothetical form. (After
http://www.ancientscripts.com/linearb.html.)

found at the end of Greek words are /s/, /n/, or /r/, so these sounds are
often left off. So is terminal /i/. When two consonants come together, the
reader has to swallow the vowel. For example, classical *tripos*, "tripod," is
spelled *ti-ri-po*: The first /i/ is swallowed in pronunciation and the final /s/
is dropped in writing.

Figure 11.8 gives examples of transliterations of some Linear B words.
The first column gives the Linear B signs; the second gives the conventional
transliteration according to Ventris's grid, the actual theoretical phonetic
information encoded in the sign; the third gives a theoretical reconstruction of how the whole word might have sounded in the Bronze Age;
the fourth column shows how the word would have been written in the
classical Greek alphabet (transliterated into Roman script); and the fifth
column gives the meaning of the word (and some modern derivations).
When the scribe reads, for example, *i-qo* (our conventional rendering), he

ko-ri-ja-do-no

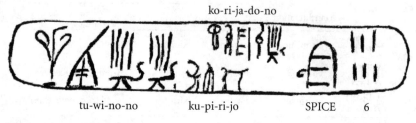

tu-wi-no-no   ku-pi-ri-jo   SPICE   6

Figure 11.9   An accounting tablet from Cnossus. (KN Ga 676.)

knows that *hippos* is meant, because the phonetic clues are close enough that he, a native speaker, can guess from the context of the writing what is intended.

Let us consider an actual example of a leaf-shaped Linear B tablet from Cnossus (Fig. 11.9). The first four signs, left to right, transliterate as *tu-wi-no-no*, evidently a man's name in the dative case (the dative ending /i/ is not written), perhaps "to Twinon" (a classical *Sinon* might be a descendant). Next, in smaller characters on the lower level, *ku-pi-ri-jo*, that is, *kyprios*, perhaps modifying "coriander": Either the spice comes from Cyprus or is meant to be shipped there (but some think *ku-pi-ri-jo* is a name, the "Cypriote"). Above *ku-pi-ri-jo*, in small characters, *ko-ri-ja-do-no*, or *koriandron*, our own "coriander" (the same plant, cilantro or coriander, whose leaves are used in a modern salad). Then a logogram ⟨logogram⟩ meaning "spice," and six strokes. Evidently Twinon has received an allotment of 6 units of spice(s) from (or for) Cyprus, of use in the ancient perfume industry.

Some scholars denied the decipherment because the writing did not fulfill the expectations of alphabet users. The undeciphered, and probably undecipherable, "Cretan hieroglyphs" and Linear A prove that the Cretan family of scripts was used from the beginning to manage the collection and distribution of commodities. For this purpose, we have four desiderata: the name of the donor or seller; the place where it came from; the name of the commodity; and the quantity exchanged. For these purposes Linear B, and no doubt its predecessors, was well designed.

Casting away the nonphonetic elements so important to Mesopotamian writing, the Minoan inventor of Cretan writing fashioned a purely phonetic syllabary capable of recording the important sounds in the name of any person or thing. Such syllabic records accompanied logographic or semasiographic nonphonetic signs that designate commodities, but such commodity signs were not part of the self-contained syllabic system, which had only phonetic signs. Linear B writing was far more economical than its cuneiform model and the comparable tradition in Egypt, and we might view it as an advance in the technology of writing. Yet couched in the older logosyllabaries arose powerful traditions of abstract thought, of mathematics, religion, ritual, and literature, whereas in Cretan writing we have only temporary tabulations of worldly goods.

Syllabic Writing on Cyprus

The powerful tool of Cretan writing did not disappear with the collapse of the Bronze Age c.1200 BC. Minoans had long had connections with CYPRUS, the geographical direct intermediary between Crete and the riches of Eastern culture, which in the Bronze Age poured into the Mediterranean over the international emporium of Ugarit, 75 miles due east from Cyprus (for more on Ugarit, see Chapter 12). Minoans were living on Cyprus, as Greeks did later and Phoenicians too. By the middle of the second millennium a Cretan-style syllabary, based on Linear A, was used on Cyprus, called Cypro-Minoan. The undeciphered Cypro-Minoan records an unknown language or even languages; there are three types of the script. The underlying language or languages must have belonged to early inhabitants of Cyprus. Few examples of Cypro-Minoan survive, some from Cyprus and others from Ugarit on the Syrian coast.

According to Greek tradition, Greeks came to Cyprus after the Trojan War. According to archaeological finds, Mycenaean Greeks were living there by 1200 BC, especially in the west of the island. The temple to Aphrodite in the southwest was so important to Greek religion that Aphrodite was, simply, the Cyprian. The occupying Greeks who came in the Late Bronze Age must have modified the Cypro-Minoan syllabic script, itself modified from Linear A, to create the deciphered script that we call the Cypriote syllabary.

A single inscription in the Cypriote syllabary, a name on a spit, survives from the eleventh century BC, then nothing until c.800 BC, a curious lacuna that is hard to explain. After 800 BC come many inscriptions in the Cypriote syllabary. The Macedonian invasion in 333 BC brought a preference for the Greek alphabet. The script was gone by c.200 BC, after being used for hundreds of years side by side with linear West Semitic and the Greek alphabet.

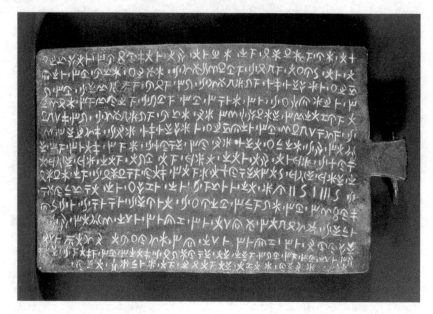

Figure 11.10   The bronze tablet of Idalion, imitating the shape of a writing board, c.480 BC. (Paris, Louvre.)

Evidence for the Cypriote syllabary emerged in the middle of the nineteenth century with the collecting efforts of a French numismatist, one Duc de Luynes. In 1852 he published a native Cypriote script based on writing on coins and on a single long text that de Luynes bought on the antiquities market, the famous Idalion tablet (Fig. 11.10). The tablet is an imitation in bronze of a wooden writing tablet and is still by far the longest example of Cypriote syllabic writing. Idalion was an important center (modern Dali) in east-central Cyprus. The inscription records a contract between a family of physicians and the people of Idalion to treat those wounded in a Persian assault sometime in the early fifth century BC.

De Luynes attempted to penetrate the script by guessing the meaning of a word repeated on many coins. Then in 1869 a Phoenician/Cypriote bilingual inscription was found at Idalion. A German scholar, Moritz Schmidt (1823–88) published a full decipherment in 1874, about 20 years after the Duc de Luynes discovered the script, demonstrating that the script encoded Greek (but not revealing how he reached his conclusions).

The syllabary is constructed in a similar way to Linear B, with five vowels and a similar (though not always identical) repertoire of consonants (see Fig. 11.11). The spelling rules allowed for somewhat greater phonetic

Figure 11.11 The Cypriote syllabary. In different parts of the island some signs had different shapes

accuracy than had Linear B. For example, final /n/, /s/, and /r/ are encoded by means of a sign that has the appropriate consonant + /e/. Distinction is made between /l/ and /r/, but /n/ in a consonant cluster is still not written. Here are a few examples, first the transliteration, then the classical Greek form in Roman characters, then the word's meaning (see Fig. 11.12).

a-po-to-li-se
ha ptolis
"the city"

a-to-ro-po-se
anthropos
"human"

ml-si-to-ne
misthon
"fee"

to-no-ro-ko-ne
ton horkon
"the oath"

Figure 11.12 Examples of words in the Cypriote syllabary

Most surviving documents in the Cypriote syllabary are dedications of only a few words. The tablet from Idalion proves, however, that complex texts were possible in Aegean syllabic writing, although nothing comparable has been found.

12

The West Semitic Revolution

Map 4   Places important in Chapter 12

In the broad picture, in the late fourth millennium came the Sumerian logosyllabary, engendered in order to manage an ever more complex economy and society made inevitable by irrigation agriculture, followed closely by the Egyptian logosyllabary, which the Sumerian inspired. From these two logosyllabaries grew several syllabaries, in ways never clear. But within the tradition of cuneiform writing itself, and without leaving it, appeared numerous writings whose signs were mostly syllables, with only a few common logograms and determinatives. These writings never achieved the concision and devotion to phonetic qualities of the Aegean and West Semitic syllabaries, but as a subset we might nonetheless refer to them as cuneiform syllabaries.

Cuneiform Syllabaries

Semitic-speaking Assyrian merchants living in Cappadocia, in the eastern portion of the great Anatolian upland, around 1800 BC used Mesopotamian cuneiform writing but with a high percentage of the signs encoding sylla-bles. This is the so-called Old Assyrian period, the first phase of Assyrian international presence and power. The merchants lived in a special quarter of KANESH, a settlement about 15 miles northeast of modern Kayseri.

The Kanesh tablets were preserved in a destruction level. They preserve the oldest writing ever found in Anatolia. Envelopes marked with cylinder seals enclosed some tablets. The tablets record economic transactions and correspondence with associates away back home in Assur on the upper TIGRIS RIVER, hundreds of miles to the east. The texts also contain some "Hittite" words (see below), and hence are the earliest evidence for the great Indo-European family of languages.

Later in Anatolia, cuneiform writing was applied to three other Bronze Age languages, preserved on tablets found in HATTUSA, capital of the Hittite power in north central Anatolia, northeast of modern Ankara. Terminology pertaining to the Hittites is, however, more confusing than usual, even desperately complex. Hattusa, a settlement in Anatolia, is so called after the Hatti, the name of an indigenous non-Indo-European people living in north–central Anatolia. Hittites is a biblical term, but derivative of the word "Hatti" and not the name by which the Hittites, who conquered the Hatti, actually called themselves. That name was Nesites, after their home city of Kanesh. Sometimes scholars do call the Hittites "Nesites," but here I retain the conventional usage. Around 1600 BC the Hittites/Nesites appear to have moved northwest from Kanesh and occupied the site of Hattusa, where the Hatti were already living.

What are the languages in Anatolia encoded by forms of the imported Mesopotamian cuneiform writing, in addition to the foreign Semitic Assyrian language?

First, there are words and names of people and places in Hattic itself, the language of the indigenes. We do not know to which family this language belongs, except that it was not Semitic or Indo-European. In fact the language does not survive, but only shadows of it embedded in names in other documents.

Second, there are documents in "Hittite," the Indo-European language of the occupiers from Kanesh (the Hittites/Nesites). This variety of cuneiform kept closely to the Akkadian complex practice of using several hundred signs with many logograms and determinatives.

Third, some cuneiform texts quote ritual passages in a Bronze Age Anatolian language called Palaic, "of the people of Pala," a dialect of unknown affinity probably spoken northwest of Hattusa.

Fourth, a complex form of cuneiform like that used to record "Hittite" encodes *Luvian*, a language related to Hittite, evidently spoken south and southwest of Hattusa. The Luvian language appears to be the ancestor of Lycian spoken in south–central Anatolia during the classical period. Some inscriptions of it in the Greek alphabet survive. Luvian was also spoken in northern Syria and in the far west, the LYDIA of the Greeks. Some think that Luvian was the language of TROY.

Luvian was also encoded in a special script unrelated to cuneiform, commonly called "Luvian hieroglyphs" (or Anatolian Hieroglyphic or Luvian Hieroglyphic) (Fig. 12.1). Partially deciphered in 1960, "Luvian hieroglyphs" are a logosyllabary written boustrophedon with about 500 syllabic, logographic, and semantic signs. Some think it is related to Aegean traditions because its syllables, by far the most commonly used signs, stand mostly for a single vowel (V) or for a consonant plus a vowel (CV), like Aegean signs. "Luvian hieroglyphs" first appear c.1300 BC and were used until c.600 BC. A bronze seal inscribed in "Luvian hieroglyphs," with two partial names, one of a man and one of a woman, was recently found at Troy, the only writing ever found there.

Also during the mid-second millennium the powerful and numerous Hurrians, of unclear ethnic and linguistic affiliation, used a cuneiform writing reduced mostly to syllables. To judge from names in cuneiform texts, the Hurrians were widespread in the Ancient Near East from at least the third millennium. Between c.1500 and 1300 BC they established their own kingdom in the KHABUR RIVER Valley off the upper EUPHRATES, and archaeological remains have been found there recently. The Egyptians called these influential people the Mitanni. One of the wives of the magnificent pharaoh Amenhotep III (c.1385–1350 BC) was a Mitannian princess, and some have thought the famous Nefertiti, wife of Amenhotep III's successor, the monotheist pharaoh Akhenaten, to be of Mitannian descent.

Figure 12.1 "Luvian hieroglyphs" on a stele from Carchemish on the Upper Euphrates, c.1000–700 BC. It is the end of a text that describes how three principal gods will punish the doer of evil. (Oxford, Ashmolean Museum.)

Meager pieces of the Hurrian language survive on tablets from Hattusa; in UGARIT on the Mediterranean coast (see below); and on one of the longest of the cuneiform letters on clay tablets found at AMARNA in Egypt. There the reformist Akhenaten built his religious and administrative capital, c.1350 BC. King Tushratta of Mitanni dictated the letter to Akhenaten's father, Amenhotep III, the only long Hurrian text known until a collection of tablets in Hurrian with a cuneiform Hittite translation was unearthed at Hattusa in 1983. Nearly all the cuneiform signs in the Hurrian texts are syllabic. The Hurrian language was perhaps related to that of the sophisticated Urartians who, much later in the first millennium BC, lived in the mountainous plateau of Armenia near LAKE VAN. The Urartians, too, used a simplified form of Akkadian cuneiform, but we do not know to what language family either Hurrian or Urartian belonged.

In ancient ELAM in southwest Iran appeared another highly syllabic variation of the Akkadian cuneiform. The language of Elam was also unrelated to other known languages (as was Sumerian and Hurrian), yet we can to some extent understand it because of multilingual texts (as with texts in Sumerian/Akkadian), above all the famous trilingual inscription that Darius the Great had carved high at BEHISTUN in 520 BC. The other two parallel texts at Behistun are in standard Akkadian cuneiform, which used around 600 signs, and the unrelated Old Persian script and language, which had 36 syllabic signs and a few logograms (see Chapter 6). At Behistun Elamite is recorded c.520 BC in a modified Akkadian cuneiform in which the sign repertory is reduced to around 130 signs, most of them syllabograms. SUSA in Elam became a center for Achaemenid Persian administration after Cyrus the Great took the city in 538 BC, and no doubt for this reason Elamite written in a modified Akkadian cuneiform continued as a script and language of such importance to Persian administration that it joined Babylonian cuneiform and Old Persian on the Behistun monument.

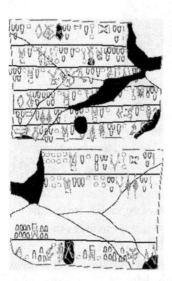

Figure 12.2 A tablet with proto-Elamite writing recording cereal rations for two gangs under two supervisors, c.2900 BC. (After R. Englund, http://www.cais-soas.com/CAIS/History/Elamite/proto_elam_history.htm.)

Before the introduction of Elamite cuneiform c.1200 BC, the inhabitants of lowland Elam, especially those in Susa, used an unrelated script called protoElamite, c.3050–2900 BC, the oldest writing from Iran and nearly as old as the nearly contemporary protocuneiform tablets from Mesopotamia (Fig. 12.2). ProtoElamite consists of around 1,000 mostly undeciphered markings. Few are pictorial, most are entirely abstract and we can make little sense of them. The complex accounting system that these markings served, by contrast, is now understood to some extent. The accounting system is related to, but different from, that used on the protocuneiform accounting tablets from Uruk to the west, which precede the protoElamite tablets by at least one hundred years. Some protoElamite signs may be derived from protocuneiform. Although many sign combinations, made of abstract designs, appear to record names, we cannot be sure that the writing is lexigraphic (though it probably is) any more than the mysterious undeciphered signs of the Indus Valley civilization (c.3300–1700 BC), with which protoElamite is sometimes compared (some think that Dravidian is the underlying language).

Later, around 2150 BC, appeared a second short-lived Elamite script unrelated to cuneiform, of around 80 abstract signs. Though called Linear Elamite, its relationship to the earlier proto-Elamite cannot be determined and the two scripts may support separate languages. Only 22 tablets of Linear Elamite survive, but because several Linear Elamite/Akkadian cuneiform bilinguals survive, scholars can make out some meanings. Still, we do not know the underlying language. By the end of the second millennium, a form of the Mesopotamian cuneiform writing had replaced the native traditions.

The West Semitic Syllabaries

Various experiments in simplification took place during the second millennium BC in the eastern portions of the Fertile Crescent among writers of Mesopotamian cuneiform on clay tablets and wax-coated folding wooden tablets. Such simplifications were encouraged by the script's passing from one people or language to another. In the West, in a similar way, the most radical transformation of the principles of lexigraphic writing since its invention one thousand years before took place. The invention of the West Semitic writing was the second great moment in the history of writing, or in the history of civilization, after the invention of the logosyllabaries at the end of the fourth millennium at the two tips of the Fertile Crescent.

Whereas the logosyllabaries had needed 600–700 signs to function, the West Semitic "consonantal syllabary," as we may call it, consisted of 22–30 signs without word-signs or determinatives. The momentous simplification, and reduction of the writing entirely to phonetic elements, with the enhanced risks of ambiguity and misunderstanding that radical phoneticism incurs, took place in lands dominated by the papyrus-using Egyptians. While in the Mesopotamian tradition the scribe might compose on a wax-coated tablet, then transfer the material to clay, in the West Semitic tradition, which also used waxed tablets (unlike the Egyptians), the writer would transfer the material to papyrus, occasionally to expensive leather. Because of the perishability of papyrus (and leather), we have fewer than one hundred examples of West Semitic writing from the Levant surviving from between 1000 BC and the time of Christ, inscribed on the rarely used stone, metal, and ceramic (additional inscriptions come from Punic Carthage). The Hebrew Old Testament is couched in a West Semitic script and survived the ancient world through the custody of the Jews, after the Roman destruction of the second temple at JERUSALEM in AD 70; from a potpourri of different kinds of documents from different periods, some as late as the second century BC, the rabbis fashioned a religion unattached to sacrificial cult at Jerusalem. Epigraphic testimony to the Greek alphabet, by contrast, begins almost from the time of its invention c.800 BC, before swelling into an ocean of epigraphic remains, of which new examples appear every year.

Egyptian writing in some way inspired West Semitic writing, as it handed on papyrus as a medium for writing. It is regrettably common to refer to the 22 to 30 linear signs of the West Semitic writings as an "alphabet," just as Alan Gardiner did for Egyptian uniliterals, but the term is inaccurate and has led to extreme confusion. The Egyptian uniliteral signs we examined earlier (Chapter 9) are not an "alphabet" embedded within a logosyllabary, because the uniliterals stood for syllables whose vowel was unexpressed, just as one needed to fill in the vowels for the biliterals and the triliterals. Nonetheless there must be a connection between the Egyptian repertory of around 24 uniliteral signs, artificially abstracted from the whole system, and the highly similar inventory of sounds represented by West Semitic writing. We wonder how this might have happened.

"West Semitic" refers to a family of scripts that share a common internal structure and not to a dialect of spoken Semitic. In closely related West Semitic scripts appeared all sorts of Semitic dialects spoken from Syria to Arabia and, later, ETHIOPIA, although we never know how such dialects sounded: West Semitic writing does not inform the reader of the sounds of speech, but provides phonetic hints that will enable a native speaker to guess at what the sound might be. Such was the high price for reducing the signary to around 25 signs; the Aegean syllabaries, with around 80 signs, did a far better job of informing the reader of the sounds of the words encoded.

On the flimsy basis of variations in consonantal structure, we may divide the West Semitic dialects into two broad categories, Northwest Semitic dialects (including Phoenician, Hebrew, Aramaic) and Southwest Semitic dialects (including North and South Arabic and Ethiopic). East Semitic dialects are simply those forms of local speech couched in Mesopotamian cuneiform, usually called Akkadian, which includes Assyrian in the northeast and Babylonian near where the rivers converge. East Semitic scripts are the standard cuneiform scripts.

As we have seen, Mesopotamian cuneiform scripts also couched numerous languages unrelated to Semitic speech. The family of West Semitic scripts, too, will include such close relatives as the scripts used in India and Southeast Asia to this day, where languages are unrelated to Semitic. Of course the Greek alphabet was based on West Semitic writing.

The "Ugaritic Cuneiform Alphabet"

When was West Semitic writing invented? Our earliest certain attestation of it comes from the polyglot Late Bronze Age stronghold of Ugarit, which flourished c.1450–1200 BC at the same time as the Mycenaean Greeks. Ugarit was a powerful and independent kingdom just north of modern Latakia in north Syria (ancient Laodicea), south of the mouth of the Orontes, its center near the modern village of Ras Shamra.

When Ugarit was destroyed by fire around 1200 BC, probably at the hands of the Sea Peoples (whoever they were), never to rise again, the intense heat preserved an anomalous collection of clay-inscribed versions of the earliest West Semitic script. Every scrap of the probably ordinary linear examples of this script, recorded on perishable imported Egyptian papyrus, has been lost. You need a good fire for good finds of tablets when scribes are writing on clay in a rainy climate. Linear B tablets too were preserved in the fires of destruction.

In the wealthy and cosmopolitan Ugarit bold experiments with writing took place with an unprecedented and unparalleled intensity, nearly a microcosm of the widespread experimentation with writing taking place all over the Near East and in the eastern Mediterranean in the Late Bronze Age. From the ruins of Ugarit come texts in Sumerian and Akkadian "languages," in standard Mesopotamian cuneiform; the so-called Luvian language in the so-called Luvian hieroglyphic script; the undeciphered Cypro-Minoan script somehow related to Cretan Linear A; Egyptian in hieroglyphic script; and, finally, the many tablets written in the "Ugaritic cuneiform alphabet," so called but neither related to Mesopotamian cuneiform nor an alphabet, a unique nonlinear signary impressed by stylus on clay (Fig. 12.3). The first texts in the "Ugaritic cuneiform alphabet" were found in 1929, but many

Figure 12.3   Lawsuit against Shamumanu for stealing 50 shekels of silver, in the "Ugaritic Cuneiform Alphabet." Ras Shamra, Ugarit, Syria, fourteenth century BC. (The Schøyen Collection MS 1955–6, Oslo and London.)

have turned up since, including literary texts of extreme importance to biblical studies and the history of myth. The stories of the victory of Baal ("lord") over Yam ("sea"), his unsuccessful struggle against Mot ("death"), and his revivification by his sister Anat (a ferocious goddess of war, perhaps Sumerian "Madam Sky") are themes that reverberate in the Bible and in Greek myth. A principal corridor for the transmission of Eastern myth, and culture, to the West was over northern Syria.

Three scholars, two French and one German, working independently, deciphered the script within a year of the tablets' discovery. Because there were only 30 signs and because the tablets were found on the Phoenician coast, chances were high that the script encoded a Northwest Semitic dialect in the manner of scripts later used to encode the Phoenician, Hebrew, and Aramaic dialects. Word boundaries in the tablets were

marked by a vertical stroke. Several tablets began with the same sign ⟨cuneiform sign⟩

as often in West Semitic texts indications of ownership or dedications begin with the preposition /l/, "to," "for," so 𝍸 might be /l/. The sound /m/ indicates a West Semitic plural ending (as in Elohi*m*, "gods") and /t/ indicates a feminine ending (as in Ana*t*) – such was true of Egyptian too – so it was possible to experiment with such values assigned to Ugaritic signs that came at the ends of words.

Searching also for the common words *mlk* "king" and *bn* "son," the decipherers identified enough sounds for the system to become unraveled. They knew the general kind of script from the number of signs; they correctly guessed the underlying language, which is well known; and they had an abundance of material. In 1955 an unexpected and by then unnecessary confirmation of the decipherment came from the discovery of a tablet that gave Mesopotamian cuneiform syllabic equivalents of the "Ugaritic cuneiform" signary, of course always encoding vowels.

On one tablet found in 1949 appears the earliest known repertory of West Semitic signs, reading left to right, top to bottom, the ancestor of our ABCs (Fig. 12.4). We might compare this Ugaritic repertory of 30 signs, c.1300 BC, with the standard modern Hebrew repertory of 22 signs, which encodes a similar range of sounds in a similar order (see Fig. 12.5). The second line of Figure 12.5 gives a transliteration in a form conventional in Semitic and Egyptological studies: We have met some of these transliterations earlier. The exact sounds of many signs is hard to explain (we discussed some earlier), and they are, in any event, hypothetical. The third

)a b g h d h w z ḥ ṭ y k š l
m d n ẓ (p ṣ q r t
ġ t)u s₂

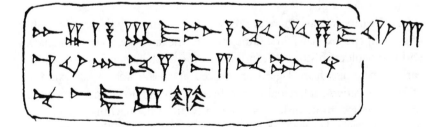

Figure 12.4   A Ugaritic abecedary, c.1300 BC, with transliteration into Roman characters. (After J. Naveh 1982, fig. 25.)

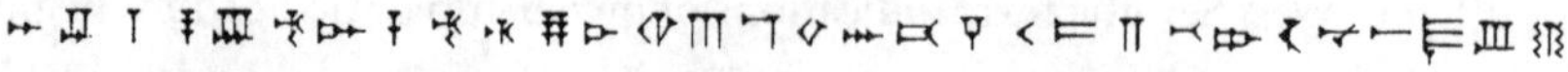

⊢ ⫫ ⟁ ⧣⫫ ⫡⋉ ⫥ ⋉ ⫏⫢ ⋉⫢ ⬡⫥⫠ ⋲ ⧈ ⧏ ⟁ ⫤ ⧈

á	b	g	ḫ	d	h	w	z	ḥ	ṭ	y	k	š	l	m	d	n	z	s	'	p	ṣ	q	r	ṭ	ǵ	t	i	ú	s
ʔa	b	g	x	d	h	w	z	ħ	t	j	k	ʃ	l	m	ð	n	ð	s	ʕ	p	ʂ	q	r	θ	ɣ	t	ʔi	ʔu	?

א ב ג ד ה ו ז ח ט י כ שׁ ל מ נ ס ע פ צ ק ר ת

Figure 12.5 The Ugaritic script, with transliterations into customized Roman characters; the International Phonetic Alphabet (IPA); and modern Hebrew signs

line gives transliteration into the IPA and the fourth line into modern Hebrew "square" characters.

Notice that in the Hebrew series, 8 signs have dropped away to make the 22 signs of the later West Semitic systems. One should not suppose, however, that the "Ugaritic language" had exactly eight more "sounds" than "Phoenician," and that the signary has been adjusted accordingly: The relationship between the number and value of signs and the actual sounds of speech is a rough and tumble game. The West Semitic system remained static with around 22 to 30 signs from the time it was created until modern times, when it still constitutes a large family of scripts.

Unlike later examples of West Semitic writing, the first sign in the Ugaritic signary ▷▷— stands explicitly for a syllable "glottal stop" /ʼ/ + the specific vowel /a/, so ▷▷— = /ʼa /, according to the chart. At the end of the Ugaritic series are three signs that do not appear in the later Hebrew signary. The first of the three stands for "glottal stop" /ʼ/ + the specific vowel /i/ = /ʼi /, the second stands for /ʼu /, and the final sign is a sibilant of unclear value used in words of apparent Hurrian origin. The need to write Hurrian words may have inspired the addition of the preceding two syllabic signs, because apart from these signs (and the first sign) all others encode consonantal values only.

The Ugaritic signary therefore presents approximately the same number of signs in approximately the same order as the later West Semitic signaries and is our oldest historical testimony to the existence of this system. The earliest examples from Ugarit are placed at c.1400 BC. Earlier examples of West Semitic script remain hypothetical. An unknown inventor placed the signs in a definite order and, evidently, from the beginning gave them names that encoded their phonetic value, a bold and brilliant innovation. Our evidence for such names, however, is not attested in the Semitic tradition until one thousand years after the tablets from Ugarit (in the third century BC Septuagint, the Greek translation of Hebrew scriptures). The ordering and naming of the signs with phonetic tag-words enabled rapid learning and was key to the writing's future enormous success. By memorizing a short sequence of names, one could control the phonetic values in a corresponding series of signs. Writing had never been so close to speech, but it remained unpronounceable, except by a native speaker.

The Phoenician Syllabary, c.1000 BC

Unique in its form, the so-called "Ugaritic cuneiform alphabet" from as early as 1400 BC cannot be the original form of the West Semitic signary, of which it is the earliest exemplar; other and always later varieties of it are linear – the signs are made up of lines, of strokes. The ordinary practice must have been to write with linear forms on Egyptian papyrus, which has not survived. Multiliteralism – the scribe's competence in more than one script and more than one language at the same time (see Fig. 0.1) – was the rule in the Near East from the time of the Akkadian Semites' adoption of Sumerian cuneiform in the mid-third millennium. The scribe who invented the "Ugaritic alphabet" was literate in Mesopotamian cuneiform, which he wrote with a stylus on clay. Wishing to write on clay the ordinarily linear West Semitic, he invented new graphic forms suitable for impression in clay. We need not look for a clearer example of the limited importance of outer form and the all-importance of internal structure when studying the history of writing.

Our earliest example of the linear style in West Semitic writing comes from the sarcophagus of a king, Ahiram of BYBLOS, now dated usually to c.1000 BC. The date, however, is contested because the French excavators found artifacts of Ramses the Great (c.1279–1213 BC) in the tomb (Figs 12.6a and b). Beneath an Egyptian-style lotus-frieze the relief shows the king on a sphinx-sided throne before a table of offerings in an Egyptian style of funerary representation. A procession of women and courtiers approach him, paying respect. The sarcophagus rests on four lions. The writing is a curse inscription engraved along the edge of the lid. Reading from right to left, the whole inscription means something like:

The coffin that Esbaal, son of Ahiram, King of Byblos, made for Ahiram his father as his house in eternity. And if any king or any governor or any army commander attacks Byblos and exposes this coffin, may the scepter of his rule be torn away, let his royal throne be overthrown, and let peace flee from Byblos. And as for him, let [somebody] efface his inscriptions!

Figure 12.6a   Sarcophagus of King Ahiram of Byblos, c.1000 BC; arrows indicate the inscription along edge of lid. (G. Eric and Edith Matson Photograph Collection, Prints and Photographs Division, Library of Congress.)

Figure 12.6b   Transcription of the first few words on the sarcophagus, which read from right to left. In a left-to-right transliteration they read *'rn zp'l [pl]sb'l bn'ḥrm mlkgbl l'ḥrm 'bh*, "A coffin that Esbaal, son of Ahiram, king of Byblos, made for Ahiram his father . . ."

More than one king of Byblos was called Ahiram (= Semitic "high-born"); the celebrated Ahiram of Tyre (969–936 BC) had dealings with Solomon (1 Kings 7:13–15). Nor does the name Esbaal give us good information about the inscription's date.

Figure 12.7 is a chart of the Phoenician signary underlying the Ahiram inscription, in standardized forms; one version of conventional names; and hypothetical values in a conventional customized Roman script (here given in brackets).

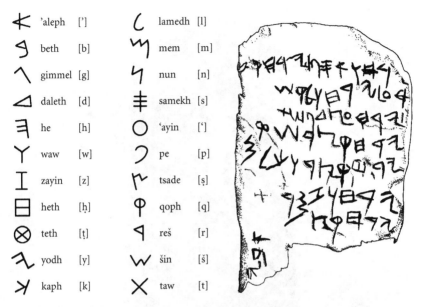

⪢	'aleph	[']	⟨	lamedh	[l]
⪦	beth	[b]	ᶆ	mem	[m]
⟍	gimmel	[g]	⪦	nun	[n]
◁	daleth	[d]	≢	samekh	[s]
⪥	he	[h]	○	'ayin	[']
Y	waw	[w]	⊃	pe	[p]
I	zayin	[z]	⪡	tsade	[ṣ]
⊟	heth	[ḥ]	φ	qoph	[q]
⊗	teth	[ṭ]	٩	reš	[r]
⪡	yodh	[y]	W	šin	[š]
⪡	kaph	[k]	X	taw	[t]

Figure 12.7 Linear Phoenician forms of the West Semitic signary, with conventional names and transliterations

Figure 12.8 Drawing of the Gezer "Calendar," c.950 BC. (After Naveh 1982 fig. 54.)

Of the very few other early examples of linear West Semitic writing we can mention several inscribed bronze arrowheads with names on them, but they are impossible to date. Early in the twentieth century a tablet seemingly almost as old as the Ahiram sarcophagus was found in Gezer, a town northwest of Jerusalem, that appears to refer to a calendar, hence it is called the Gezer Calendar (Fig. 12.8). Claimed as the oldest example of "Hebrew writing," it is simply the West Semitic system applied to a local Northwest Semitic dialect. The document seems to attribute various duties, such as planting or harvest, to the months of a year, but because of the ambiguity of West Semitic writing, and the ineptness of the inscriber, it can be understood only partially. Some have wondered whether the "Gezer Calendar" is the text of a popular song; others think it is a tax document!

A celebrated monument of the early West Semitic writing, 150 years or more younger than the sarcophagus of Ahiram, is the Mesha Stele, a black basalt stone bearing an inscription by King Mesha who ruled over MOAB, the strip of mountains that run along the eastern side of the Dead Sea. It

Figure 12.9   The Mesha Stele, c.850 BC. (Paris, Louvre Museum.)

is from the ninth century BC (Fig. 12.9). King Mesha erected the stele as a memorial of his victory in a revolt against Israel. Discovered in 1868, the inscription of 34 lines is the longest ever found in Palestine. Fearing the stone's loss when scholars discovered it, the local Arabs built a fire around the stele and doused it with water, shattering it into many pieces. Fortunately, a paper squeeze – a papier maché impression – had been made of the writing, so we can read it today. Moab is a long way from Phoenicia, and the stele was inscribed over a hundred years later, but the script and "language" is the same as on the Ahiram sarcophagus. Scribes are using an identical script and "language" over a wide area, through a long extent of time. They do not attempt to distinguish local dialects (as did archaic Greek alphabetic writing), which the vowelless script is hardly suited to accomplish.

13

What Kind of Writing Was
West Semitic?

We want to understand how West Semitic writing worked and where it came from, but the topic is complex and muddled with imprecise terminology and theory. We have touched on this problem repeatedly, but must now face it directly. In life we speak loosely of the "alphabet," of the "Ugaritic cuneiform alphabet," the "Hebrew alphabet," the "Arabic alphabet," and of the "Cherokee alphabet," but in such expressions "alphabet" means only "a system of writing." The Egyptians had their alphabet, so did the Hebrews, so did the Mayans, and so do we.

What Is an Alphabet?

When discussing the "Ugaritic cuneiform alphabet," general studies explain that in spite of the name the signs are really "consonantal," except, of course, for the three syllabograms at the end of the series not found in later West Semitic signaries, and also the syllabic first sign in the series, as discussed above. When we transliterate the Egyptian signs

 as *ḫwfw* to spell Khufu, we do so on the theory that

the same nonvocalic, consonantal repertory of sounds that lurks behind the West Semitic repertory also stands behind the Egyptian hieroglyphs. Being "alphabet-users," as were the users of West Semitic writing, we can recast logosyllabic writing into "alphabetic" equivalents and so begin to understand what is being said – in just this way were Egyptian hieroglyphics deciphered.

Our unspoken assumption is that alphabetic signs represent something objective in human speech that can be wrested from the ancient, recalcitrant lexigraphic systems of writing. Yes, they are all "consonants" – odd, but a fact. In trying to understand the Egyptian text we superimpose on it an alien technology, our own, which did not exist in the days of the Egyptians, whose writing was made up of word-signs, syllable-signs, and semantic complements. We falsify essentially the Egyptians' own experience of writing in order to understand it, but are glad to do this because early attempts at decipherment failed through ignorance of the phonic aspects to Egyptian writing. And we express phonic aspects in any system of writing graphically by means of "alphabetic signs."

The problem of the nature of West Semitic writing cannot be separated from the problem of its origin. Not from any formal similarity between Egyptian writing and West Semitic writing, but from the similarity between the phonological structure of Egyptian writing and of West Semitic writing do we conclude that West Semitic traditions of writing must descend from Egyptian writing, and not from the far more widely used and more influential Mesopotamian cuneiform writing. The syllabograms of Mesopotamian cuneiform *did* encode vocalic qualities (except for a few signs, where the vowel remains unspecified), and there were signs for pure vowels.

If the West Semitic repertory is similar to the 24 Egyptian uniliterals – and even modeled on it in some way – and the West Semitic signary was an "alphabet" – then an "alphabet" existed already within the Egyptian logosyllabary. In fact Alan Gardiner's monumental *Egyptian Grammar* (1957) made that claim (Fig. 13.1). Gardiner's category "alphabet" comes from his recognition of the phonological similarity between the 24 Egyptian uniliterals, artificially separated from the other kinds of Egyptian signs, and the repertory of West Semitic signs long familiar from Aramaic, Hebrew, and Arabic scripts and commonly called "alphabetic." Modern Egyptian grammars continue to refer to the "alphabetic" signs within the Egyptian logosyllabary. It is a practical category, but does not represent the history of writing.

Not that Egyptologists believe that the uniliteral Egyptian signs represent what linguists call *phonemes*, the small particles of sound that make a difference in meaning, for then all Egyptian signs would have to represent phonemes, because the function of the uniliterals within Egyptian writing is, as we have seen, not distinguished from the function of the biliterals and triliterals, whose values uniliteral signs often reinforce as phonetic

THE ALPHABET

SIGN	TRANS-LITERATION	OBJECT DEPICTED	APPROXIMATE SOUND-VALUE	REMARKS
	ꜣ	Egyptian vulture	the glottal stop heard at the commencement of German words beginning with a vowel, ex. *der Adler*.	corresponds to Hebrew א *ăleph* and to Arabic ا *'alif hamsatum*.
	i	flowering reed	usually consonantal *y*; at the beginning of words sometimes identical with *ꜣ*.	corresponds to Hebrew י *yōdh*, Arabic ى *yā*.
(1) ⃒⃒ (2) \\	y	(1) two reed-flowers (2) oblique strokes	*y*	used under specific conditions in the last syllable of words, see § 20.
	ꜥ	forearm	a guttural sound unknown to English	corresponds to Hebrew ע *ʿayin*, Arabic ع *ʿain*.
	w	quail chick	*w*	
	b	foot	*b*	
	p	stool	*p*	
	f	horned viper	*f*	
	m	owl	*m*	
	n	water	*n*	corresponds to Hebrew נ *nūn*, but also to Hebrew ל *lāmedh*.
	r	mouth	*r*	corresponds to Hebrew ר *rēsh*, more rarely to Hebrew ל *lāmedh*.
	h	reed shelter in fields	*h* as in English	corresponds to Hebrew ה *hē*, Arabic ه *hā*.
	ḥ	wick of twisted flax	emphatic *h*	corresponds to Arabic ح *ḥā*.
	ḫ	placenta (?)	like *ch* in Scotch *loch*	corresponds to Arabic خ *ḫā*.
	ẖ	animal's belly with teats	perhaps like *ch* in German *ich*	interchanging early with ḏ *š*, later with ḥ, in certain words.
(1) (2)	s	(1) bolt (2) folded cloth	*s*	originally two separate sounds: (1) *z*, much like our *z*; (2) *š*, unvoiced *s*.
	š	pool	*sh*	early hardly different from *h*.
	ḳ	hill-slope	backward *k*; rather like our *q* in *queen*	corresponds to Hebrew ק *qōph*, Arabic ق *ḳāf*.
	k	basket with handle	*k*	corresponds to Hebrew כ *kaph*, Arabic ك *kāf*. Written in hieratic.
	g	stand for jar	hard *g*	
	t	loaf	*t*	
	ṯ	tethering rope	originally *tsh* (*š* or *tj*)	during Middle Kingdom persists in some words, in others is replaced by *t*.
	d	hand	*d*	
	ḏ	snake	originally *dj* and also a dull emphatic *s* (Hebrew צ)	during Middle Kingdom persists in some words, in others is replaced by *d*.

Figure 13.1   Gardiner's "alphabet" of uniliteral signs embedded within the Egyptian logosyllabary. (*Egyptian Grammar*, p. 27.)

complements. Scholars nonetheless justify a claim that the West Semitic tradition of writing, first attested historically in Ugarit, was "alphabetic" because (1) the signs come in a row, *aleph, beth, gimel* and (2) the signs allegedly stand for phonemes, "individual sounds," as they always do in an alphabet. According to this manner of thinking, we might define an alphabet as "a graphic system whose signs come in a certain order and represent phonemes."

The West Semitic signs do come in a row, but the word "alphabet" is in fact Greek in origin, from the names of the first two letters of the Greek series, which came in the same order as signs in its Semitic model. In Greek the names, attested by the fifth century BC, are gibberish and are clear distortions of Semitic originals (which are not themselves always meaningful). We must wait two hundred years more for first testimony of the Semitic names (in the Greek Septuagint of the third century BC). The arrangement of the signs in a series is in any event a formal convention, invaluable for learning, but independent of how the writing functions, and probably should not be taken as a criterion for what we mean by alphabet. For that we need to understand how the writing functions to "represent phonemes."

The Phoneme

<u>P</u>OT

<u>R</u>OT

RO<u>O</u>T

ROO<u>F</u>

Figure 13.2 Change of meaning through phonemic transformation

Speech is made up of sound and phonemes are "pieces of sound." A phoneme is a sound that makes a difference in meaning. So *pot* and *rot* mean different things because they begin with different phonemes, encoded in the letters *p* and *r* (Fig. 13.2). Different languages have different repertories of phonemes, but only a limited number of phonemes exist, dependent on the physical construction of the human mouth, throat, and vocal cords. These sounds are now graphically indexed in the IPA (Fig. 13.3). In graphic combination, this limited inventory of individual speech sounds makes up the endless variety of human speech. No wonder that the alphabet-using Greeks used the same word for alphabetic sign, *stoicheion* – "something in a row," that is, of signs – as they did for an atomic element, just as they imagined that the structure of their writing paralleled the structure of the phenomenal world. Still today in physics we accept the Greek atomic description, in general terms.

To those who think that West Semitic writing was an "alphabet" like the Greek alphabet (except without signs for vowels), the signs of the West Semitic signary stood for phonemes just as much as did the Greek signs, except for some reason they were always consonants. Had the Western Semites really discovered how to encode through graphic means the phonemic inner structure of speech, the true purpose of writing according to the commentators cited in Chapter 1? Because that is what an alphabet does and is.

THE INTERNATIONAL PHONETIC ALPHABET (revised to 1993)

CONSONANTS (PULMONIC)

	Bilabial	Labiodental	Dental	Alveolar	Postalveolar	Retroflex	Palatal	Velar	Uvular	Pharyngeal	Glottal
Plosive	p b			t d		ʈ ɖ	c ɟ	k ɡ	q ɢ		ʔ
Nasal	m	ɱ		n		ɳ	ɲ	ŋ	N		
Trill	B			r					R		
Tap or Flap				ɾ		ɽ					
Fricative	ɸ β	f v	θ ð	s z	ʃ ʒ	ʂ ʐ	ç ʝ	x ɣ	χ ʁ	ħ ʕ	h ɦ
Lateral fricative				ɬ ɮ							
Approximant		ʋ		ɹ		ɻ	j	ɰ			
Lateral approximant				l		ɭ	ʎ	L			

Where symbols appear in pairs, the one to the right represents a voiced consonant. Shaded areas denote articulations judged impossible.

CONSONANTS (NON-PULMONIC)

Clicks	Voiced implosives	Ejectives
ʘ Bilabial	ɓ Bilabial	' as in:
ǀ Dental	ɗ Dental/alveolar	p' Bilabial
ǃ (Post)alveolar	ʄ Palatal	t' Dental/alveolar
ǂ Palatoalveolar	ɠ Velar	k' Velar
ǁ Alveolar lateral	ʛ Uvular	s' Alveolar fricative

VOWELS

	Front	Central	Back
Close	i y	ɨ ʉ	ɯ u
	ɪ ʏ	ʊ	
Close-mid	e ø	ɘ ɵ	ɤ o
		ə	
Open-mid	ɛ œ	ɜ ɞ	ʌ ɔ
	æ	ɐ	
Open	a ɶ		ɑ ɒ

Where symbols appear in pairs, the one to the right represents a rounded vowel.

OTHER SYMBOLS

ʍ Voiceless labial-velar fricative
w Voiced labial-velar approximant
ɥ Voiced labial-palatal approximant
ʜ Voiceless epiglottal fricative
ʢ Voiced epiglottal fricative
ʡ Epiglottal plosive

ɕ ʑ Alveolo-palatal fricatives
ɺ Alveolar lateral flap
ɧ Simultaneous ʃ and x

Affricates and double articulations can be represented by two symbols joined by a tie bar if necessary.
k͡p t͡s

SUPRASEGMENTALS

ˈ	Primary stress	ˌfoʊnəˈtɪʃən
ˌ	Secondary stress	
ː	Long	eː
ˑ	Half-long	eˑ
˘	Extra-short	ĕ
.	Syllable break	ɹi.ækt
|	Minor (foot) group	
‖	Major (intonation) group	
‿	Linking (absence of a break)	

TONES & WORD ACCENTS

LEVEL		CONTOUR	
e̋ or ˥	Extra high	ě or ˬ	Rising
é ˦	High	ê ˆ	Falling
ē ˧	Mid	e᷄ ˀ	High rising
è ˨	Low	e᷅	Low rising
ȅ ˩	Extra low	e᷈	Rising-falling
↓ Downstep		↗ Global rise	etc.
↑ Upstep		↘ Global fall	

DIACRITICS

Diacritics may be placed above a symbol with a descender, e.g. ŋ̊

̥	Voiceless	n̥ d̥	̤	Breathy voiced	b̤ a̤	̪	Dental	t̪ d̪
̬	Voiced	s̬ t̬	̰	Creaky voiced	b̰ a̰	̺	Apical	t̺ d̺
ʰ	Aspirated	tʰ dʰ	̼	Linguolabial	t̼ d̼	̻	Laminal	t̻ d̻
̹	More rounded	ɔ̹	ʷ	Labialized	tʷ dʷ	̃	Nasalized	ẽ
̜	Less rounded	ɔ̜	ʲ	Palatalized	tʲ dʲ	ⁿ	Nasal release	dⁿ
̟	Advanced	u̟	ˠ	Velarized	tˠ dˠ	ˡ	Lateral release	dˡ
̠	Retracted	i̠	ˤ	Pharyngealized	tˤ dˤ	̚	No audible release	d̚
̈	Centralized	ë	̴	Velarized or pharyngealized	ɫ			
̽	Mid-centralized	e̽	̝	Raised	e̝ (ɹ̝ = voiced alveolar fricative)			
̩	Syllabic	l̩	̞	Lowered	e̞ (β̞ = voiced bilabial approximant)			
̯	Non-syllabic	e̯	̘	Advanced Tongue Root	e̘			
˞	Rhoticity	ɚ	̙	Retracted Tongue Root	e̙			

Figure 13.3 The International Phonetic Alphabet (IPA)

The Phoneme as a Projection of Greek Alphabetic Writing

It is not improbable, but impossible that the West Semitic signs encoded phonemes, as they appear to in our own alphabetic and prejudicial transliterations. We read Egyptian well, but we do not know how it sounded, because its writing gives no information about the vibration of the vocal cords, but only about the various forms of obstruction made by mouth, lips, and teeth in the pronunciation of human speech. (We cannot pronounce the logosyllabic Akkadian either, but for different reasons.) While we call such obstructions "consonants," consonants do not exist in nature as separable sounds; the syllable is the smallest unit of sound in nature. The syllable may consist of the naked vibration of the vocal cords, for example /a/, /e/, /i/, /o/, /u/, or the vibration of the vocal cords in conjunction with a certain pattern of obstruction (stops) or partial obstruction (sibilants, fricatives) in the mouth, for example /be/, /ba/, /bo/, /bi/, /bu/ or /se/, /sa/, /so/, or /fe/, /fa/.

Instinctually we believe that speech is made up of consonants and vowels because the Greek alphabet, the basis for our education, has separate signs for forms of obstruction (consonantal signs) and qualities of vibration (vocalic signs) and a rule that these two categories of signs must work together. From this graphic distinction between consonants and vowels in alphabetic writing, such as appears on this page, comes the illusion that such separable sounds, existing in nature, are capable of discovery any time. But any spectrograph shows that real speech is a continuous stream of sound with surface variations that follow a wave-like pattern (see Fig. 13.4). There are no separable atoms, or particles, that make up the molecules of speech.

The graphic isolation of the consonantal sounds of human speech in Egyptian writing, associated with an unspecified vowel, was therefore an intellectual achievement of the very highest order, but in spite of alphabetic transliterations from Egyptian into Roman characters, the Egyptian signs never stood for consonants as in the IPA. They stood for syllables whose sounds we cannot recover. West Semitic systems, modeled on the Egyptian, must have worked in the same way, to form an odd and much compressed form of syllabary, a view that I. J. Gelb first argued in 1952.

Through deliberate analysis we can reduce speech sounds to syllables, and many early systems of lexigraphic writing did this by artificially and deliberately breaking up the continuous wave of real speech. Analysis of

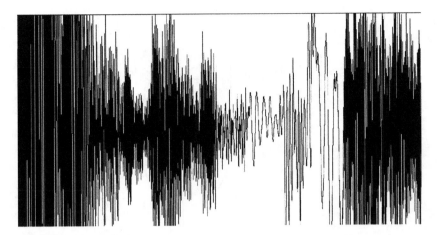

Figure 13.4 Spectrograph of "row, boat, row," reading left to right

the sounds of speech beyond the syllable is not, however, possible without special training, as repeated experiments in the field have shown. For example, it is impossible for a Chinese literate in the strange and nonalphabetic Chinese writing (see Chapter 15) ever to make phonemic distinctions. By contrast, Chinese who have learned *pinyin*, "spell-sound," make such distinctions easily. Pinyin is an *alphabetic* system for teaching nonMandarin speakers – that is, hundreds of millions of Chinese – how to pronounce Chinese in the Mandarin dialect; it was not designed to communicate other information.

Because in nature speech is not made up of particles but is a wave (Fig. 13.4), the letters of the Greek alphabet do not represent speech directly. The Greek letters *are* particles that through a kind of trick allow the reconstruction of a wave. The Greek alphabet functions in a very different manner from the West Semitic writings, where the signs *are not particles* by means of which the reader can construct a phonetic equivalent to the graphic markings. For this reason we cannot pronounce West Semitic writing any more than we can pronounce hieroglyphics or cuneiform; only a native speaker can find an equivalent in speech of the graphic markings. Even then he will not be certain, and other readers will reach other reconstructions. Scholarly reconstructions of the actual sound of ancient languages are inventive and clever but often imaginary and based on poor understanding of the relationship between speech and writing in the real world.

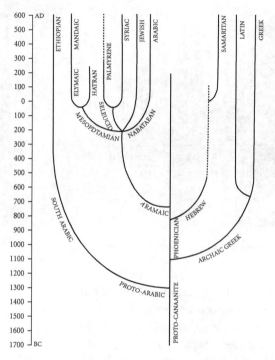

Figure 13.5 Chart of the descent of the "alphabet," of which Greek is an "offshoot." (After J. Naveh 1982, fig. 1.)

The Greek alphabet, which we will examine in Chapter 17, did not therefore reveal the secret structure of speech, but defined our illusions about it, on which the science of linguistics rests uncertainly. If phonemes are not discrete objective elements of speech, but only a way of talking about speech dependent on the historically conditioned and somewhat haphazard structure of the Greek alphabet, the first writing that allowed the reader to reconstruct the actual sounds of speech, West Semitic writing was not "alphabetic," as described in such common charts as Figure 13.5. The Greek alphabet is not a branch of the great tree ALPHABET, parallel and analogous to ProtoArabic, Aramaic, and Hebrew as in Figure 13.5, but is an entirely different tree, related historically to the West Semitic systems, yet different in kind.

We can pronounce Greek alphabetic writing without knowing any Greek (as Greek teachers know!), but when we transliterate a Ugaritic "alphabetic" text into Roman characters, in this case a tablet with a vertical and a horizontal line of characters (no. 357, Schaeffer 1939), we will write

vertical line: *ʒnt ṭpn dkm lʒbb mn 8*
horizontal line: *šmʿʒ mrʒ rb ʿ[prm]*

and translate

Thou, O Shaphan, collect from Ababa eight minas
Shimea, groom of the chief of car[avaneers?]

Asked to read aloud, a student says *"anet tchepen dekem elabeb men* 'eight.' *Shemaa mera reb a[perem],"* inserting a colorless vowel between each sign to enable pronunciation, meaningless to anyone who spoke a Semitic dialect in ancient Ugarit.

From time to time (but never in Phoenician script) the scribe might use the *aleph, yod,* and *waw* signs to suggest a vowel, but never in a consistent way or with consistent vocalic qualities. So *yod* can suggest /i/ or /e/, *waw* can suggest, /u/ or /o/. Grammarians call West Semitic signs used in this way *matres lectionis,* "mothers of readings," a device to help make sense of a writing system deeply ambiguous about phonetic qualities and bereft of the old-fashioned aids from semantic signs. But *matres lectionis* never evolved into a system for vocalic representation like the Greek system.

Users of a West Semitic script could not have come to the modern theory of the phoneme because recognition of the phoneme depends on the structure of the Greek alphabet and not on objective phenomena. Persistent disagreement about the meaning of *alphabet,* touching upon sometimes unscholarly claims about invention in culture, is confined to users of the Greek alphabet. Users of a West Semitic script could not follow any such conversation. Just how Greek writing came to atomize speech, we will discuss in Chapter 17.

West Semitic signs, then, designate the smallest analyzable unit of speech, the syllable, as did their Egyptian model, whose vocalic value remains unspecified but is implied in the sign (or there is no vowel if the sign closes a preceding syllable: Only a native speaker could know this). It is easy to see how scholars misunderstood the realia behind the writing. Thus the Phoenician grapheme that we call by the Hebrew name *mem* "water"

ᱬ does not have the phonetic value /m/, but the value /ma/, /mi/, /me/,

/mu/, whatever syllable the reader knows from experience of Semitic speech will make the best sense. In this way we treat the few signs in Mesopotamian cuneiform that appear to stand for a consonant alone; for example, a sign with the value /w/ that Assyriologists transliterate as /wa/, /wi/, /we/, /wu/, as context dictates, but never as /w/. The use of a diacritic sign called *shewa* (= Hebrew "emptiness") in several West Semitic systems agrees with the historical understanding of West Semitic signs as representing syllables, because the *shewa* means "there is no vowel here," where ordinarily we expect to provide the vowel. In the Ethiopic and various Indian writings, too, derived from versions of West Semitic, the naked sign alone stands for a consonant + the vowel /a/, whereas adjustments to the shape of the sign allow for the same consonant + other vowels (see below). In other words, the basic "naked" sign in Ethiopic, derived directly from a West Semitic model, stands for a syllable.

What could the Phoenicians and other users of West Semitic writing have been thinking in the way they used their writing? Surely they *did* attempt to indicate phonic aspects of speech, but not *consonants* in a theoretical sense, because consonants are phonemes that "sound along" (Latin *consono*) with vowels, and "vowels" as separable units that sound along with consonants are a way of speaking about human speech dependent upon the structure of the Greek alphabet. When commentators claim that West Semitic writing had no signs for the vowels and only encoded the consonants, they describe Phoenician writing as lacking something not yet invented.

Some scholars do now speak of the "West Semitic syllabaries," but unhistorical descriptions of Phoenician writing and its Greek congener, as in Figure 13.5, fashion a theoretical confusion. Caught in the prism of our expectations, alphabet-users define the goal of writing to be phonographic verisimilitude (see Chapter 1), which it never was, then wonder to what extent the preGreek, but certainly related, West Semitic Phoenician writing realized, or failed to realize, an ideal that did not then exist.

Abjads, Abugidas, and Other Monsters

To one scholar, the West Semitic writings were an "alphabet"; to another, they were a "consonantal alphabet"; to another, they are a "consonantal writing"; to others, a "consonantry"; to another, a "consonantal syllabary." To whatever category the West Semitic writings belonged they did not work like the Greek alphabet, always qualified as the "first true alphabet" or something similar.

Inspecting only the external features of a writing, and mindful of the controversy, one scholar has suggested the term *abjad* for the West Semitic writings, an acronym from the first four signs in the Arabic signary *Alif, Ba, Jim, Dal*, according to an order of the signs no longer observed in modern Arabic (grouped according to letter shape). The order appears to be very old, but how old is hard to say, perhaps a variation on an unattested ancient Phoenician series *aleph, beth, gimel, daleth*. Now one encounters this term on Wikipedia and even in print. Arabic writing is, of course, a West Semitic writing, in which only the long vowels are notated within the otherwise consonantal system, much as functioned the ancient *matres lectionis*. Unfortunately, to call West Semitic writing an *abjad*, a Semitic equivalent to the Greek *alphabetos*, does not clarify its inner structure or place the writing within a general theory of how writing systems are related historically and how as types they are related to the elements of speech.

Just as well the neologism *abugida*, offered by the creator of "*abjad*" to categorize the scripts of Ethiopia and India and other similar scripts, further obscures that such writings are minor modifications of the ancient West Semitic syllabic system. The term *abugida* is based on a medieval Ethiopic signary, a contraction of the Semitic names *aleph, beth, gimel, daleth* (**abugida**) or however they might have sounded in Ethiopia around AD 1000. Again, it is the Greek word *alphabetos* with a Semitic accent.

In "*abugidas*" the basic sign is said to stand for a consonant + /a/, then the same consonant with different vowels is designated by diacritic marks added to the basic sign, as in the Ethiopic writing mentioned above: The medieval Ethiopic writing, c. AD 1000, based on a Southwest Semitic version of West Semitic script, worked in this way. So did the much older syllabic Indian Karosthi and Brahmi scripts. The Karosthi script appeared in the third century BC in the Punjab (modern Pakistan) under the influence of earlier Persian bureaucratic use of the West Semitic Aramaic script and language. Karosthi script died out in the third century AD, when the still earlier Brahmi script also disappeared. Short examples of Brahmi script have recently been found from the fifth or even sixth century BC. Karosthi and Brahmi scripts appear to be independent developments from the West Semitic Aramaic. The Brahmi syllabic script is the ancestor of all modern "native" scripts in India, including Devanagari script ("sacred script of the city"), in which today are written Hindi, Marathi, Pali, Sindhi, and many other South Asian languages. Brahmi script was also the ancestor of

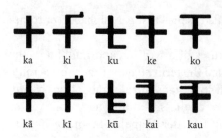

Figure 13.6 Syllabic signs in the Brahmi script

scripts in Tibet, Mongolia, and Southeast Asia.

The earliest extended documents in Brahmi are edicts published by King Ashoka, who ruled 273 to 232 BC and included in his empire most of modern India, parts of Afghanistan and Persia, and portions of Bengal. He accepted the teachings of Sakyamuni the Buddha and installed 33 edicts, which ringed all of India, about the need to follow *dharma*, "righteousness," in his kingdom, and to follow other Buddhist social and moral precepts. The Edicts of Ashoka are in fact the earliest testimony to Buddhist teachings. While the edicts in the east were in Brahmi script in an eastern Indo-European language (Magadhi, probably the language of the Buddha), edicts in the west were in Karosthi script and a western Indo-European language (an ancestor to Sanskrit). Figure 13.6 is an example of Brahmi

script. The basic sign **╋** = /ka/ is modified by the addition of attached diacritics to alter the quality of the vowel; its model, Aramaic, must have been syllabic too, unless we believe that the inventor of Brahmi script rejected the "phonemic" analysis of West Semitic signs to encode syllables instead. The Greek alphabet, and its revolutionary system of vocalization, was two hundred years old in c.600 BC, if Brahmi script goes back that far, but the inventor of Brahmi script clung nonetheless to the syllabic structure of his model.

Such writings as West Semitic and Ethiopic and Brahmi are not "*abjads*" or "*abugidas*," nomenclature based solely on external features, but old-fashioned syllabaries answering to the human faculty to break down speech into syllabic units. Such was the inner structure of these writings.

14

The Origins of
West Semitic Writing

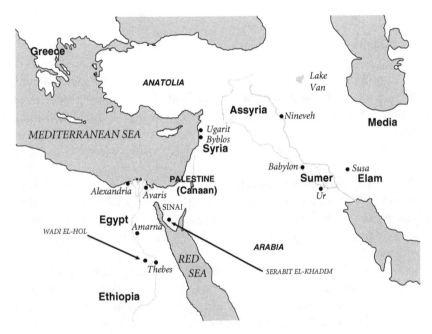

Map 5   Places important in Chapter 14

Faced with the puzzle that West Semitic writing encoded the obstructions of tongue, lips, and throat, and left the reader to supply appropriate qualities of the vibrating vocal cords, many commentators have suggested that it is to the structure of Semitic languages, in which vowels never begin a word and in which unchanging consonantal triliteral roots are subjected to complex vocalic alteration in order to fashion different parts of speech and different verbal aspects, that this odd feature owes. According to this argument, the structure of the writing reflects the structure of Semitic speech. For example, in Arabic the triliteral combination *ktb* always has something to do with writing. In a rough transliteration, with Greek vowels inserted, we might witness the following transformations upon the skeleton *ktb*:

> katab = "he wrote"
> katubti = "I wrote"
> katabu = "they wrote"
> jiktob = "he will write"
> 'ektob = "I will write"
> katob = "write!"
> koteb = "writing"
> katub = "being written"
> maktaba = "library"

A good deal of preIslamic poetry depends on just such changes rung on a common triliteral root, a kind of game in which the reader must supply the missing sounds from context. Did the inventor of West Semitic writing consciously understand that obstructions and formations of the mouth remain constant while vibration of the vocal cords keeps changing to create the lexical forms of Semitic speech? Did he, for simplicity's sake, discard all graphic information about the sounds of the vibrating vocal cords and the variety of lexical forms built on a common root, to confine himself to graphic expression for formations and obstructions in the mouth, thus ridding his writing of information about tense, person, voice, and part of speech?

We have already answered this question in tracing West Semitic writing to an Egyptian model. The inventor of this approach to lexigraphic writing was not a Semitic speaker suiting the script to his language, but an Egyptian who lived in the late fourth millennium. We wonder what impelled the legendary Thoth. The ancient Egyptian language, as far as we can reconstruct it, shared with Semitic languages the same habit of a triliteral consonantal root, so perhaps, after all, such analysis underlay the invention. The Egyptian Thoth must have known cuneiform, which, having no interest in consonantal roots, was content with constant interruption by inappropriate and inaccurate vowel qualities, especially in encoding words with final consonant or with consonant clusters. Understanding the principles of phonetic representation within a logosyllabary, did the inventor of Egyptian writing simply see the advantages in economy of graphic expression that silent vowels can bring? He spoke Egyptian and knew how it sounded, and so would his readers.

Origins of West Semitic Writing: The Epigraphic Finds

The persistent uncertainty about what is West Semitic writing has made it hard to know when we have found the earliest epigraphic evidence. Certainly it existed before the fourteenth century BC, when we date some tablets in the "Ugaritic cuneiform alphabet," but how far back? How, exactly, does the tradition spin off from the prior Egyptian logosyllabary?

On November 13, 1999, the *New York Times* reported a find of the oldest "alphabetic graffiti" ever found, in the WADI EL-HOL ("Gulf of Horror"), in the desert west of Egyptian Thebes. Nearby the two graffiti, according to their discoverers, are hieroglyphic inscriptions datable to the late Middle Kingdom, c.1850–1750 BC (Fig. 14.1). The two inscriptions were carved along an ancient desert road linking Thebes to the south and the sanctuary of Osiris at Abydos in the north, a sort of short-cut across the great bend in the river north of Thebes.

The inscriptions cannot be read, but to many they "look like" they may be antecedent to the later West Semitic syllabary, as first claimed in the *New York Times*. The characters are evidently based on Egyptian hieroglyphic or hieratic signs, but they are certainly not hieroglyphic writing. For example, ⌐ᴸᵤ looks like the Egyptian "water" sign ∿∿∿ with the value in Egyptian of /n/. Perhaps ℓₒ may be based on the uniliteral sign for "tethering rope" ℗⇒ with the value in Egyptian hieroglyphs of /ṭ/ (a /ch/ sound as in "church"). The simple cross ✗ has various possible

Figure 14.1 Two undeciphered early inscriptions based on Egyptian hieroglyphs from the cliff face in the Wadi el Hol, "Gulf of Horror," west of Thebes in southern Egypt c.1850–1750 BC. (After http://en.wikipedia.org/wiki/Middle_Bronze_Age_alphabets.)

models in hieroglyphic and hieratic. The sign ⟨⟩ may derive from hiero-glyphic "face" ⟨⟩, a logogram/biliteral for /ḥr/, a strong aitch + /r/, and so forth.

However, Egyptian phonetic values make no persuasive sense of the Wadi el-Hol writing. Evidently someone is using Egyptian hieroglyphs in support of a separate system, but we cannot be sure of the nature of that system or the underlying language. A nearby hieroglyphic inscription (hence intelligible) refers to one "Bebi, general of the Asiatics." Asiatics are likely to be Semitic speakers, so is the underlying language Semitic?

We are not even sure that all signs are phonetic. For example, the sign ⟨⟩, which appears in both inscriptions, looks like the Egyptian "man with arms raised" ⟨⟩ or "dancing man" ⟨⟩, but in Egyptian these signs are determinatives and never have phonetic value. If the Wadi el-Hol inscriptions are in the direct line of descent of the West Semitic Writing systems, we cannot prove it.

The Proto-Sinaitic Inscriptions

Similar uncertainty attaches to signs long known from the Egyptian turquoise mines at remote SERABIT EL-KHADIM in the southwest SINAI Peninsula. The great British archaeologist Flinders Petrie found them in 1905. The Sinai is a long way from the Wadi el-Hol, but Semitic slaves may have worked the turquoise mines there too, opened already in the Third Dynasty (c.2700 BC), especially active in the Middle Kingdom (c.2100–1750 BC), and again in the early Eighteenth Dynasty (c.1600–1500 BC) where most scholars place the badly weathered inscriptions.

A few dozen inscriptions of a strongly iconic character survive. They seem to consist of 20 to 30 Egyptian hieroglyphs, although like the Wadi el-Hol inscriptions they cannot be read (see Fig. 14.2). In Figure 14.2, in the vertical line, we recognize signs that also appear in the Wadi el-Hol inscriptions, the bull's head ⟨⟩, the enclosure, ⟨⟩, and the water sign ⟨⟩. In the lower line, reading from right to left, we can make out water signs again, the bull's head, human heads, an eye, an enclosure.

In 1916 the British Egyptologist Alan Gardiner, whose category "alphabet" for the subset of Egyptian uniliteral signs we examined earlier (see Fig. 13.1), noticed a series of signs repeated four times among the approximately 2,000 preserved signs of protoSinaitic. These he interpreted as standing for the Semitic *el Balat*, "to the lady," that is to Hathor, the eminent Egyptian goddess of fertility and love. Hathor was the tutelary goddess of the turquoise mines at Serabit el-Khadim, where substantial ruins from her temple survive.

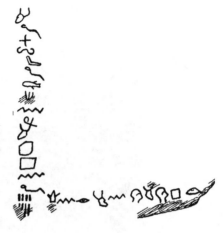

Figure 14.2 Proto-Sinaitic inscription on a boulder. One line is vertical and one horizontal. (After Albright 1966, fig. 27.)

Gardiner reached his influential conclusion in the following way. The name of Hathor is written in ordinary hieroglyphs on one side of a sphinx made (but not necessarily inscribed) in the Middle Kingdom, c.1800 BC. On the other side is a proto-Sinaitic inscription and the combination of signs that Gardiner worked with (Fig. 14.3):

Gardiner ingeniously proposed that Semitic-speaking workers at the mines took Egyptian hieroglyphic "pictograms," discarded their phonetic values in Egyptian writing, gave Semitic names to the pictograms, then reduced *their* values to the first sound of the Semitic name according to the so-called "acrophonic principle." And this is how the "alphabet" came into being.

So the protoSinaitic sign is said to be a "crook," for which a Semitic word is *lmd*, hence through the "acrophonic principle" the value of is /l/, the first sign in *lmd*. ProtoSinaitic is the picture of "house,"

Figure 14.3   Sphinx c.1800 BC with proto-Sinaitic inscription. (British Museum, EA 417148.)

which in Semitic is *bt*, hence the value of ⬜ is /b/. Proto-Sinaitic 𓂀 is an "eye," which in Semitic is /ʿn/, usually called ʿ*ain*, so the value is /ʿ/ (a guttural sound). Proto-Sinaitic ⚹ might be almost anything, but may resemble the later Semitic letter *tau*, doubtfully explained as meaning "mark" with the value /t/. The sequence of consonants /lblt/ is intelligible in Semitic as "to Baalat," the female counterpart of the Levantine storm god Baal, for which Egyptian Hathor would be a logical equivalent.

However, Gardiner could decipher no other words by continuing to proceed according to what was in effect a method of decipherment based upon the theory of the "acrophonic principle," and in spite of one hundred years of hard work on these important inscriptions, including long labor by the great biblical scholar W. F. Albright, the script remains undeciphered. "El Balat" is hard to resist, but if Gardiner's "acrophonic principle" were real as an explanation for the formation of what he took to be West Semitic writing from the preexisting Egyptian writing, we should have made more headway.

Exactly the same "acrophonic" method has been applied to the Wadi el-Hol inscriptions, with suggested readings of the inscriptions in the upper photo of Figure 14.1 coming out as (writing left to right for the right-to-left inscription)

r ẖ m ʿ ʾ ḥ m p w h w m w q b r

But nothing certain can be made of this transliteration, or of the second Wadi Hol inscription either, any more than the "acrophonic principle" has yielded further results for the protoSinaitic inscriptions.

Discarding the "Acrophonic Principle" in the History of Writing

Most general books on writing, with evident piety, agree to the "acrophonic principle" as the explanation for the origin of the letter names in West Semitic writing, and the sound-values implicit in these names, hence of the very writing itself. But if the signs did not begin as pictures, as Egyptian "pictograms," then we must abandon the acrophonic principle as a strategy for explanation. In the following discussion I will refer to the Semitic signs by their conventional modern names: We do not know how the names sounded in 1000 BC, though we assume that they existed.

The "acrophonic principle" assumes that the West Semitic linear signs, intelligible as a system beginning with the Ahiram sarcophagus c.1000 BC, began as pictures named as the thing represented. But lexigraphic writing did not begin as pictures, as semasiography. Lexigraphic writing began with the rebus, when graphic markings, whether iconic or more often not, ceased to refer to things and instead referred to units of sound in speech.

According to the theory of the origin of West Semitic writing through the "acrophonic principle," in protoSinaitic a square is a picture of a house, which in Semitic is *bet*, hence the value of this sign is /b/; an eye in Semitic is ʿ*ain*, so the phonetic value of a picture of an eye is /ʿ/. In a similar way, in later linear West Semitic, the first sign ⅄ is supposedly called *aleph*, "bull," because once it was the picture of a bull. The second sign in the series 𐤁 is called *beth* "house," because once it was the picture of a house, and so forth down the list. However, the linear forms of the West Semitic signs have no pictorial character as we have them, and scholars cannot agree about what pictures might stand behind many of the signs. We do not interpret the sign 𐤀 as an oxhead because it looks like an oxhead – it is an abstract open angle with a vertical slash – but because its name is *aleph*, which means "ox": then we look for face and horns. Similarly, no one thinks that 𐤁 looks like a house, which it does not, but because its name is *beth*, which means "house," it is so explained. At least four signs in the West Semitic repertory bear names that mean nothing in any Semitic language (*he*, *heth*, *teth*, *sadhe*, probably *samekh* too). Furthermore, some signs have different names at different times and places. For example, the sign called *nun* 𐤍 = /n/ in the northern tradition of West Semitic writing means "fish," which it in no way resembles, but is later called *nahash*, "serpent" in Ethiopic, which descended from the southern tradition of West Semitic writing. It is hard to imagine how 𐤂 *gimel* = "camel" can be derived from the picture of a camel (it may show his hump, or his head and neck!) or how 𐤒 *qoph* may derive from the picture of a monkey, if that is what *qoph* means. In Arabic *qaf* = "nape of the neck," so some explain this sign as deriving from the picture of a head and neck. The sign called *lamed* 𐤋 hardly suggests a "goad," which the word might mean, but is a simple rotation of 𐤂 *gimel* = "camel."

Perhaps the strongest evidence that some at least of the signs in the West Semitic signary did not begin as pictures are pairs of signs both phonetically and formally similar. For example, *nun* "fish," with the value /n/, is 𐤍, while the phonetically close *mem* "water" = /m/ is 𐤌, that is, the same shape with an additional squiggle. The sign called *teth*, meaning unknown, standing for a "strong" /t/, is drawn as a cross in a circle 𐤈

while the other, less emphatic /t/ sound called *tau* is drawn as a simple cross ✗ without the circle. The sign called *he* , meaning unknown, with the value of /h/, is a simple variation of the sign called *heth* , meaning unknown, with the similar value of a strong /h/ (transliterated as [ḥ]). The sign called *zayin* "weapon?" with value of /z/ or something similar, is a simple variant on another sibilant *samekh* , meaning unclear, with a theoretical value of /s/. Evidently someone in the second millennium BC has understood to some extent the phonology of ancient West Semitic speech and in these cases has fashioned similar signs to reflect similar sounds. These signs cannot descend from pictures.

According to the explanation of West Semitic writing as deriving from application of the acrophonic principle to named pictures drawn from Egyptian hieroglyphs, we must imagine that a Semitic speaker has searched hieroglyphic writing, selected a small number of pictures, discarded the Egyptian phonetic value of these pictures if they had any, then renamed the pictures in Semitic speech, then derived the value of the sign from the first sound in the new name. How lucky that the inventory so produced closely matched the phonology of Semitic speech! "In other words, the Semites were supposed to have named things before they had acquired any meaning!" as Gelb put it (Gelb 1963: 141).

Where the evidence is clear, one of three things may happen when a new writing appears. It may take the forms, values, and names from its model, as Greek did when invented on the basis of the Phoenician model. It may take the forms and values but not the names, as when Latin took over the Greek alphabet and the Greek *alpha* became /a/ and the Greek *beta* became /bē/. Finally, the forms and values may be a free creation, as with Norse runes or Glagolitsa, the oldest Slavic system of writing, invented c. AD 855 by SS Cyril and Methodius. Thus in runic writing, called *futhorc* after the initials of the names of the first five letters, names are applied to the characters, after their invention, as a mnemonic device: *feoh* = "money"; *ur* = "auroch"; *thorn* = "thorn"; *rad* = "voyage"; *cen* = "torch." In the Slavic Glagolitic, the first letter, with the value /a/, is called *az*, which means "I"; the second letter, with the value /b/, is called *buki*, which means "letter"; the third sign, with the value /u/, is called *vedi* = "wisdom," and so forth.

We are accustomed to such usage in the modern International Telephone alphabet where one spells my own first name as **Benjamin Alfred Robert Robert Yellow**, or in the Military Phonetic Alphabet as **Bravo Alpha Romeo Romeo Yankee**. We learn them much earlier, as children. **A** is for **Apple**, **B** is for **boy**, **C** is for **Cat**; or, just as well, **A** is for **Ape**, **B** is for **Bear**, **C** is for **Carrot**. It is hard to find clear examples of the "acrophonic principle" anywhere in the history of writing, and (though it is oft repeated) we should reject it in our attempts to understand the origins of the West Semitic family of writings, and in our attempts to decipher unknown linear writing in the Egyptian sphere of influence.

The Invention of West Semitic Writing

The names of West Semitic signs, first attested in the third century BC, seem to have been tag names to enable learners to remember the associated sounds. They do not preserve the names of primordial pictograms that later took on phonetic value. A Semite, educated in Egyptian writing, must consciously have understood the possibilities inherent in the 24 uniliteral Egyptian signs, that they might constitute a wholly phonetic signary capable of notating the rough structure of personal names and perhaps places and things. The notion of a purely phonetic repertory may have come from outside, even from the Aegean, where, on Crete, a self-contained phonetic repertory exists at least from the time of the Egyptian Middle Kingdom, c.1800 BC. There was contact between Crete, Cyprus, and the Levant, and the Philistines of southern PALESTINE, visible by the twelfth century BC, appear to have been Mycenaean refugees from Crete (their pottery is Mycenaean, *tout court*).

Taking the *values* of the preexisting phonetic repertory of uniliterals, this great genius, a second Thoth, created abstract linear signs for each sound, then assigned Semitic names to the signs as a mnemonic device. By remembering the name, you could remember the associated sound. Some names are meaningful, but some like *he* and *heth* are made up from the pre-assigned sound. Some letters, like *nun* or *nahash*, have more than one name. Not pictures, but sounds came first in the invention of the seminal family of West Semitic scripts.

We do not know where this invention took place, except in the sphere of the Egyptian bureaucracy. It is unlikely to have happened in the remote deserts of Wadi el-Hol or the Sinai. Of course we do not expect to find the very earliest exemplars of any writing. The linear West Semitic script is a free invention based on the phonology of the Egyptian uniliterals. It is plausible, but unprovable, that the need to record the personal names of Semitic slaves working for the Egyptians led to the adoption of such a wholly phonetic system of writing, of which the Wadi el-Hol and Serabit el-Khadim inscriptions from the Middle Bronze Age (or later) could be early exemplars, even if they are not the direct predecessors of West Semitic writing. A powerful need drove the invention of a system so ambiguous, so closely tied to the vagaries of real speech. The need to record personal names would provide that motivation, as it seems to have led to the discovery of the phonetic principle in Mesopotamia in the first place, over one thousand years before.

Other Levantine Epigraphic Finds from the Bronze Age

As we saw above in the discussion of Ugarit, the Late Bronze Age, the second half of the second millennium BC, was a time of rich experiment in the history of writing. Pieces of unfamiliar writings are also found over a large area in Palestine and the Lebanon, from considerably before the Hebrew invasion of perhaps c.1200 BC. Surviving inscriptions, however, are so few and short that we can rarely make sense of them. Most finds from this time and area, called *protoCanaanite*, are on pots or pieces of pots and sometimes preserve a similar though not identical script to proto-Sinaitic (Fig. 14.4). Sometimes scholars speak as if the protoCanaanite scripts, like the proto Sinaitic, are a direct ancestor of the linear historical West Semitic script first attested around 1000 BC on the Ahiram sarcophagus. In fact we cannot establish a direct link between West Semitic writing and the earlier finds, although there may well be one.

Other mysterious undeciphered texts survive from the Late Bronze Age in the Levant. Well known is the "pseudo-hieroglyphic" script from BYBLOS, roughly contemporary with protoSinaitic and protoCanaanite, so called because about one-fifth of the signs resemble Egyptian hieroglyphs; other signs resemble the later West Semitic linear forms. Byblian "pseudo-hieroglyphic" is known from ten inscriptions found in Byblos, two on bronze tablets, hammered and not scratched, and others on bronze

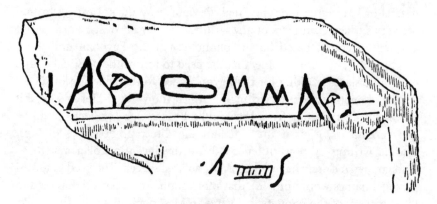

Figure 14.4   Undeciphered protoCanaanite inscription from Shechem, c.1600–1500 BC. (After Gelb 1963, fig. 18.)

"spatulas" (probably tags attached to votive offerings) and several on stone. They are uncertainly dated to the second millennium BC, probably between the eighteenth and fifteenth centuries BC. Because there may be somewhat more than 100 signs, the Byblian "pseudo-hieroglyphic" is no doubt a syllabary, however it worked.

We must wonder at what social conditions led, as in the case of the Byblian inscriptions, to the creation of a writing that had no clear forebears and no successors. We naturally look to the Aegean for the model of a purely phonetic syllabary, if that is what Byblian "pseudo-hieroglyphic" is. Did someone understand how Aegean writing worked, restructure it, borrow signs from Egyptian hieroglyphic, then fashion new ones that resemble later linear West Semitic? Why, and who?

From this extraordinary age two other unique inscriptions turned up in Byblos, one on a statue and three lines on a tablet. Additional undeciphered short unique linear inscriptions come from the Egyptian oasis of the Faiyum (c.1900 BC?), and from Jordan (c.1300 BC?), on a black basalt stele. Truly, as I. J. Gelb put it, there were "many attempts to create systems which everywhere in this period began to spring up like mushrooms after a rain" (Gelb 1963: 127).

15

Chinese Logography

We have so far explored all branches of our tree of structural relationships (see p. ii), save for the final leg, ALPHABETIC WRITING, which we will address in Chapter 17. Remarkably, this development has taken place within a single tradition. No one is certain how long humans have lived on this planet, because human self-consciousness and moral sense leave scant remains in the fossil record: possibly one million years. It took a long, long time before anyone discovered the phonetic principle in graphic representation, what we have called lexigraphic writing, and we might wonder that it was ever discovered. Of course semasiography precedes lexigraphy, but we cannot say by how many millennia.

Knowledge of the human past is exiguous and always exaggerated. The evidence for early periods is so slim as barely to exist. Not until we know men's thoughts, with the beginning of writing in the fourth millennium BC, can we begin to illuminate the mystery. The cultural developments in Mesopotamia were seminal for all humankind and unexpected, and we do not know why what happened there did happen, or why it happened when it did.

So extraordinary were the achievements of Mesopotamian culture that we live under its direct influence every day. Egypt was mighty and influential too, but provincial in many ways. The Greeks imitated Egyptian buildings and statuary but in their thoughts and literature drew their life from the Land of the Two Rivers. Logosyllabic, then syllabic writings underlay the mighty achievements of Mesopotamia. Was lexigraphic writing discovered only once, then, in the human past? in Mesopotamia?

In fact two other traditions, the Chinese and Central American, appear to be separate developments, although the Chinese may owe something to Mesopotamia. If our chart of the categories of writing accurately describes universals in the relationship between graphic sign and thought, between graphic sign and speech, we should be able to describe such systems in similar terms. Let us first examine Chinese writing, and in the next chapter look at Mesoamerican writing.

Chinese Writing

Everyone knows about Chinese writing because it adorns Chinese restaurants and informs the tourist that he or she is now in Chinatown. Because one of every four human beings is Chinese and because the writing has been in continuous use for over three thousand years, it is of paramount historical importance. Yet most Chinese read a limited number of characters. The full repertory of characters, in the largest dictionaries, runs to an incredible 50,000 signs, but no one knows them all any more than any one knows all the words in the *Oxford English Dictionary*. In order to read 90 percent of a Chinese newspaper you need to know around 1,500 signs. Those who know 3,000 signs can read most of the newspaper and write most words, but those with a university education (a very small percentage) should know around 4,000 signs. Apologists claim that knowledge of some signs is widespread among all the Chinese, but the average Chinese can never have comprehended complicated texts. In the Western world, in stark contrast, we learn around 30 alphabetic signs; at least, such was the figure before the advent of semasiographic computer icons.

In China, if anywhere, we expect to find the logography that our schema for understanding the structures of writing suggests might be possible. Yet it is a special form of logography where most signs contain phonetic elements; other signs have no phonetic elements. Chinese is so complex, arbitrary, and inconsistent in its functioning that experts, both Chinese and Western, disagree even about the principles on which it operates. The classic Chinese writing, used roughly from the second century BC until around AD 1900 (and to some extent still used today), may have been tied to speech, but speech of so long ago, and so haphazardly attached, that when pronounced according to conventional rules this writing was not intelligible to anyone not trained in these rules: Just because you spoke "Chinese," and had studied writing, did not mean that you could pronounce even a simple written text. Classic Chinese writing is a separate language in its own right and guaranteed governance by a tiny elite, just as had the ancient Near Eastern logosyllabaries.

Recognizing how writing stood between the Chinese people and the modern world, Chinese reformers began in the early twentieth century to advocate reform of the ancient and antiquated and obscurantist system. Some wished to discard it entirely and replace it with an alphabet – that is, a graphic system in which the signs stand for phonemes, like the Greek alphabet. Unfortunately, there are so many homophones in Chinese – words with the same or similar sounds but different meanings – that a purely phonetic description of speech would leave the reader bewildered. Various alphabetic systems were nonetheless devised, although Chinese characters are not phonetic so there could be no question of transliteration: rather, transcription, or interpretation. A system of Romanization called Wade-Giles was formalized in the second half of the nineteenth century and was standard throughout the twentieth century. In 1958 a new Roman alphabetization called *pinyin*, "spell sound," was devised in order to facilitate the establishment of the modern Beijing dialect, a local variety of the much wider-spread Mandarin dialect, as the correct way to pronounce Chinese characters. Pronunciations in *pinyin* are the new standard ("Peking" is Wade-Giles, "Beijing" is *pinyin*). Today in China *pinyin* is widely used in early education, although not as a means for encoding and communicating information among adults, except occasionally how to pronounce something in Beijing dialect.

Neolithic Finds

Because of official Chinese political indifference to evidence in the study of the past, and the world's most powerful tradition of honoring the past by imitating it, we can never be sure, in dealing with Chinese artifacts, that we are not dealing with fakes. Much earlier signs than anything we find in the Near East are reported on pottery from the seventh millennium, from a Neolithic site in the valley of the Yellow River called Jiahu (Fig. 15.1). Somewhat similar signs are inscribed on pottery from the later Neolithic site of Banpo, dated to c.5000 BC, near the ancient capital of Xian (where the subterranean army of terra-cotta warriors c.240 BC was found); I have seen these inscribed pots in the museum there (certainly reproductions). Banpo is also claimed to be a "matriarchal village," where women ruled, according to the social and historical theories of Friedrich Engels. Are these signs writing? The Chinese excavator of Jiahu writes:

Figure 15.1 Neolithic markings from Jiahu, Henan Province, China, c.6500 BC. (After *Nature*, April 28, 2003; cf. http://en.wikipedia.org/wiki/Image:Jiahu_writing.svg.)

Here we present signs from the seventh millennium BC which seem to relate to later Chinese characters and may have been intended as words. We interpret these signs not as writing itself, but as features of a lengthy period of sign-use which led eventually to a fully-fledged system of writing . . . The present state of the archaeological record in China . . . does not permit us to say exactly in which period of the Neolithic the Chinese invented their writing. What did persist through these long periods was the idea of sign use. Although it is impossible at this point to trace any direct connection from the Jiahu signs to the Yinxu characters [that is, those found at a capital of the late Shang Dynasty, c.1200 BC, three hundred miles south of Beijing], we do propose that slow, culture-linked evolutionary processes, adopting the idea of sign use, took place in diverse settings around the Yellow River (Li, Harbottle, Zhang, and Wang 2003: 31, 45).

We cannot read these signs, nor is the author sure what he means by "writing." In our own terminology, he seems to mean that in China semasiography preceded lexigraphy, hardly surprising, but there is no need for lexigraphy ever to grow from semasiography. If the signs do refer to words, as this scholar suggests, such logographic signs would be already a form of lexigraphy, three millennia older than finds from Mesopotamia. Such would be a startling result and against common consensus that "true writing," that is, lexigraphic writing, first appeared in Mesopotamia about 3400 BC in the logosyllabic systems of Sumer and Akkad, and not in China c.6500–5000 BC.

Oracle Bones and the Problem of Origins

Whatever the nature of such Neolithic markings, there does appear to be continuity between lexigraphic inscriptions first attested from the late Shang Dynasty around 1200 BC, called oracle-bones, and the Chinese writing still used today. A mass of these oracle-bone inscriptions was found in large deposits from an archaeological site near Anyang in northern China, carved on the scapulae (shoulder-blades) of cattle and on the plastra (belly pieces) of tortoise shells. About 150,000 examples exist, many of them small pieces with only a few signs. Scapulomancy, attested for the Neolithic in China, must have been an important industry from an early time. Casual finds of these bones were long used in Chinese medicine; in 1993 I saw one for sale at a market in Dunhuang in the Gobi Desert (if it was genuine). Similar inscriptions from Anyang also appear on contemporary bronzes, where they have been carved into the clay around which the bronze was cast. A few signs also survive on shell, jade, and pottery. The script is by no means primitive, but fully developed with from 3,000 to 5,000 logographic signs. Because of the similarity to later forms, one-third to one-fourth of the signs are intelligible.

The oracle bones are remnants of the sorcerer's art. Depressions were first drilled into the back of a turtle plastron or the bovine scapula. A question was asked, for example, will the coming week bring disaster? The sorcerer/scribe, or the king himself, then placed a hot metal instrument to the depression in the shell or bone, causing a network of cracks, the work of prescient spirits. The plastra or bones must have been stored, with the question and date of the interrogation written on them, until the event transpired, when the result was also recorded. Many bones have no inscription, however, or only the date and question but not the outcome.

Figure 15.2 is an elaborate example, the rubbing of a plastron from the reign of Wu Ding, a king of the Shang Dynasty. The plastron mentions a Lady Hao, a consort of Wu Ding whose tomb is the richest ever found from the Shang Dynasty, filled with hundreds of precious jade vessels, some inscribed. The writing on the plastron appears in columns beginning on the right; the left half of the plastron repeats the inscription, somewhat foreshortened. The signs in the far right-hand column give the date, the act of divination, and the name of the man who did the divining as Que, and can be translated as "Crack-making on the day *Jiashen*, Que divining."

Figure 15.2   Rubbing of turtle plastron with early inscriptions, c.1200 BC, from an ancient capital of the Shang Dynasty near modern Anyang in the Yellow River Valley. (After Zhang Bingquan, *Xiaotun, di er ben: Yingxu, Wenzi: bingbiang*, Part 2 (1). Taibei: Institute of History and Philology, Academia Sinica, 1962, no. 247.)

The last sign (broken) is "Lady," continued at the top of the second column with "Hao, childbearing lucky?" Most oracle bones end here, but this one continues with the king's interpretation of the cracks and the outcome: "If the child is born on a *ding* day, lucky. If on a *geng* day, enormously auspicious." *Ding* and *geng* are names from the Chinese 10-day week. The king himself interprets because a subordinate's unfavorable prediction might be treason. Evidently the question has been repeated over and over, for there are 11 cracks on the shell (hard to see), numbered on the bottom left from one to five, and on the bottom right from one to six. The inscription must be a digest of a long procedure. Then we learn what happened: "Three weeks one day later on day *jiayin* child born. Unlucky. A girl."

Scholars have asked what the purpose of the oracle bones was, but no good answer has been given. Perhaps they formed a display, but why would the king display a record of an unpropitious omen? Perhaps they are documents to be read by the spirits of the ancestors, who would belong to same literate elite as the king and his family. Just as uncertain is what the bones mean to the reconstruction of the history of Chinese writing. Some think that because the earliest Chinese writing is divinatory or dedicatory (on some inscribed bronzes) it was invented for this purpose. However, we must assume an earlier development on such perishable substances as strips of bamboo tied together to form a mat that can be rolled into a scroll: Actual examples survive from the fifth century BC and later. The characters were written vertically down the strips with a brush and ink. The Anyang inscribed bronzes can attempt to reproduce the ductus of signs made with a brush.

When, where, and why Chinese writing was invented are unknown. There is no evidence before the Anyang period once we exclude the Neolithic markings. In Mesopotamia the earliest uses of lexigraphic writing were restricted to accounting; in Egypt, significantly, for display of the king's prerogatives, but not until five hundred years later, c.2700 BC, did either system present a connected discourse, which texts on the oracle bones, and occasional records of military exploits, was already able to do. Some scholars imagine the same socio-economic pressures as existed in the ancient Near East in the fourth millennium to lie behind the creation of the Chinese writing: the need to keep track of economic information and assist trade and empire. Certainly whole categories of Chinese writing are lost that must once have existed – for example, the documents and aids that students require. No writing can exist without formal means for training new scribes; 10 percent of surviving Sumerian tablets are school exercises with lists of words of similar meaning or function, and "literary" texts copied, recreated by memory, or taken down by dictation. Not a scrap survives from the scribal schools of early China, by contrast. The ordinary medium for writing must have been perishable and Wu Ding's enormous collection of inscribed oracle bones must reflect an idiosyncrasy.

How Chinese Writing Works

One critic remarks that "The Chinese script came into being, probably in the second millennium BC, as a largely pictographic and logosyllabic writing system comparable to archaic Sumerian and Egyptian" (Parpola 1994: 39). The bête noir "pictography," however, in the sense of drawing pictures of what you mean, is never important in Chinese writing and is already lost in the Neolithic markings, whatever their true character might be (see Fig. 15.1). The meaning of not one single Chinese sign in use today is obvious from its shape. Nor was Chinese writing a "logosyllabic writing" like Sumerian cuneiform or Egyptian hieroglyphs.

About 90 percent of Chinese characters are *complex*, made up of two elements whose separate existence is not obvious, but capable of discovery through analysis. One of the two elements in a complex sign, the "radical," is a sematogram, a determinative or semantic complement referring to a category or concept. There are about 540 radicals according to a classification from the first century AD, but only 214 according to a classification completed in AD 1716.

The second element in a complex sign contains phonetic information, but the element does not encode a certain (if often variable) phonetic value as in the logosyllabic and syllabic systems earlier examined. Rather, the second element of the sign, called the "phonetic," gives a hint through the rebus about the sound of the word meant. The semasiographic radical, combined with the phonetic, constitutes a unitary logogram tied to a specific word. As we have the system, in place by 200 BC, the radical and phonetic work together, and scholars disagree about which came first. Chinese never became a logosyllabary because the phonetic signs were never organized into a standardized system for phonetic representation. It is our only historical example of a full logography, although it works in unexpected ways.

An Example of a Chinese Complex Character

A common radical is the sign 木 , supposed to be a stylized tree according to the Chinese tradition of finding pictures in abstractions in order to facilitate learning the sign, very much as Semitic speakers applied names to their signs to aid learning. As a "tree," the sign refers to anything made of wood or having to do with wood, very like the semantic complement "tree" 𓆸 in Egyptian hieroglyphics. Taken not as a radical, which has no phonetic value, but as an independent simple graph, a logogram, 木 is pronounced /mu/ in Beijing Mandarin, which means "wood." Now the sign 安, fancifully said to represent a woman beneath a roof, is a logogram for "peace," which in Mandarin is /ān/. The horizontal line over the [ā] in the transliteration does not refer to the length of vowel, but means that the sound has a "steady tone." By attaching the semasiographic sign for "something made of wood" to the bottom of the logographic "peace," reduced to the sound /ān/ through the rebus, you create a character meaning "table" 案 pronounced as /àn/ in the Beijing dialect, a near homophone for /ān/ = "peace." The grave accent indicates a "descending tone." The tone in Chinese speech is not a decoration; it is phonemic. That is, /ān/ and /àn/ sound different, but the "tree" radical means that the radical and phonetic combined together are to be taken as the word /àn/ = "table."

The character 案 = /àn/ "table" is a single grapheme, not obviously made up of two separate graphemes at all, one hinting at the sound /àn/ and the other placing the object in the class "things made of wood," and even the learned reader will not ordinarily resolve the complex sign into semasiographic/logographic components, on the one hand, and phonetic components, on the other, but will recognize the whole sign right away as /àn/, Beijing Mandarin for "table." In a similar way we recognize the different meanings of the homophonous *write, rite, wright, right* without isolating phonetic and semantic elements. If, however, one wishes to look up an unknown sign in one of the big Chinese dictionaries, the learned reader will then need to recognize, or guess at, the radical in the unknown sign, because such dictionaries are organized, first, according to the radicals and, second, according to how many strokes are required to draw the phonetic portion of the character.

A standard example of the use of near homophones to suggest the meaning of a character is the writing of the word for "mother" /mā/ with "steady tone" by means of the radical 女 = "female" (a sematogram) combined with the phonetic 馬 = "horse" (a logogram), which in

Mandarin is /mǎ/ with "descending and ascending tone." In this case the radical, the first sign, and the phonetic, the second sign, are easily distinguishable:

女 ＋ 馬 ＝ 媽 "mother"

The syllables /mā/ and /mǎ/ are different sounds with different meanings in Chinese speech, but close enough to suggest that the reader understands the sign /mǎ/ "horse" 馬 as a rebus for /mā/ "mother" with steady tone, to which the semasiographic 女 "something to do with females" must refer. Given to playful explanations about their writing, a Chinese may explicate the combination as in origin meaning a "female horse," as if in satiric reply to the eternally baffling question, "Tell me, what is a woman, really?"

Chinese Logography

Nine out of 10 signs in the Chinese repertory work as complex signs, resolvable into radical and phonetic hint, and already in the oracle bone inscriptions over 50 percent of the decipherable signs work in this way. The other *simple* signs are either radicals (sematograms) or phonetics (logograms) standing alone. It is hard to be sure whether the radical in a complex Chinese character is really a sematogram, with meaning not tied to speech and directing the phonetic element toward a certain category of meaning, or whether it is sometimes a logogram, referring to a precise element of speech, to which the phonetic stands as a phonetic complement. In any event the two elements are unified graphically and written in invisible boxes that come one after the other in columns reading top to bottom and right to left or, today, usually in lines reading from left to right across a page. There is no punctuation or word division or other diacritic information. The unified characters are virtual logograms, each standing for a monosyllabic morpheme, that is, a word in Chinese, a unit of sound with meaning, but never informing the reader just how the word is to

	Pronunciation	Meaning of character	Semantic component	Meaning of semantic component
堯	/yáo/	'legendary chief'		—
澆	/jiāo/	'water (verb)'	水	'water'
僥	/jiǎo/	'lucky'	人	'man, human'
蹺	/qiāo/	'lift foot'	足	'foot'
翹	/qiáo/	'lift up'	羽	'quill'
驍	/xiāo/	'good horse, valiant'	馬	'horse'
曉	/xiǎo/	'dawn'	日	'sun'
燒	/shāo/	'burn'	火	'fire'
譊	/náo/	'shout, quarrel'	言	'word, speech'
橈	/náo/	'oar'	木	'tree, wood'
鐃	/náo/	'bell, cymbal'	金	'metal'
撓	/náo/	'disturb'	手	'hand'
嬈	/ráo/	'graceful'	女	'woman'
蕘	/ráo/	'brushwood'	艸	'grass, plant'
蟯	/ráo; náo/	'roundworm'	虫	'insect, reptile'
饒	/ráo/	'abundant'	食	'eat, food'
繞	/rào/	'coil'	糸	'silk, thread'

Figure 15.3 Chart of complex Chinese characters built on a single phonetic /yáo/ combined with 16 radicals to create 16 different logograms. The "accents" over the vowels indicate pitch. (After H. Rogers 2005, chart 3.1.1.)

be pronounced. The reader must learn through education. We do not expect to find phonetic elements locked within logograms, but here we certainly do.

Although phonetic elements are present in the complex signs, very many signs are required for the overall system because of the lack of a consistent system of phonetic representation (Fig. 15.3). For example, in Figure 15.3 the simple sign 堯 at the top of the first column is a logogram for "legendary chief," which, in Mandarin, is /yáo/ (with ascending tone on the *a*), so through the rebus this sign can suggest a phonetic value. The characters in the rest of the column are made up of this same sign, now a phonetic, plus the radicals listed in the fourth column, whose governing category is given in the fifth, right-hand column. The sounds of the many different, but similar, words represented in this way are given in the second column and the meaning of the complex sign in the third. It is easy to see from this chart how imprecise is the phonetic component of a complex sign!

The phonetic portion of a complex sign therefore fulfills its function in an indiscriminate even slapdash fashion. In reading most signs the reader plays a game called "guess the word" through, first, knowledge of the "radical," the semasiographic portion of the sign; and, second, through knowledge of the sound suggested through the rebus by the logographic portion of the sign. In most cases the original relevance of the radical has long been lost, even if the radical can be isolated within the often intricate grapheme. The sound of the phonetic has also changed, often greatly, since it was first formalized into a written character as long as two thousand years ago. Mostly the reader does not understand Chinese signs through analysis into radical and phonetic, but must learn each sign on a case-by-case basis, opening it to the charge by unfriendly critics as the "worst system of writing ever devised."

Chinese Writing and Chinese Speech

We might think of Chinese writing as a gigantic repertory of the morphemes in Chinese speech. All the meaningful monosyllabic units in Chinese have been assigned to one or other sign. Hence the illusory impression that Chinese speech is monosyllabic, although the difficult question remains mixed up with the obscurity of the word "word." We exist and live by them, but cannot define them. Chinese speech is in fact given to the formation of compounds, and some scholars understand two-thirds of Chinese speech as consisting of more than one morpheme, as a polysyllabic "language." Yet in the Chinese language there is not even a word for "word," only for "syllable" (*tzu*), that is, the monosyllabic morpheme to which signs in Chinese writing refer. Supporters of the Romanization of Chinese writing can never decide whether to write Chinese words as monosyllables separated by spaces, as in Western alphabetic systems, or as solid words, as when we write "meadowlark" or "grandmother" or "Schadenfreude." The name of China in *pinyin* is *Zhongguo*; in the older Wade-Giles, it is *Chung-kuo*.

By those without expert training, including Chinese, the Chinese writing is easily confused with the Chinese language, with which it bears only an indirect factual and a tangled historical relationship.

The grammar taught in Chinese schools is the grammar of written style. The ability to write properly, together with a knowledge of the rules of pronunciation, are felt to be enough to enable any Chinese to speak Putonghua ["common language," that is, the Beijing dialect of Mandarin] with facility. Little direct attention is paid to standards for speaking. Putonghua grammar is defined in terms of written Chinese, not spoken Chinese. (Ramsey 1987: 49)

Spoken Chinese is fairly easy to learn because there are no cases, tenses, gender, or moods. The root vowel is always the same, never varying to fashion linguistic difference, as in our own *sing, sang, sung*. Its simplicity sets it solidly against Chinese writing, learned only through agonizing labor, in reality never mastered. In spite of twentieth-century efforts to tie Chinese writing to the Mandarin dialect of Beijing, the writing still stands at a far remove from any real Chinese speech ever spoken.

The distance of the Chinese grapheme from the sounds of speech makes it difficult to write the names of foreigners, which of course mean nothing in Chinese, as well as imported foreign words. When necessary to write the name, for example, of an American president the name is fashioned solely through the rebus, discarding the meaning of a character but preserving its sounds, of course never in a consistent way and never getting very close to the real sound of the name. Different characters can and do spell the same name. Such difficulties offer plenty of opportunity for play. It is common to find multisyllabic foreign imports as composed of meaningful syllabic units. "Coca-Cola," for example, can be written with signs that imitate phonetically the name and also mean "tasty and enjoyable."

Attempts at Reform

Apologists for this famously cumbersome system complain that homophony is so common in Chinese speech that two Chinese speakers of the same dialect, standing face to face, may in some cases actually not understand one other. In such cases one Chinese may inscribe in the air the character that designates his meaning! For in Chinese writing, a different graph is assigned to every different meaning that a single syllabic sound might have, a homophonous morpheme. Thus we write *their* and *there* or *might* and *mite* to indicate different but homophonous words. But many

Chinese homophones have *many* meanings or even dozens and in one case 146 different meanings! One wag made up an entire story about a poet who hunted and ate lions in which every single word has the sound in Mandarin dialect of /shi/ (but ignoring the four "tones" – steady, ascending, descending and ascending, descending – that are phonemic in Chinese speech).

Because of its simplicity as a spoken language, wherein nearly all syllables are morphemes (meaningful units), Wilhelm von Humboldt (1767–1835) famously classified Chinese as the archetypal "isolating" language, set against "agglutinative" languages like Turkish and "inflecting" languages like Greek, Latin, and German. Von Humboldt's famous schema looked like an evolutionary model, in which language advances from simple and primitive, like Chinese, to intricate and advanced, like Greek, Latin, and German. Many Chinese intellectuals who studied in Europe began to see their own language and writing and its hallowed tradition in just this way, as deeply inferior to European languages and traditions of writing.

Hence arose many efforts at reform, but really to change Chinese writing would be to lose the sacred and ancient Chinese culture encoded in it, and represented by it, and especially the opportunities for calligraphy and its associated claims to aesthetic enjoyment and social superiority that justify Chinese social behavior. As we saw, even mass-murderer Mao Zedong (1893–1976) bragged about his fine handwriting and set up a model of it in Tiananmen Square on the granite Monument to the People's Heroes, which still stands. Mao lacked the power to discard the clumsy ancient system but following the reformers he simplified the writing. In 1956 and in 1964 the Chinese Communist Party promulgated lists of simplified signs. By reducing the number of strokes in a character, a dubious benefit to the writer, you do not necessarily make the character easier for the reader. Breakaway Taiwan and the large communities of Chinese spread throughout the world (except for that in Singapore) did not follow the Communist example. The result of reform was to produce two mutually unintelligible forms of Chinese writing.

The groundwork for such well-meaning interference was laid in the early twentieth century when Putonghua, the Beijing dialect of Mandarin, was established as the official dialect behind the writing, extinguishing the scholarly and artificial classical Chinese "language" as a living system for symbolic communication and expression as it was for two thousand years. The Chinese development is a moral lesson. Because writing is conventional, "improvements" bring the loss of intelligibility. As a conventional system, Chinese writing is abhorrently complex, but professionals and even ordinary people can and do master its conventions, and it has served humankind in a noble way.

China's Influence

In the eighteenth century more books were printed in Chinese than in all European languages combined. As West Semitic phonography dominated the West and today the world, from the Chinese writing derived the still more complex Japanese writing, which uses two systems intermixed, a pure syllabary (called *hiragana*, "ordinary signs," because they are not Chinese logograms) and imported Chinese logograms (called *kanji* "Chinese writing"), but associated with Japanese words. The Japanese might easily encode their "language" in writing by means of the syllabic *hiragana* alone, but they take pride in the traditional system that boasts, together with one of the most complex writings ever devised, one of the highest literacy rates in the world.

In Korea three adaptations of the Chinese writing took place, always closely tied to classical Chinese language. In 1444 a Korean king invented an interesting alphabetic system, called *Hangeul* ("great writing") in which the shape of the signs imitates the position of the tongue and mouth during articulation; but Hangeul has by no means replaced *hanji*, the old-fashioned "Chinese writing." Still today in South Korea a high-school student may master 1,800 Chinese logographic characters, and even more in North Korea. Similarly in Vietnam, controlled by China for most of the first millennium AD, classical Chinese writing and language was the official medium until 1918, when exams were no longer administered in Chinese writing. Since then the Greek/Roman alphabetic system taken from Portuguese Jesuits in the seventeenth century has mostly replaced the Chinese writing that both suited and determined traditional Asian social structure for over three thousand years.

The structure of the Chinese writing is so dissimilar to the logosyllabic systems of the ancient Near East that one doubts a direct historical connection, which is sometimes assumed. If the Neolithic signs from the seventh or fifth millennia are lexigraphic, a historical connection would be ruled out in any event. If the writing was invented at the same time as the Mediterranean Late Bronze Age, c.1500 BC, the idea of lexigraphic writing may have come to China over what was later called the Silk Road, a network of trails passing up the Yellow River Valley and north of the Himalayas before descending over central Asia into Mesopotamia. China was never completely isolated from the Near East.

In the Mesopotamian and Egyptian traditions, three kinds of signs are admixed in a continuous text. Syllabic signs have a roughly predictable phonetic value. In a second category, logograms refer to words but have no phonetic value. In a third category, semantic indicators or determinatives place the word into a class. Signs from each category are written alone; they do not combine into a single grapheme. The phonetic component of logo-syllabic Mesopotamian cuneiform and Egyptian hieroglyphs enabled these writings to come far closer to speech than Chinese writing ever did, and allowed a reduction of the signary to 600 or 700 signs. However, Near Eastern logosyllabic writing's far closer, although still far distant, proximity to speech made the writing less suitable to govern a broad empire than did the Chinese writing. The scribal class must always be bilingual or trilingual, as Mesopotamian scribes ordinarily were and Chinese scribes never were. In fact an empire comparable to China's never arose in Mesopotamia except the short-lived empire of Sargon in the third millennium, marked by significant administrative and scribal reform.

Chinese Writing and Poetic Expression

The sinologist A. C. Graham remarked that "when a Chinese poet writes abstractly it is nearly impossible to make him interesting in English" (Graham 1965: 13). Let us see what Graham might have meant, and what we learn about the relationship between Chinese writing and a partly imaginary Chinese speech. Let us take two lines from the famous "Autumn Meditation" series by China's greatest poet, Du Fu (AD 712–70), in which Du Fu contrasts one statesman's meager accomplishments with those of a great statesman of olden times. Here is an alphabetic phonetic transliteration accompanied by an English translation. The very important aesthetic pleasure from the fine drawing of the characters is of course gone, and for this reason a Chinese could never recognize our version as in any sense a form of poetry. The phonetic transliterations (in Wade-Giles) are in CAPS and the English equivalents are in *italics*:

K'UANG	HENG	K'ANG	SU	KUNG-MING	PO
K'uang	*Heng*	*write-frankly*	*memorial*	*Success*	*slight*
LIU	HSIANG	CH'UAN	CHING	HSIN-SHIH	WEI
Liu	*Hsiang*	*transmit*	*classic*	*Plan*	*miss*

We can understand these lines in the following way. Du Fu is complaining about his own inability to make a lasting achievement either as statesman or as scribe. As statesman, he is like K'uang Heng, an adviser to the emperor who failed; as littérateur, he is less than Liu Hsiang, a famous scholar who edited many classical texts in Chinese literature. A. C. Graham (1965) renders this bewildering couplet as:

> A disdained K'uang Heng, as a critic of policy.
> As promoter of learning, a Liu Hsiang who failed.

Alphabet-users, like ourselves, do not live in the same world as the literate Chinese. The Chinese poem will always be something essentially different from alphabetic imitations, because the Chinese reader sees a sequence of beautifully drawn symbols in whose beauty, as much as anywhere, lies the emotive power of the poem. Graham's version is no translation, but an interpretation, a new kind of literary artifact fixed now within an alphabetic tradition. To the alphabet-user, this is dreary stuff. Yet the native Chinese is as puzzled as we in thinking about the poem and puzzled partially in the same way.

The Chinese original works by presenting a sequence of images, triggered in the mind of the reader, invoked by logographic signs that have no consistent phonetic value. The sounds potentially have meaning, rhythm, maybe rhyme, but the reader cannot reach those levels of aesthetic pleasure without the formally unique characters that guide him to distinguish meaning in the Chinese homophonic wilderness. The poetry is simply not separable from the graphic signs. It does not exist in the sounds, as, for example, it did in the poetry of Homer. The absence of inflection, number, gender, and tense in Chinese speech encourages this style of imagistic poetic expression, as such features no doubt affect Chinese morality and politics.

The characters have magical force and intrinsic power. In this sense they are roughly similar to the Egyptian hieroglyphs. Chinese characters can even draw religious devotees. A sacred shrine in south China (in Xiamen, that is, Amoy) is devoted to a gigantic Chinese character *fo*, which means

Figure 15.4 The Buddha as the character *fo*, in Xiamen, c. seventeenth century AD. (Photograph © Wang Miao/Paris, Agence de Press, ANA.)

"Buddha." In the Chinese fanciful tradition of seeing pictures lurking in the characters of their writing, the sign is taken to portray the Buddha in cross-legged meditation (Fig. 15.4).

Summary

In a way Chinese writing *is* the Chinese language, as everyone believes. "After all, the modern Chinese dialects are really more like a family of languages, and the Chinese of the first millennium BC is at least as different from the modern standard language as Latin is from Italian or French" (Norman 1987: 1). Although in contemporary education the Chinese learn to pronounce Chinese writing as if it were the Beijing dialect of Mandarin, the writing does not in fact represent any one dialect or language and it never has. In the long history of China the writing made possible the great Chinese Empire. Scribes across a vast area, where many languages were spoken, could all understand the writing and so remain in communication with the center of empire in northern China. Like Egyptian hieroglyphs, it served the needs of political power as a standardized graphic system for the exchange of information across dialect or language barriers. So did Egyptian writing unify the Nile Valley, where a plethora of local dialects certainly existed, undetectable in the writing.

No doubt the bizarre Chinese writing has long stood between China and modern ideals, suitable or not for all people, of universal education and democratic self-governance. The global computerization of intellectual culture only heightens the tension. Our difficulties in understanding Chinese writing derive from our own alphabetic culture. Chinese writing, like other lexigraphic writings, is a system for symbolic thought parallel to speech, making use of the resources of speech, but very different from speech. Nonetheless, to be literate in Chinese is something outside our own experience.

16

Lexigraphic Writing in Mesoamerica

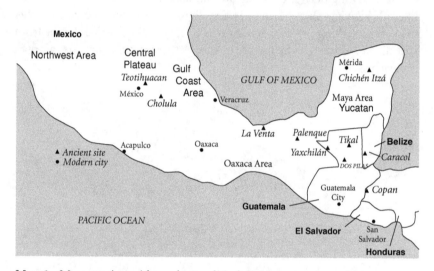

Map 6   Mesoamerica, with modern political divisions, towns, and important archaeological sites

Controversy about the time of arrival of humans in the Americas continues vigorously, with the old-fashioned date of c.12,000 BC constantly pushed back by new finds, including stratified finds from Chile going back to c.35,000 BC. Certainly the native inhabitants of the Americas came over the Bering land strait at some time, which has risen and sunk repeatedly in recent geological history. While the indigenous populations of the Americas resemble in some way the East Asians with whom they must once have associated, they are nonetheless racially distinct from Asian populations. Whenever they arrived, the American Indians were separated for many millennia from the cultures of the Old World and offer a case study in efforts to separate what is irreducibly human from what is shaped by culture.

Remarkably, a form of lexigraphic writing appeared in Mesoamerica that can have had no connection with developments in Mesopotamia or China. Yet the writing mimics in some ways the functioning of the Old World systems, while in others it defies them. Some think Chinese writing the worst ever devised because of restrictions that complexity and ambiguity place upon the refinement of thought and on popular literacy; but Mesoamerican writing went a step beyond.

Slouching toward Decipherment

In AD 1519 Hernán Cortés, a Castilian, landed near VERACRUZ in the Gulf of Mexico. By 1521 he ruled MEXICO. The Roman Catholic Spaniards, horrified by the indigenous culture of ritual human sacrifice and cannibalism began – after collecting the gold and decimating the population through disease – systematically to destroy every trace of the devil's handiwork. The Maya Indians of the northeast lowlands, in the YUCATAN, at this time had many books made of the inner bark of the fig tree, covered in a lime slip, then painted with figures and characters. In July of 1562 the bishop Diego de Landa (1524–79) ordered the destruction of every single one. But three (or four) survived.

Not until three hundred years later, in the early nineteenth century, in the flush of the Romantic movement that idealized the life of natural man, were the American Indians of Mesoamerica again a topic of interest. European and American travelers now visited the jungle-covered ruins of the Maya in what are today the countries of BELIZE, GUATEMALA, EL SALVADOR, and Mexico. They made drawings of the monuments and the odd figures often carved on them, although the figures were often overgrown and decayed. The conventions of Maya art are so baroque that it was hard to see what was represented. In 1810 the great German scholar Alexander von Humboldt (who classified all languages into types) made an important advance when he published pages from what is called the Dresden codex, purchased by the royal library of the court of Saxony in 1739. Labeled Aztec or Mexican, its Maya origins were at first unknown (Fig. 16.1). Later, three other codices were found: one in a library in Madrid, evidently once belonging to Hernán Cortés himself; one in a Paris trash can, of mysterious origins; and one, if it is genuine, found c.1970 in a cave and called the Grolier codex.

Figure 16.1   Page 9 of the Maya Dresden Codex, from an 1880 edition
by Ernst Förstermann. The codex contains astronomical observations and
calculations, especially of the planet Venus, and also ritual prescriptions and
many dates. Six full pages are devoted to calculating, with great accuracy, the
cycle of Venus. There may be calculations for the movements, too, of Mars,
Mercury, and Jupiter

In 1862 the French cleric who was to discover the Madrid codex also
discovered in the Spanish royal archives a manuscript by the same Bishop
de Landa who three hundred years before exercised such energy in de-
stroying native superstition that even the Spanish brought him to trial.
In his defense, de Landa wrote his *Relación de las Cosas de Yucatán,*
"Description of the affairs in Yucatan," which contained a description
of how the Mayan writing worked (Fig. 16.2). In the *Relación* de Landa
includes drawings of various Mayan glyphs and assigns to them letters in
the alphabet, sometimes syllables. The French cleric thought that he had
found a Rosetta Stone for Mesoamerican writing, but no one was able to
make sense of available texts by inserting de Landa's alphabetic values. The

Figure 16.2 Bishop Diego de Landa's description of how the Mayan writing worked, the *Relación de las Cosas de Yucatán*. (After http://upload.wikimedia.org/wikipedia/commons/2/2f/De_Landa_alphabet.jpg.)

topic was soon forgotten. De Landa must have had something wrong, as in fact he did.

In the meanwhile, scholars in the late nineteenth and early twentieth centuries attempted to explain the writing by working with the available codices and with accurate drawings now coming out of Mesoamerica, and to a large extent were able to puzzle out the astonishingly complex Maya calendrical system based on the number 20. One portion of the calendar is called the Long Count, a day count from a fixed date in the fourth millennium BC, as recorded both in the Dresden codex and on monuments. Nonetheless, even the nature of the writing remained unknown. About Mesoamerican writing I. J. Gelb wrote:

> The best proof that the Maya writing is not a phonetic system results from the plain fact that it is still undeciphered. This conclusion is inescapable if we remember the most important principle in the theory of decipherment: *A phonetic writing can and ultimately must be deciphered if the underlying language is known.* Since the language of the Mayas is still used today, and is therefore well known, our inability to understand the Maya system means that it does not represent phonetic writing. (1963: 56)

To such views the voluminous writings of the highly influential British-born J. Eric Thompson, one of the twentieth century's most accomplished Mayanists, lent support. It was Thompson who first correlated the Maya calendar with the Gregorian. He developed the numerical system for cataloging the Mayan glyphs still used today. But Thompson doubted that the glyphs had important phonetic components and thought that they could not record historical information. Instead they embodied philosophical speculations on time and prophecy by a pacific scribal priestly elite, no bloodthirsty gang of intoxicated cultists given to self-immolation, the consumption of psychotropic mushrooms, human sacrifice, and the eating of the still-living victim. He wrote in the first edition of his classic *Maya Hieroglyphic Writing: An Introduction,*

> It has been held by some that Maya dates recorded on stelae may refer to historical events or even recount the deeds of individuals; to me such a possibility is well-nigh inconceivable. The dates on stelae surely narrate the stages of the journey of time with the reference befitting such a solemn theme. I conceive the endless progress of time as the supreme mystery of Maya religion, a subject which pervaded Maya thought to an extent without parallel in the history of mankind. In such a setting there was no place for personal records, for, in relation to the vastness of time, man and his doings shrink to insignificance. To add details of war or peace, of marriage or giving in marriage, to the solemn roll call of the periods of time is as though a tourist were to carve his initials on Donatello's David. (Thompson 1950: 155)

Thompson spent his career on the Maya, was knighted for his labors, but fundamentally misunderstood them. He was as wrong about the Maya as

Arthur Evans was about the Minoans, another moral lesson: Before you can read the writing, you cannot know what it will reveal.

To Thompson's credit, in the third edition of his *Maya Hieroglyphic Writing* (1970) he backed away from his earlier severe hostility to the presence of phonetic elements in Mayan writing, persuaded partly by the work of an independent scholar named Heinrich Berlin, who lived in Mexico City and supported himself as a businessman. In 1958 Berlin published a paper showing that unique glyphs characterized each archaeological site. Such glyphs must be the names of the sites. He called them "emblem glyphs." If the sites were named, then the writing could not be devoted *wholly* to astral speculation, as Thompson believed.

Shortly after Berlin's paper appeared a Russian-born scholar living in America, Tatiana Proskouriakoff (1909–85), greatly strengthened the historical hypothesis. Trained as an architect, she worked in COPAN (in Honduras) and in YUCATAN (in Mexico) and in 1960 published an article showing how systems of three dates on individual monuments suggested the span of an individual's career: the time of his birth, accession to power, and death. She recognized a sequence at one site of seven rulers who ruled over two hundred years, evidence against Thompson's position that the glyphs contained no historical information.

The first persuasive evidence of systematic phoneticization in Mayan writing came with a paper by Yuri Knorosov (1922–99), published in 1952 (the same year as Ventris's decipherment) in Russian in Leningrad (now once again St Petersburg), but because of the Cold War unknown to Western Mayanists for many years. Knorosov had served in the Red Army during the Battle of Berlin in 1945. According to the story, from boxes crated by Nazi authorities and awaiting shipment in the halls of the Prussian State Library he helped himself to a rare publication of the Dresden, Madrid, and Paris codices. From this moment began his obsessive interest. Knorosov set forth his views in papers read to the Russian Academy of Science in what was then Leningrad.

Being a student of Egyptian hieroglyphs, Japanese, and Arabic, Knorosov knew in a practical manner something about the different ways that lexigraphic writing can work and that universal principles may govern the history of writing. He argued that on the analogy of the structure of ancient Near Eastern systems we should expect to find phonetic mixed with semantic elements in Mayan writing. He guessed that when de Landa interrogated a Maya informant, he placed what he heard within his own alphabetic system of understanding, like a tourist who goes to the Egyptian trinket shop and buys a personal name written in "the Egyptian alphabet" within a cartouche.

But the sounds associated with certain Mayan signs cannot have been alphabetic (any more than were Egyptian signs or Japanese signs or Arabic signs or Hebrew signs), because we never find alphabets that do not depend in some way on the Greek alphabet, the first writing that isolated phonemes in graphic representation (see Chapter 17). The signs must therefore stand for syllables, the smallest phonetic unit that the untrained ear can isolate. In fact de Landa gives syllabic values for several of the Mayan signs. When de Landa asked his informant to write the letter "B" pronounced in Spanish as /bay/, the informant wrote a sign with the value /bay/.

Knorosov's second proposal, based on the spelling conventions we find in such other ancient systems as the Cypriote Syllabary (Linear B had only just been deciphered) is that words ending in a consonant will probably be written with a sign whose vowel sound is the same as the vowel sound in the preceding sign (Mayanists call this "synharmony"). Because most words in modern spoken Maya end in consonants, this vowel sound will regularly be suppressed in pronunciation, but present in theory. If true, we will have a system for discovering the phonetic values of unknown signs, if we can discover the value of a preceding sign. J. Eric Thompson, trapped by his use of the treacherous word *ideographic*, by which he characterized the Mayan glyphs, ridiculed Knorosov's suggestions, embedded as they were in the usual obnoxious Communist cant. But intensive subsequent work has shown Knorosov to have been correct in both cases.

Knorosov's first example was based on signs in the Madrid codex. According to de Landa's notebook the sign 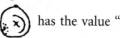 has the value "cu" (in Spanish). This sign appears in the Madrid codex (though drawn differently, such variation is usual) (Fig. 16.3). In one dialect of Maya speech the word for "turkey" is *kutz*, a meaning apparently confirmed by the picture of a turkey tied by a rope in the Madrid codex. The sign after /ku/ should therefore have the value /tzu/, according to Knorosov's theory that the vowel following a terminal consonant is the same as that in the preceding sign (synharmony). He seems to have deciphered the phonetic value of a previously unknown sign.

Then in the Dresden codex Knorosov found the same sign as the one following /ku/ in the Madrid codex, namely 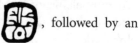, followed by an

ku

tzu

tzu

lu

tzul, "dog"

Figure 16.3 Excerpt from the Madrid codex containing the word for "turkey." (After M. Coe, fig. 34.3.)

Figure 16.4 Excerpt from the Dresden codex containing the word for "dog." (After M. Coe, fig. 34.7.)

unknown sign (Fig. 16.4). Because the signs are written over the picture of a dog, and because in Maya /tzul/ can mean "dog," he concluded that

the new sign must have the value /lu/, according to the same

principle of the harmony of vowels. Now he has deciphered the phonetic value of a second previously unknown sign.

In this way a select group of scholars has, in the last 40 years, puzzled out wholly or partially an impressive number of signs, though very many remain unknown or obscure. To everyone's surprise – a popular refrain in the study of writing! – the Mesoamerican writing turned out not to be philosophical speculation on the mystical properties of time, but earthly records of self-congratulation and pride in mutilation of the enemy.

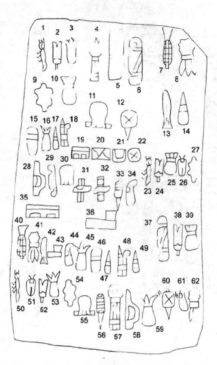

Figure 16.5   Drawing of the so-called Cascajal block, c.900 BC, an Olmec block bearing marks of unknown meaning, discovered in the 1990s but not published until 2006. The 62 figures are numbered in the drawing. (*Science*, September 15, 2006, 313 (5793): 1610)

Origins of Maya Writing

The origins of Mesoamerican writing are even more obscure than are those of other forms of writing, but it was no Maya invention. The earliest Mayan inscription comes from the third century BC, but inscriptions as early as 900 BC were reported in 2006 from Olmec territory on the southern edge of the Gulf of Mexico (LA VENTA is an Olmec site) (Fig. 16.5). Some of the 62 characters are repeated, one four times, and it "looks like writing," but some doubt that it is lexigraphic writing. None of the signs resemble signs in later Mayan writing. In any event, although we know little of the Olmecs, who flourished c.1200–400 BC, they may well be the inventors of Mesoamerican civilization, hence of the tradition of writing that we later find in the Maya lowlands. Two other important finds, of uncertain date but certainly BC, reflect Olmec achievement in the arts of writing: one on a four-ton basalt stele discovered in 1986, with hundreds of characters and a figure expertly carved in a traditional Mesoamerican style (the La Mojara stela). These examples are often grouped together as "Isthmian scripts" (because found on the isthmus joining Yucatan to the central Mexican plateau).

By c.600–400 BC (?) there are calendrical inscriptions from the hill-top site of Monte Albán in the valley of OAXACA, where the Zapotec Indians still live. We are never sure what language stands behind these early undeciphered "Zapotec" inscriptions, however, or if they are lexigraphic writing at all. Throughout Mesoamerica there is a remarkable continuity of culture from an early time up to the European conquest, shared by its traditions of writing. Similar styles of art, patterns of agriculture, and religious behavior characterize Mesoamerican peoples of different languages and ethnicities. Mesoamerican writing was inseparable from Mesoamerican culture and must somehow be a single tradition, even though we cannot understand its scant early testimonies.

The Nature of Maya Writing

The topic is difficult. Mayan "hieroglyphs" are only partly deciphered and will never be understood as we understand Old World cuneiform or Egyptian hieroglyphic documents. Certainly the writing contains phonetic elements, but we are on uneasy ground in reconstructing the Mayan "language" that stood behind the writing. Linguists divide the Mayan language into two main branches, the Cholan (spoken in southern Mexico) and the Yucatecan, but our earliest information about these languages is from the sixteenth century, seven hundred years after the close of the Classic Maya period c. AD 900. Historical Mayan language is to Classic Mayan rather as Coptic was to Pharaonic Egyptian. Furthermore, modern linguists identify 31 separate living Mayan "languages"! Even in theory, it is asking a lot to imagine that we can reconstruct the "real sounds" behind the phonetic elements in Mayan writing. Nonetheless, phonetic reconstructions of Mayan speech behind the writing can appear remarkably like modern Mayan speech, which Mayanists think is closest to the modern Cholan family of dialects.

The writing seeks and enjoys an exasperating complexity for its own sake, reminiscent of the enigmatic hieroglyphs of the Ptolemaic Egyptians. We rarely recognize a pictorial origin of individual signs. We can view the writing as a logosyllabary, but one that has a taste for substitution of different signs for the same value, homophones, and many values for the same sign, polyphones, far surpassing anything found in the Near East. Mayan writing was a learned game designed not to communicate information but to conceal it, while memorializing through arcane arts the life and achievements of kings and their wives.

The whole situation is extraordinary and baffling. The Mayan writing made exhausting use of calendrical and astronomical information to memorialize the mighty men of the day, but the writing had no other purpose, as far as we know, except sometimes as labels on cups. Virtually all sentences are in the third person singular, the barest reporting of the doings of a great man. There is no trace of economic documents; nothing about the economy of Mesoamerica required written records, where there was no irrigation agriculture and no very large units of power. Many kinglets dotted the land. Still, the cultivation of maize enhanced the vitality of these peoples and increased their numbers enormously, as it did in the preColumbian southeastern United States, the outer fringes of the Mesoamerican maize culture.

Recent finds of Mayan writing may go back to the third century BC and the latest come from the time of the Spanish conquest in the early sixteenth century AD, but by far the great majority of the surviving 10,000 inscriptions are from the so-called Classic Period, c. AD 200–900. While most inscriptions are on pottery or on stone stelae, they are written on many other substances and surfaces too. There are about 800 basic signs (some say 1,000), what one expects in a logosyllabary, but probably only 200–300 were used at one time. These basic signs recombined with one another with flexibility and variability into complex, or compound, signs. About 200 phonetic elements have been identified, but many are homophones. Just as in Near Eastern systems, the same sign can function in different capacities, too. For example can be a syllabogram with the value /ku/ or as a logogram stand for KUN, "stone" or "year."

To see how Mayan writing works, and its exorbitant frustrations, let us consider a phonetic rendering of the word for the Maya month *Mac* (Fig. 16.6). First one looks for the *main sign*, the one in the center or the biggest; the subordinate signs on top, bottom, front, and back are called *adfixes*. As Knorosov suggested in the 1950s, the basic phonetic value of phonetic signs is the open syllable, a consonant plus a vowel (CV). Also

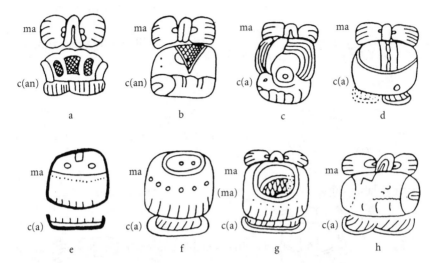

Figure 16.6 Different ways of spelling *Mac*, a Maya month. (After Thompson 1950, fig. 18.)

as Knorosov predicted, the final consonants common in Mayan speech are represented by a sign with the same vowel (not to be pronounced) as that attached to the preceding sign.

Thus in (a)  the sign for /ma/ is a

syllabogram, an adfix placed on top of the main sign ![main sign], a

logogram standing for an object pronounced something like /can/ or /chan/, giving us the combined value /mac/ once we have dropped the /an/ from the word suggested by the logogram.

In (b) 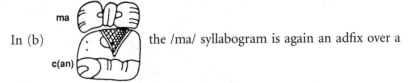 the /ma/ syllabogram is again an adfix over a

different main sign ![main sign], evidently another logogram standing for

/can/ as in (a). Notice that the /ma/ is drawn differently in both (a)

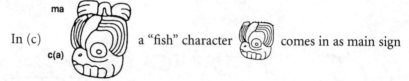 and (b) and in fact differently every time it

occurs.

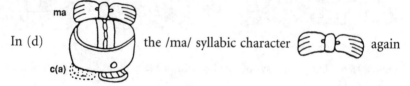 a "fish" character comes in as main sign

with syllabic value /ca/ = /c/ to provide the terminal consonant.

In (d) the /ma/ syllabic character again

is an adfix, but now over another logogram as main sign , with

unknown value. Fortunately the "comb" character , which
also has the value /ca/, is added as an adfix to the bottom of the main sign
to guarantee the terminal consonant. Both the /ma/ and the

/ca/ adfixes probably serve as phonetic complements to the

Mayan word attached to the logogram of the main sign.

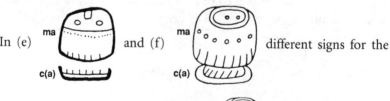 different signs for the

syllable /ma/ are introduced, and , now as main signs to

which again is attached the "comb" sign in (e) and 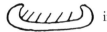 in

(f), both of which have the value of /ca/.

Finally, (g) is a variant of (d) 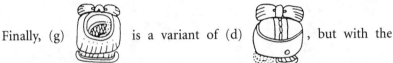, but with the

logogram of the main sign drawn differently and containing within it still

another syllabogram with value /ma/, and (h)  is a variant

of (d) .

Another example of the mutability of form is a spelling of the verb
tsa-pa-h(a), which means "was set up," said of rulers coming into power
(Fig. 16.7). In the first character, the syllable /tsa/ appears as an adfix over

the main sign , a syllabogram with the value /pa/, and a second

adfix /ha/ concludes the expression (but do not pronounce the /a/).

In the second character in Figure 16.7 what was the main sign is now

sandwiched in between two elements of the /tsa/ sign that has taken

on a vertical orientation. In the third glyph, a typically bizarre and demonic figure with an enormous nose replaces the /pa/ sign as he cradles
in his arm the glyph for /tsa/; the /h(a)/ is not represented. The substitution of grotesque faces and full figures for signs is common in Mayan
writing.

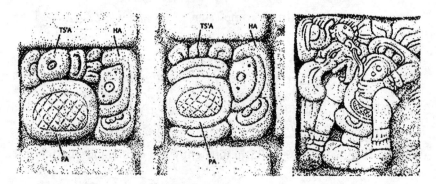

Figure 16.7 Three ways of writing *tsa-pa-h(a)*, "was set up." (After D. Stuart, S. D. Houston, http://images.google.com/imgres?imgwd.)

The Earliest Historical Text

The earliest historical Mayan inscription, one bearing real information about someone who once lived, is a famous artifact in Leiden called the Leiden Plaque. A carved bronze pendant once worn by a Maya great man, it bears a date in the Gregorian calendar of September 17, AD 320, (Fig. 16.8). The pendant, which comes from TIKAL in northern Guatemala, commemorates the accession of a ruler, shown on one side in full dress regalia, resplendent in feathers and ennobling accoutrements that, to our eyes, appear a mass of wiggles and loops, a nest of worms from which peer shrunken heads. The ruler stands over a captive, no doubt soon to sanctify the ruler's accession by drowning an altar from his gushing, still living heart.

On the other side is the date of the accession and the name of the ruler.

The first sign is a common glyph that introduces a statement,

but its exact meaning is unknown. The adfix ⬚ attached to the bottom of the main sign has the value /tun/, meaning "year," and the main sign is the head is of the god of the month Yashkin, perhaps when this event took place.

The personification of units of time, a curious kind of logography, is a striking feature of Mayan writing and determines the next five signs,

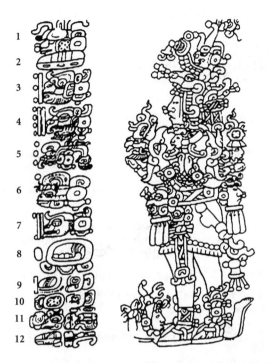

Figure 16.8   The two sides of the Leiden Plaque, drawing by Linda Schele. (After Schele and Miller 1986, fig. 12.)

whose dominance in the overall inscription reflects the central importance given to the difficult but accurate Maya calendar and the correlation of political events with it.

Here is how the signs work: First we learn the date in the Long Count through a system compared to cogs of different sizes interlocked in a cosmic machine. The glyphs numbered (3) to (7) represent five of these cogs, each one smaller than the preceding according to multiples of 20. Every day is unique, counted from the beginning of the Long Count on August 13, 3113 BC. In each character dots or dots and vertical bars precede stylized faces that stand for the different cogs in the machine of cosmic time: a bird, another bird, a reptile, a fish, a monkey.

Hence sign (3) 〔glyph〕 (a bird) notes that eight periods of the fifth magnitude have passed since the beginning of the Long Count

(144,000 days each period): The dots stand for single units and the bars for five.

Sign (4) (a bird) notes that 14 periods of the fourth order

of magnitude have passed (7,200 days each); sign (5)  (a

reptile) says three of the third order have passed (360 each); sign (6)

(a fish) that one of the second order of magnitude (20 days

each) has passed; and sign (7) (a monkey) that 12 of the

first order have passed (one day each). Thus 1,253,912 days have passed since the beginning of the Long Count, dating the inscription in our calendar as September 17, AD 320.

Sign (8) refers to a different calendrical calculation from that of the Long Count. The sign combines two logograms: a dot that means "1" and a logogram that stands for the month called "Eb." The event took place on "One Eb," a date in a 260-day calendar that ran concurrently with a 365-day solar calendar, again a smaller cog rotating within a larger one. The 260-day calendar is itself the product of two smaller cogs, one consisting of 13 days and one of 20 days, all of them with their own names and glyphs. Because 13 × 20 = 260, on day 261 the cycle begins anew.

The solar cog is turning and within it the 260-day cog is turning so that they return to their original positions every 52 years, when dates on both calendars will coincide, a time of extreme astrological importance. The 52-year cycle reflects the interacting of the 260-day and 365-day calendars and is called the *Calendar Round* (the place on the 52-year Calendar Round, used in conjunction with the Long Count, ought to be the "Short Count," but the term is not used).

The glyphs now are arranged in two columns of smaller characters. The first character (9) gives still more information about when this event took place: It is the glyph for the particular "lord of the night" who rules on this date. There are nine such lords who rule one after the other in rotation. This is a logogram for the fifth of the nine, but we do not know his name.

The second sign at position (9) and the first at position (10)

give the date in the present calendrical year, namely "0 Yashkin," which is arrived at in the following way. In the Maya solar calendar there are 18 months of 20 days each and 5 additional days to make up the 365-day year. The second sign, in position (9) , is a

compound sign. The main sign , called the "seating glyph," is a logogram that could stand for either the word /chul/ or /chum/; the adfix

= /mu/ functions as a phonetic complement, indicating that we are to take the word as the Mayan *cum*, which means something like "seated" or "seating." The first sign in position (10) is made up of two logograms, the first suggesting the value /yash/, which means "blue green" or "first," and the second suggesting the value /kin/, which means "sun" or "day," to spell *Yashkin*, the name of the Maya seventh month. Taken together, the "seating [of] Yashkin" refers to the last day of the preceding month (which is Shul), the day on which the coming month Yashkin was "seated" or "inaugurated," so really this day is the 20th of Shul; by convention it is called "0 Yashkin," which comes out to the 120th day of the Maya solar year.

The second sign in position (10) is once again the "seating

glyph" as main sign, now with a different adfix than in position (9) just above it. Its phonetic value identifies this form of the logogram "seat" to be in the passive voice, giving the meaning "was seated" for the compound sign, that is, the man portrayed on the other side of the pendant.

His names and titles follow in positions (11) and (12), but

we cannot read them as such.

Translating a Mayan Text: A Historical Inscription from DOS PILAS, Mexico

A second example, this time commemorating a military exploit, will give a better understanding of how Mesoamerican lexigraphic writing worked as a conventional system of markings that communicate information (Fig. 16.9). Such a continuous text is read from left to right, top to bottom, but by double columns, so first you read E1, then F1, then E2, then F2 and so forth. Mayanists work in stages from the glyphs to a translation. First they make a transliteration, writing down the probable phonetic values of syllabograms and writing the Maya words for logograms. Here is a transliteration in which the phonetic elements are in lower case and the logograms in CAPITALS (['] = glottal stop).

E1: ju-b'u-yi / **F1:** u-to-k'a /
E2: u-pa-ka-la / **F2:** nu-na /
G1: JOL / **H1:** CHAK-ki /
G2: u-KAB'-[ji]ya / **H2:** b'a-la-ja /
I1: CHAN-na / **J1:** K'AWIL-la /
I2: u-CHAN-nu / **J2:** TAJ-MO'-o

Because the signs are highly unclear about the exact sound of any human speech, the Mayanist next attempts to recast the information from the transliteration into a hypothetical form of Mayan speech that might really have existed over one thousand years ago. On this shaky basis, the researcher now makes a first translation of such a recasting:

Figure 16.9 A passage from hieroglyphic stair four, step five, at Dos Pilas, in the province of Petén, Guatemala, c. AD 660. (Drawing by Stephen Houston, in Kettunen and Helmke 2005, app. 1, p. 67.)

got downed, (the) flint, (the) shield of mediation? (the) head of Chaahk; (the) overseeing of Kawiil who hammers sky, (the) guardian of Torchy Macaw.

Such gibberish (reminiscent of translations of Chinese poetry!) requires careful interpretation. Taking the obscure "mediation head of Chaahk," "hammers sky," and "Torchy Macaw," as parts of names, one can create a second stage of translation:

The flint and the shield of Nun Ujol Chaahk got toppled; it was overseen by Bajlaj Chan Kawiil, the "guardian" of Tajal Mo.

Evidently a military exploit is celebrated in which a certain Bajlaj Chan Kawiil, who watches over a place called Tajal Mo, overcame his opponent Nun Ujol Chaahk, whose army fought with flint-tipped spears and shields. Now the Mayanist may attempt a third stage of translation:

Bajlaj Chan Kawiil, the captor of Tajal Mo, overcame the army of Nun Ujol Chaahk, who fought with shields and spears tipped with flint.

Summary

The Mesoamerican writing presents many puzzles, but it seems to have supported abstract thought only in the formation of elaborate arithmetical calendrical calculations. There is something astonishing about the Mesoamerican obsession with the cycles of time, and one wonders how they came up with the Long Count and how exactly they decided on its base date and when, and how such calculations were performed. The Mesoamericans were and remain a mysterious people, but the partial decipherment of their partly phonetic script has utterly changed earlier perceptions of them.

The Egyptians, too, were thought to be a philosophical people, steeped in ancient wisdom, until decipherment of their script showed them to be a nation of bureaucrats with a taste for priestly fantasy. Once thought to be awash in speculation about the harmonies of eternity, a partial decipherment of Mayan writing shows them to have been cruel, masochistic, and filled with braggadocio. Mayan writing glorified the warrior and social elite by recording, in an opaque and obscurantist script, their titles, their lineage, and their place in the cosmic progression of time – dates of birth, accession, death, and of victory in war, when they captured the enemy for the hangman's bloody hands.

We wonder who read this script. We imagine the scribal elite explaining to the great lords how the glyphs are read and what they mean. Perhaps they were read aloud in public display, as some speculate. In only that limited sense can Mesoamerican writing have been a medium for the transmission of information to anyone outside a minuscule and self-aggrandizing class. We must imagine this writing, like Egyptian writing, to have possessed magical power to eternalize men on stone monuments, as the precise astronomical observations and calculations preserved in the Dresden and other codices enabled the scribal elite to guide the local lord in decisions about war, sacrifice, and marriage.

As a writing system, the Mesoamerican is a logosyllabary, but the signs are far more variable in form and ambiguous in phonetic value than we find in any Near Eastern system, including the maddening Akkadian cuneiform. The determinative or semantic complement, so characteristic of Egyptian hieroglyphs and of Mesopotamian cuneiform, appears in Mayan writing, especially in cartouches and pedestals associated with day-signs, but by no means forms so important a role. Although elements of the writing are tied to speech, the writing never rises above simple statements of fact. Mesoamerican writing was a form of Mesoamerican art, which it always complemented. Maya artistic taste for curlicues and thingamajigs, for demonic beings, skulls, and eerie threatening beasts also governed the forms of the writing, which for so very long resisted every attempt to penetrate it.

17

The Greek Alphabet: A Writing That Changed the World

Map 7   Places important to the background of the Greek alphabet

We know something about the man who invented West Semitic writing. He came from the Egyptian school because the phonic aspects of Egyptian writing, too, ignored the vibrating vocal cords to concentrate on hints about how in speech the stream of sound is obstructed. We cannot pin down the date of the earth-shattering invention of the wholly phonetic West Semitic syllabary, which sprang from the Egyptian logosyllabary. The famous Sinaitic inscriptions of perhaps 1500 BC, or recent similar even earlier finds from Egypt, even if not in line of direct descent, push back experimentation toward the Middle Bronze Age.

The circumstances of the invention of West Semitic writing are of course elusive but may be to record the names of Semitic subordinates, as some think. The need to record names is an initial and driving force in the history of writing. The enormously innovative concentration on phonic elements to the exclusion of other signs, an extreme anomaly in the history of writing, may have come from the Aegean, either through southern Palestine where Mycenaeans are later visible as the Philistines, or through UGARIT, whence comes our earliest finds of the West Semitic tradition in the "Ugaritic cuneiform alphabet," really syllabary. In Bronze Age Ugarit appeared just that cosmopolitan blend of Egyptian, Aegean, Anatolian, and Mesopotamian writing that we might require as background for an extraordinary invention.

In any event, along the north Syrian coast – not in Palestine, Egypt, Crete, or Asia Minor – was prepared the division between East and West, with the Greek alphabet-users on one side, the Greeks and the Romans, and the nonalphabet users on the other, the peoples of the Near East, ancient, medieval, and modern. Modern political configurations directly reflect ancient divisions in the technologies of writing. The Greek alphabet-users were unable to cross the veil of writing technology to reach directly the intellectual cultures encoded in Mesopotamian cuneiform, Egyptian hieroglyphic, and West Semitic syllabic writing, whereas after Alexander's conquests Easterners learned Greek alphabetic writing as a matter of course, absorbed Greek alphabetic culture, and made important contributions to it.

Background to the Invention of the Greek Alphabet

The transmission of cultural forms from East to West – and the deep division that transmission entailed – appears to have taken place near or across the ORONTES estuary and littoral. Emerging from SUMER in southern Iraq in the fourth millennium BC, cultural forms early moved on commercial routes up the Euphrates, then turned west. There are three ways to reach the coast from the Euphrates valley. A southern route led across open desert through what later was the oasis-kingdom of PALMYRA, but camels were required. Of the two northern routes one headed across to ALEPPO, critically positioned equidistant between the Euphrates and the Mediterranean, mentioned in texts from MARI on the Euphrates from the end of the third millennium. Aleppo lay variously under Amorite (a Semitic people west of the Euphrates), Bronze-Age Hittite, Egyptian, Hurrian, and Iron-Age Hittite rule, until conquered by the Assyrians in the eighth century BC.

From Aleppo the trade route led west to the Plain of Antioch where the north-flowing Orontes bends back on itself to run southwest into the sea through a pass between the Amanus range to the north and the northern extension of the Lebanon Mountains to the south. In Hellenistic and Roman times the metropolis of Antioch (modern Antakya in Turkey) stood south of the river, near this bend, about twenty miles from the sea. In the Iron Age, from the ninth century on, the nearby port town of AL MINA served as a major emporium for the exchange of Greek and Eastern products. Euboeans, the most aggressive and wealthy Greeks of the late Iron Age, may have been living there – at least their pottery is found there – and some have suspected Al Mina as the very place where writing passed from East to West.

The second northern route led somewhat south of Aleppo, in the third millennium across the great archaeological site of Ebla, 33 miles southwest of Aleppo, then south to modern Homs in the Orontes Valley, the ancient Emesa where Elagabulus became Roman emperor. From Homs the route leads west through the "Homs gap" in the Lebanon Mountains, where crusaders built the great castle Krak des Chevaliers. Bronze-Age Ugarit stood somewhat north of where the road through the Homs gap meets the Mediterranean coast. The Egyptians held close relations with this coast from at least the third millennium BC and acquired timber from the forests of western Lebanon, including planks to fashion the enormous royal bark found beside the pyramid of Cheops (c.2600 BC).

From Ugarit in the Bronze Age, in modern Syria, and from Al Mina in the Iron Age, seafarers headed west to CYPRUS, a mere 75 miles across the sea. Overseas trade was encouraged by an unremitting Assyrian pressure in the Iron Age against the mixed Semitic Aramaean (Aram = DAMASCUS) and the Indo-European Hittite populations of north Syria. The Semitic Aramaeans built a permanent settlement in southwestern Cyprus by c.900 BC at KITIUM, only miles from the Greek colony of Salamis to the north, founded about the same time.

Leaving Cyprus, merchants cruised along the Cilician coast (where Bronze Age shipwrecks are found on the southern coast of Turkey) to RHODES, thence across the Cyclades to Euboea and mainland Greece, or on the southern route over Karpathos to Crete, the Ionian isles, Sicily, and the Italian mainland. There in Latium, not so far from ancient Rome, astonishingly, was recently found the earliest known Greek alphabetic inscription, part of a word stratigraphically dated to 775 BC.

The transmission of writing from north Syria, or "Phoenicia," to Greece over this route is remembered in Greek legend in the story of Cadmus, founder of the city of Thebes in the Boeotian plain, near Aulis and the narrow crossing to Euboea. Herodotus writes:

> The Phoenicians who came [to Thebes, in the plain of Boeotia near EUBOEA] with Cadmus, among whom were the Gephyraei, introduced into Greece, after their settlement in the country, a number of accomplishments of which the most important was writing, an art until then, I think, unknown to the Greeks. At first they used the same characters as all the other Phoenicians, but as time went on, and they changed their language, they also changed the shape of their letters. At that period most of the Greeks in the neighborhood were Ionians. They were taught these letters by the Phoenicians and adopted them, with a few alterations, for their own use, continuing to refer to them as the Phoenician characters [*Phoinikeia*], as was only right, because the Phoenicians had introduced them . . . In the temple of Ismenian Apollo at Thebes in Boeotia I have myself seen cauldrons with inscriptions cut on them in Cadmean characters, most of them not very different from the Ionian. (Histories 5.58)

By "Ionians" Herodotus must mean the nearby Euboeans, who spoke an Ionian dialect. The Boeotians spoke a dialect akin to Doric. "Cadmus" means in Semitic "man of the East" (*kdm*) and in mythical chronology belongs in the Bronze Age, though the alphabet is much later. Herodotus must have seen some archaic inscriptions in the temple at Thebes.

"Phoenicians" is not a term known from the coastal Semites, but is a Greek name, presumably "the red ones," based (as many think) on the red hands of the purple-dyers who lived along the Lebanese and north Syrian coast. This is the celebrated "Tyrian purple," the most precious dye of the ancient world, made from a shellfish that once lived along these coasts (billions of discarded shells can still be seen today near ancient Phoenician sites). The Phoenicians did not exist as a people or a culture. Simply, they were the mercantile, seafaring Western Semitic-speakers who controlled the only ports in the East Mediterranean. Like all Semitic-speakers, the Phoenicians were of admixed ethnicities and politically diverse. Homer some-times calls them Sidonians, after the port of Sidon, receptors of an ancient and variegated Semitic influence – Akkadian, Babylonian, Aramaean, and Assyrian – and of an Indo-European Hittite influence who, after the Bronze Age, occupied large districts in northern Syria and left impressive monuments there. On the basis of various geographical details, the famous myth of the battle between the sky god and an enormous monster (Typhon in Greek) evidently came into Greek literature from the Hittites who in the Iron Age lived near the Orontes estuary.

The Adapter's Achievement

A great mystery has surrounded the transmission of writing from Syria to Greece, made impenetrable by misleading theories about the history of writing. Many commentators have supposed that the "alphabet" came to Greece at some time or other as a Phoenician import, acquired signs for vowels, which the Phoenician system mysteriously lacked, was used for various purposes, and, at some time along the way, recorded 28,000 lines of Homer's hexametric verse – and thousands by Hesiod as well – and that was the beginning of the Western world and of modern times. Although once widely circulated, such a view cannot be accurate.

As noticed earlier, humans cannot distinguish sounds in speech smaller than the syllable unless trained in some form of the Greek vocal alphabet. Nor is human speech made up of little pieces, of phonemes awaiting graphic representation, as alphabet users want to believe, although illiterates *can* separate out syllabic units when prompted. Speech is nonetheless a wave, a continuum. What was the nature of the radical shift in the technology of writing that made possible the reconstruction of human speech from graphic symbols, even if the speech is not understood? I. J. Gelb coined the term "grammatography" for the new form of writing (see chart opposite title page), to balance "syllabography," but we can probably never get rid of "alphabet." Preferable might be the German *Vokalalphabet* to refer to the Greek alphabet, because that was the principal feature to this writing (see chart opposite title page), that it informed the reader, in a rough way, of the actual sounds of speech.

The Greek alphabet was a single invention that took place at a single time. All writing systems, as far as we know, were invented by single men, never by groups or committees. The early logosyllabaries appear to have undergone evolution, but only after someone had set down principles of symbolization. According to one tradition Cadmus brought *phoinikeia* to Greece, but according to another the inventor of Greek writing was Palamedes, the clever Trojan-era enemy of Odysseus, who unmasked Odysseus when he simulated madness. Palamedes invented other things too, and may be the adapter's actual name.

It is inaccurate to say that the inventor of the Greek alphabet "added vowels" to a previously vowelless script, when the concept "vowel" depends on how the Greek alphabet functions and not on objective features of human speech. The inventor of the Greek alphabet did not "add vowels," therefore, but remade the internal structure of his model by means of two deliberate innovations.

First, he divided the entirely phonetic signs of the very old and very short West Semitic signary, in which all signs were of a single nature, into *two unequal groups* of signs of different natures.

Second, he established the rigorous *spelling rule*, never violated, that a sign from the smaller group must always accompany signs from the larger group.

The five signs in the small group, which represented a selection of five vowel qualities (Latin *vox* = "voice") from a larger range in Greek speech, were pronounceable by themselves, as vowel signs had been in Aegean and cuneiform writing. But the signs in the second and larger group, the "consonants," were *not pronounceable by themselves*, as they had been in West Semitic writing. These signs were incomplete without an appended sign from the smaller group, with which they could "sound along" (Latin *consono*). The inventor's spelling rule, devised for a practical purpose, inadvertently created the illusion that speech consists of particulate phonemes and the prejudice that writing exists to record speech.

In fashioning a short set of characters different in kind from the long set, the inventor assigned vowels to earlier Phoenician syllabic signs (Fig. 17.1). To Phoenician *'aleph*, a glottal stop = /'/, the adapter assigned the vowel /a/, which to his ears may have sounded something like a glottal stop; to *he*, a "strong" /h/ of some kind, he assigned the perhaps phonetically similar vowel /e/; to *yod* = /y/ he assigned the vowel /i/, for which the *yod* sometimes stands in the West Semitic *matres lectionis*, the use of consonantal syllables to suggest vowels (but the Phoenicians never used *matres*); to the Semitic *ʿayin* = /ʿ/, a pharyngeal sound absent from Indo-European languages but conspicuous in modern spoken Arabic, he

Phoenician symbol (c.700 BC)	Semitic name	Approximate Semitic sound + unspecified vowel	Greek symbol (c.700 BC)	Greek sound	Greek name
	'aleph	glottal stop (catch in voice)	A	a	alpha
	beth	b	B	b	beta
	gimel	g in glory	Γ	g	gamma
	daleth	d	Δ	d	delta
	he	h	E	e	epsilon
	waw	w	F	w	wau, digamma
	zayin	z	I	ts	zeta
	heth	"strong" h	B	long e	eta
	teth	"strong" t	⊗	th	theta
	yod	y in yellow	ς	i	iota
	kaph	k	K	k	kappa
	lamed	l	Λ	l	lambda
	mem	m	M	m	mu
	nun	n	N	n	nu
	samekh	s	Ŧ	ks	xi
	'ayin	pharyngeal consonant (gagging sound)	O	o	omicron
	pe	p	Γ	p	pi
	sadhe	ts	M	s	san
	qoph	"rough" k	Φ	q	qoppa
	resh	r	P	r	rho
	shin	sh	Ş	s	sigma
	taw	t	T	t	tau
	waw	w	Y	u	upsilon
			Φ	ph	phi
			X	kh, ks	chi
			Ψ	ps, kh	psi
			Ω	long o	omega

Figure 17.1 The adapter's alterations to his Phoenician model to create the Greek alphabet

arbitrarily assigned the value /o/. Finally, he did an odd thing when he retained the Semitic *wau* = /w/, which the Greeks much later called *digamma* ("double gamma"), then to the same sign with a slightly altered shape (Ϝ becomes Υ) he assigned the vowel /u/. He must have heard a phonetic resemblance between /w/ and /u/. He attached this sign, originally called *u* and much later called *upsilon*, or "bald U" (to distinguish it from a diphthong that had acquired a similar sound) to the end of the West Semitic Series after *tau*, where it still is today.

The adapter also added three new signs, which grammarians called the "supplementals," namely phi Φ, *chi* Χ, *psi* Ψ, not realizing that they were part of the original system. Many technical difficulties surround attempts to explain the original values of these signs, because during the classical period *chi* Χ had the value /kh/ in Athens and /ks/ in Italy, whence comes its value in contemporary English orthography. For /kh/ the western Greeks used Ψ, probably its original value, but in Athens Ψ had value /ps/. Phi Φ, however, always had the value /ph/. The adapter seems to have attempted to fashion a coherent system of aspirated stops (pronounced with a strong breath), but because aspiration was weak or absent in parts of Greece, these signs fell into confusion and in Crete disappeared altogether.

The first system of vocalic notation was approximate, and vowel signs notated only a rather wider range of actual sounds in speech. Sometimes it is hard in English speech to hear the difference between long and short vowels (short /ă/ and long /ā/ perplex students), but evidently in ancient Greek speech long and short were strongly demarcated and they were phonemic, they made a difference in meaning. The sign later called *omega*, "big o," attached to the end of the series, is not found before the sixth century BC and is simply *omicron* "little o" (originally called *o*) broken at the bottom. Omega was not part of the adapter's system. Because of weak aspiration in the Greek spoken along the coast of Turkey, in Ionia, the sign called *hēta* Η (from Semitic *heth*, our H) was pronounced as /ēta/. According to the ancient West Semitic rule that the value of the sign was encoded in the first sound of the name of the sign, *ēta* ☐ took on

the value of long /ē/, the quality of its vowel. Because Athens was an Ionic dialect and accepted this change in the late fifth century BC, the *ēta*

☐ acquired a vocalic value in the standard Greek based on Athenian

practice. There never were single signs for the long /ī/ or the long /ū/ or the long /ā/. Nor was the Greek vocalic system confined to 10 vowels, 5 long and 5 short, any more that the English vocalic system is so confined: linguists count 27 separate vowel sounds in standard spoken English.

At first Greek alphabetic writing was written *boustrophedon*, "back and forth as the ox turns," always beginning from the right like West Semitic (although West Semitic was written in lines, not *boustrophedon*). Later the direction changed to left to right, the Romans copied them (but the Etruscans wrote right to left), and today we write left to right. Except for the devolutionary changes to the values of the supplementary signs *chi* and *psi*, the addition of *omega*, and the shift in value of *hēta* from /h/ to /ē/, no other changes ever took place to the functional elements of the Greek alphabet. The system is intact today in modern Greece, except that the sounds assigned to several characters, and especially the vowels and diphthongs, have changed.

The genius of West Semitic writing was in how it was learned, as a short list of signs in a fixed order whose phonetic values were encoded in a name, sometimes meaningful and sometimes gibberish. Mesopotamian cuneiform and Egyptian hieroglyphic writing were not so easily learned. The inventor of the Greek vocal alphabet took over the West Semitic system of learning in total, corrupting the Semitic names slightly or inventing new ones, but preserving the relationship of name to value (several, such as *upsilon*, *omicron*, *omega*, *digamma*, were named hundreds of years later). Nothing important has changed in the history of writing since the invention of the Greek alphabet, whose triumph has given it universal currency everywhere on the planet, a most potent force for unity in planetary life.

The Earliest Greek Alphabetic Writing

An inscription from c.775 BC found recently in Latium in Italy on the site of ancient GABII (modern OSTERIA DELL'OSA) holds present claim for the

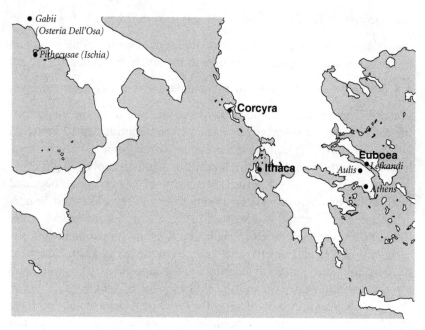

Map 8 Places important in the early history of the alphabet

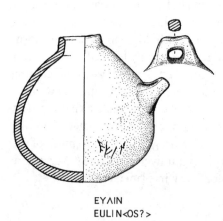

EYΛIN
EULIN<OS?>

Figure 17.2 The earliest alphabetic inscription, from Gabii (modern Osteria Dell'Osa), cremation grave 482.1, c.775 BC. (After Ridgway 1996, 87–97.)

earliest example of the division of the West Semitic syllabic signary into two categories of signs and the spelling rule about how they work together (Fig. 17.2).

However, what exactly EULIN might mean is not clear: perhaps part of a name ("the good linen maker"?). Other tiny scraps survive from about the same time from the Iron Age site of LEFKANDI on the long island of Euboea, which runs along the east coast of mainland Greece, one scrap probably as old as the EULIN inscription (Map 8). By c.740 BC, a generation or so later, we find inscriptions of

Figure 17.3   The Dipylon Oinochoe, c.740 BC. (Athens, National Archeological Museum, 192, author's photograph.)

several words and even whole sentences. Here is the actual specimen of our oldest Greek alphabetic inscription of more than a few letters, inscribed through the glaze of an Athenian Late Geometric wine jug, the famous Dipylon Oinochoe (Fig. 17.3). More has been written about this single inscription than any other in Greek. Homer may have been alive when it was made. The jug is the product of the workshop of the famous Dipylon Master, who introduced a revolutionary new art style into Greek ceramics that included human figures.

The inscription reads from right to left, a perfect hexameter (Fig. 17.4). The certainly illiterate oral singer Homer composed in exactly this rhythm, which has six strong points, then a pause, then another six strong points, then a pause, on and on, forever. It is the only Greek inscription that has the sidelong *alpha* in the West Semitic style; ever after the Greek *alpha* is written upright. At the end of the inscription are some enigmatic signs,

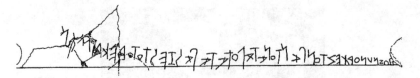

HOSNUNORXESTONPANTONATALOTATAPAIZEI
TOTODEK{M}M{N}N

Whoever of all the dancers now dances most gracefully, to him this ....

Figure 17.4   Transcription and translation of the Dipylon Oinochoe inscription. (After Powell 1991, no. 58.)

perhaps a snippet from an abecedarium (as if someone learning to write tried to write KLMN but got it wrong).

The inscription on the Dipylon Oinochoe is good evidence that the Greek alphabet was from the very beginning used as a notation for dictated oral verse. An oral poet has composed a line, "whoever is the best acrobat here, he will get . . ." He must mean "this vase," but only one line was completely written. Various technical features disagree with later Athenian writing, so perhaps the writer is an outsider showing off his skill at a new technology to the ignorant Athenians, showing how he can imprison in graphic signs the sounds of oral song. Perhaps a second hand has attempted to scratch the KLMN, a student (or the singer?) eager to learn the new art (an abecedarium written boustrophedon will break around KLMN).

Equally or more astonishing is a similarly sophisticated hexametric inscription of the same date c.740 BC, but now from the far west, from a burial on the island of PITHECUSAE (modern Ischia) in the Bay of Naples. Euboean sailors had established the earliest western colony there already by the early eighth century BC. There Phoenicians and Greeks lived together and intermarried, and some West Semitic inscriptions come from the same site. The colony on Pithecusae, "monkey-island," was a jumping-off point for Euboeans eager to exploit Western mineral resources, the western terminal of the north Syrian metals trade. The early EULIN inscription from Latium is not far from this focus of Euboean exploration.

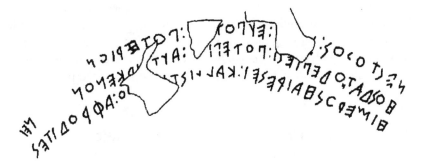

Figure 17.5 Cup of Nestor inscription. (After Powell 1991, no. 59.)

Three lines are scratched into the glaze of the cup imported from Rhodes, written from right to left in three separate lines (see Fig. 17.5). We can transliterate the inscription into modern Greek font as

Νεστορος : ε[ιμ]ι : ευποτ[ον] : ποτεριον
hος δ'α<ν> τοδεπιεσι : ποτερι[ο] : αυτικα κενον
hιμερος hαιρεσει : καλλιστε[φα]νο : Αφροδιτες

which means

I am the cup of Nestor, a joy to drink from.
Whoever drinks this cup, straightaway
the desire of beautiful-crowned Aphrodite will seize him.

The inscription seems to reflect a poetic capping game such as we know was played at aristocratic symposia in the classical period. One man sets the game by raising his cup and saying, "This is the cup of Nestor." That is a joke, because in the *Iliad* the cup of Nestor is grand and made of gold (*Iliad* 11.632–7). A second diner now spins a hexameter, an introduction to a curse formula of which early written examples are known: "Whoever steals this cup, he will fall sick and die," or the like. Instead he says, "Whoever drinks from this cup . . .". The third diner must now declare his doom, obviously in hexameter verse, and it is . . . to endure a pleasant sexual experience!
Someone far in the west in the eighth century BC knew enough about alphabetic writing skillfully to engrave these three lines on the cup, two of

them hexameters, later an heirloom buried in the grave of a ten-year-old boy. Exceedingly striking is that no trace of the use of writing for economic purposes survives among the early Greek inscriptions, not even any numbers until the sixth century BC. On the other hand, people write their names on cups and, occasionally, highly complex and sophisticated poetic verse.

The Date of the Alphabet's Invention

Because it is traditional (if thoughtless) to call West Semitic writing and its congeners an "alphabet," the question about the date of the Greek alphabet's invention can fade into a child's game. The "alphabet" could have come to Greece pretty much any time, even in 1800 BC, or 1100 BC as some actually believe, or in 950 BC, as others believe, or any date you want. Or it could have come several times in different places. Such views still color the study of archaic Greek inscriptions, whose local differences are even thought to reflect separate acts of transmission.

Once we have understood the monogenesis of the Greek writing, proven by the treatment of Semitic *wau* (divided into two characters) and other arbitrary changes to the Semitic model, including the assignment of the /o/ to the Semitic *ain* and the addition of the supplementals, we must wonder when and where the adapter lived. The method for dating the Greek alphabet (as other writing systems) is to seek the very oldest examples, then place its invention before that . . . but not too much earlier, at least in the case of the Greek alphabet, because after the few examples from the eighth century BC, in the seventh century we find many more, and in the sixth many, many more, and in the fifth an ocean of inscriptions. If the earliest examples of the Greek alphabet are c.775 BC, coming from lands intensively explored archaeologically, the alphabet must have been invented around 800 BC, give or take a few years.

The Poetic Inspiration for the Invention of the Alphabet

Many have puzzled at such sophisticated use of early Greek alphabetic writing as that found on the Dipylon Oinochoe or on the Cup of Nestor, but a unique colophon on a clay tablet from Ugarit, baked in the destruction of the city, reports how the contents of 15 tablets found in the library of the chief priest of Baal in the main temple complex, telling a story about the storm-god Baal, were taken down by a certain Ilimilku from Shubbani as they were dictated, evidently, by the chief priest, one Attanu-Purlianni, under the reign of the king of Ugarit Niqmaddu II (reigned c.1349–1315 BC). In a similar fashion the Hebrew prophet Jeremiah, who lived in the seventh to sixth centuries BC, dictated a scroll to his scribe Baruch (Jer. 36:18); perhaps all the early texts of what became the Old Testament were composed by dictation. The very odd focus on purely phonetic but unpronounceable elements in West Semitic writing, which made it unlearnable except by someone who spoke the language, may well reflect this writing's origin in dictation as a means of composition, even the shouting out of names. The composer speaks, and the scribe represents the sounds as best he can. In this way you can write anything you can say, so long as you are working with a wholly phonetic system and there is enough context for a literate speaker to reconstruct the message.

A very early attested use of the West Semitic syllabary, therefore, the direct ancestor of the Greek alphabet, was to take down a literary text by dictation. In the polyglot, racially mixed north Syrian coast, with its western connections in mainland Greece and Italy, where Greek speakers and Semitic speakers lived together and intermarried and learned each other's language, someone who inherited the West Semitic tradition of notating dictated verse seems to have tried the method with Greek oral verse. This was the heyday of the great Greek poets Homer and Hesiod, who lived during the eighth century BC, early enough to know nothing about writing, which they never mention (except once, obliquely, in Homer) in their long poems filled with descriptions of everyday technologies and behavior. Such catastrophic formations represented alphabetically as the Homeric *aaatos*, meaning "decisive," a form that could never occur in ordinary speech, suggest that any effort to notate Greek verse in the West Semitic writing could not succeed. If a Western Semitic speaker tried to apply the West Semitic syllabary to write down the first line of the *Iliad*, and separated the words by dots as Phoenicians did, it might look something like

MNN·D·T·PLD·KLS

for the Greek alphabetic

MENIN AEIDE THEA PELEIADEO AKHILEOS.

In 1991 (*Homer and the Origin of the Greek Alphabet*) I argued that at this moment the inventor of the Greek alphabet restructured his model in the way described, enabling him to preserve the rough phonic outline of the verse, as in the early epigraphic examples of the Dipylon Oinochoe and the Cup of Nestor. In writing, as in life, necessity feeds invention, and the need to preserve the powerful rhythm of poetry seems, on the evidence, to have motivated the invention of signs for vowels, which, of course, had existed in several earlier writings, and inspired the revolutionary spelling rule that one group of signs, which we call consonants, must always accompany representatives from a second group of signs, the vowels. The best candidate for the adapter's inspiration must remain the poet Homer himself, whose work was certainly preserved in alphabetic writing in the eighth century BC, in the first technology of writing capable of preserving him.

The Fortuitous Origins of Alphabetic Writing

The invention of the Greek alphabet, "the first true alphabet," was highly fortuitous and improbable in the utmost. In no sense was it the product of evolutionary forces urging the technology of writing to fulfill its destiny to achieve ever greater heights of phoneticism. First we require the anomalous and scarcely explained inattention of Egyptian writing to the vibration of the vocal cords. Then we require the mysterious interaction of undoubtedly foreign peoples, Semitic speakers, with this odd Egyptian writing to create a wholly phonetic but unpronounceable writing that has been reduced to a handful of signs. Then we require the special needs of still another foreign people, in this case the troublesome poetry-obsessed Greeks, who lived at the edge of the civilized world. Evidence is strong that the need to record Greek hexameter verse inspired the inventor of the Greek alphabet, who only behaved as he was taught in cocking his ear to phonetic distinctions encoded in abstract linear signs. The unexpected result was to make the Greek vocal alphabet as different from its model, West Semitic, as was West Semitic from its model, Egyptian.

For the first time writing communicated through a sensual intimacy with forms of speech that, in the Greek miracle, was itself rapidly transformed by the new expression that alphabetic writing offered. For the first time it was possible to make up a word in writing and expect the reader to reproduce and even understand it, an explosive power shining in the new coinages that pepper the early literature actually composed in writing (not dictated), Greek lyric and Attic tragedy.

In a reconstruction of an early text of the opening of the *Iliad* the only way to tell what it means is to extract the sounds from the signs, listen to the sounds, then recognize what is meant (Fig. 17.6). The work is tedious and hard going, but the primacy of sound is clear from the lack of word division and the absence of diacritical marks of any kind, even one thousand years after the alphabet's invention. The adapter has rigorously excluded visual semantic information from his system, a quality he shares with his West Semitic model; but even West Semitic scripts ordinarily divided the words with dots.

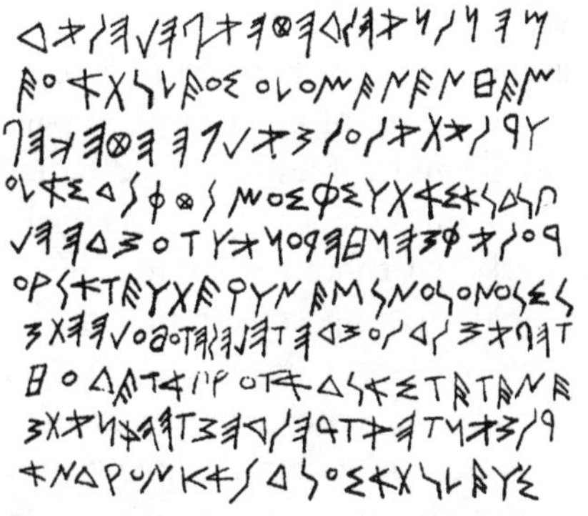

Figure 17.6 Reconstruction of the first lines of the *Iliad*. (After Powell 1991, no. 58.)

It is customary to praise the Greek alphabet for the hyperphoneticism that tied written expression to what people might say, who without training might say anything and always in a different way and with a different sound. For this reason the study of early Greek dialects requires diligence, learning, and imagination. After five hundred years, in the second century BC, the Greeks at last settled into a civilized *koinê*, "common speech," based on the dialect of Athens. Still, in the modern world, thanks to the Greek alphabet, academics must learn German, Italian, and French to discuss an obscure line in Homer. The Greek alphabet's system for phonetic representation can be applied indifferently to any human speech, a very grave problem.

After the Greek adapter's unique invention the phonetic but unpronounceable West Semitic writings stood on one side, and on the other the now pronounceable Greek alphabet and its manifold offshoots. In spite of the hyperphoneticism that closely roots understanding in a specific language and dialect, in practice alphabetic writing opened a restricted literacy to anyone who learned the very simple system. Now anyone could write his name or his wife's name on a tombstone, or that of his dead child. Suddenly by the seventh to sixth centuries BC, Etruscans, Phrygians, Carians, Lydians, and Iberians are doing just that. Only educated guesses exist for how many Athenians, say, could read and write a longer text of average complexity in the fifth century BC – 5 percent? – but by any measure an ocean of people by comparison to the minuscule social, political, and religious elites of the old Eastern societies.

Not until modern times has English and French orthography abandoned Greek hyperphoneticism to return to a partly semasiographic and logographic writing, at last rich in diacritical devices and spelling oddities of all kinds that refine thought and assist understanding. Reformers of English spelling are somehow unaware of the advantages of nonphonetic written communication, but the following example shows how far modern English alphabetic orthography has come from the practices of the Greeks:

AOCCDRNIG TO RSCHEEARCH AT CMABRIGDE UINERVTISY, IT DEOSN'T MTTAER IN WAHT OREDR THE LTTEERS IN A WROD ARE, THE OLNY IPRMOETNT TIHNG IS TAHT THE FRIST AND LSAT LTTEER BE AT THE RGHIT PCLAE. THE RSET CAN BE A TOTAL MSES AND YOU CAN SITLL RAED IT WOUTHIT PORBELM. TIHS IS BCUSEAE THE HUAMN MNID DEOS NOT RAED ERVEY LTETER BY ISTLEF, BUT THE WROD AS A WLOHE.

It is not the human mind that is responsible, but our education as small children when we learn to read from the shape of a word and to use phonetic signs only as hints and not direct representations of phonetic elements.

18

Summary and Conclusions

Evidently human beings have access to an invisible reality within which symbolization takes place. Humans can get there, nonhumans cannot. The most usual expression of this human power of symbolization is speech. Animals cannot talk, and there are no symbols in nature. It is misguided to claim, as is sometimes done in anthropological literature, that human speech first appeared tens or even hundreds of thousands of years after the evolution of the species. You cannot have humans without speech.

Such pathologies as dumbness and deafness prove that the human faculty to symbolize by means of speech is, however, by no means limited to the modulated stream of symbolic sound issuing from the human vocal cords and its reception by other sense organs. Symbolization is a faculty and speech, which is ephemeral, is only one possible tool for its expression; writing, which is material and potentially eternal, is another.

In puzzling over the origins of lexigraphic writing we must focus on the situation in Mesopotamia at the end of the fourth millennium. For thousands of years Mesopotamians kept track of commodities and of the exchange of commodities by means of abstract geometrical clay tokens. By making clay envelopes to contain tokens and asseverate a transaction, the Mesopotamians inadvertently learned to impress the token shapes into clay. They abandoned the tokens themselves and retained the shape. They flattened the envelopes into tablets and in this way clay became the medium for Mesopotamian writing. It is an unusual choice, because clay is fragile, messy, clumsy, and hard to store and to transport. The Egyptian papyrus, an immensely superior medium, was unavailable to the Mesopotamians who had such ready access to clay, the reason they had enclosed tokens in clay envelopes in the first place.

Protocuneiform, which made use of the symbolic resources of the old tokens, was a kind of logography that became a lexigraphy through application of the rebus. Without direct evidence, we can nonetheless accept that the motivation for the discovery of the phonetic principle through the rebus applied to logograms was the desire to record personal names and names of places and names of things. Personal names and place names especially are critical to the kind of economic behavior the Mesopotamians were keeping track of: Who brought this? From where? Who counted it? Who grew it? What is it? Where?

Cylinder seals, in widespread use from the middle of the fourth millennium, come from this economic environment, the single most ubiquitous artifact from all Mesopotamia. A small cylinder – usually of a hard stone, carved with a design – the seal was rolled across the clay envelope, then the clay tablet, to make the agent's signature. The practice survives today in the affixing of wax seals to important documents. At first cylinder seals bore abstract or symbolic designs, but by the third millennium they often record in lexigraphic cuneiform the names and titles of the owner.

The discovery of lexigraphic writing was a critical moment, a turning point in human life, the beginning of history. Lexigraphic writing does not come from pictures but from the conscious application of the rebus to symbols that may or may not have ever been pictures. Most of the protocuneiform signs are not pictures. The signs that *are* pictures are not "picture-writing" but logograms that stand for words. They are always potential syllabograms when the meaning falls away but the phonetic value remains. The alternation of the same sign between logogram and syllabogram takes place throughout the history of cuneiform writing and other logosyllabic writings and is an important reason for their complexity. In the theory of the history of writing the logogram is the missing link, the channel through which one passes from semasiography to lexigraphy: First the symbol stands for a thing, then it stands for a word that names the thing, then it stands for the sound of the word.

So in many instances we are not sure whether the sign functions logographically or whether only the sound remains, so that through the rebus the sign has become a syllabogram, as first we have "1, 2, 3," logograms, then "1st, 2nd, 3rd," syllabograms. Such ambiguities must have remained unresolved in the minds of the ancient practitioners, who, like ourselves, were interested in practical results and not in theory: a system of marks on a material substance with a conventional reference that communicates information.

Through application of the rebus the association between word symbol and graphic sign became so intimate that the Semitic-speaking Akkadians continued to use the alien Sumerian words to create literary and other documents: Not just "a word," but "a Sumerian word" was tied to the sign. In a similar way medieval Europeans, who spoke a cacophony of local and mutually unintelligible dialects, maintained the Latin language as a system for thought and expression that was intelligible everywhere, informed by rigorous rules of expression in the classic Roman authors. Even today Latin fulfills this function among devoted groups.

The logosyllabic systems, the Mesopotamian and the Egyptian, did not become better over time, more efficient engines for thought and for the communication of information, during the three thousand years of their dominance. In all Egyptian poetic texts, nothing surpassed the Pyramid Texts for emotive power, but they are the earliest religious texts (c.2600 BC). These systems retained their inner structure and in their operation only became more complex, riddled with single signs with many sounds and many signs with the same sound and other obscurities. Of course writing systems became increasingly complex, because a professional society controlled the technology, who devoted their lives to mastering the constant puzzles that lexigraphic writing offered. The Mesoamericans allowed this affection for self-pleasure to go very, very far. As conventional systems, scripts cannot in any event be altered without threatening intelligibility. What possible motive for reform? Such ancient writings well served the state that had given them birth and that nurtured them. It was no mission of the ancient state to spread the art of writing among the masses.

For mysterious reasons, purely phonetic writing appeared in the Aegean and in the Levant at about the same time, in the Middle Bronze Age, perhaps c.1800 BC. We are better informed about the Aegean development, because what became Linear B appears to have begun as the undeciphered "Cretan hieroglyphs," which must therefore have been a syllabary like Linear B. Cretan hieroglyphs, often found on seals, must record names used to officiate transactions according to the ancient Mesopotamian custom. The need to record Semitic names may, likewise, have inspired the West Semitic invention, as many believe. Early names are found on bronze arrowheads.

In both the Aegean and the Levant the inventors appear to be building on the earlier logosyllabic writings. Crete is closely tied to Mesopotamia in its use of clay tablets to make economic records to manage the complexities of a palace redistributive economy; they also kept records on papyrus and, perhaps, on parchment, to judge from fragments found on clay sealings. Whoever invented Cretan writing knew something about cuneiform, which also had signs for open syllables like /ba/, /be/, bi/, /bu,/ and signs for pure vowels. So did the Cretan writing. But the inventor of the Cretan writing worked across linguistic and national lines to build a new system consisting of phonetic elements alone.

Something similar happened among the speakers of West Semitic languages, who were working with the Egyptian system, but it is unlikely that the West Semitic revolution in phonetic representation was not in some way connected with the parallel Aegean development. They happened at about the same time. The astounding discovery in the 1990s of Minoan frescoes of c.1500 BC (at first dated earlier) in the Egyptian city of Avaris in the northeastern Delta (Tell el Daba), once capital of the invading Semitic Hyksos, awaits explanation, but implies the presence of Cretans in a city with Semitic traditions. At Ugarit occurred similar cosmopolitan conditions.

The Aegean and West Semitic syllabaries were really a new idea in writing, because in discarding most semantic elements they tied the conventional system of physical markings closely to speech, which the logo-syllabaries had never done. Neither writing, however, informs the reader of how it is pronounced. That you must infer from your own knowledge of the living speech.

Cretan writing was highly influential, and a form of it, the Cypriote Syllabary, was used down to the third century BC, if only on Cyprus. The Cypriote syllabic writing seems to have inspired the "Luvian hieroglyphs" for the recording, on monuments and seals, of Indo-European Luvian in Anatolia. Still, the future lay with the West Semitic tradition. The syllabograms with unexpressed vowels of West Semitic are a rough inventory of Semitic consonantal speech sounds, meant to suggest to a Semitic speaker some word in his language solely through phonetic clues. Lacking information about the vowels, the writing was phonetically so ambiguous that similar spellings could be understood by speakers of widely different dialects, a great advantage, for the consonantal structure of words differently pronounced remained the same. But this very flexibility, maintaining a desirable looseness between graphic sign and speech sound, also inhibits precise description and original expression. There is no room for neologisms; they will not be understood. Although strong poetic expression and rich historical description are possible, as in the Hebrew scriptures, the only long West Semitic document to survive from the ancient world, everything has a kind of flatness to it when compared with alphabetic expression.

No similar developments took place in Asia. The enormous prestige of Chinese high culture made *de rigueur* the use of Chinese logograms in the derivative Korean, Vietnamese, and Japanese writings. The Asian traditions are deeply imbued with the vice of calligraphy and can never separate the aesthetic function of graphic signs from their need to communicate information. To take away calligraphy from Chinese writing and its dependents is to take away historical culture, fine feeling, and abundant opportunities to make class distinctions. In the fifteenth century a Korean king designed an ingenious alphabetic system, called *Hangeul*, but it made little headway until recent times. Although China today must face an international Internet culture, which is predominantly alphabetic, it is unlikely ever to abandon its ancient logography "for important things."

Our prejudgments about the nature of lexigraphic writing depend on the history of the decipherment of ancient Near Eastern scripts, achieved by alphabet users who assigned alphabetic values to signs in unknown scripts. Egyptian hieroglyphics are still read according to Champollion's explanation, which isolated alphabetic elements in order to reconstruct an unknown language whose sounds were also unknown (pharaonic Egyptian), then theorized about the semantic value of such reconstructions by comparison with an ancient language preserved in the Greek alphabet (Coptic), then translated the alphabetic reconstruction into a modern European language. The many nonphonetic signs assist in the semantic reconstruction, but scholars mostly set them aside in reading Egyptian.

It only appears surprising at first that the inspiration for the invention of this miraculous alphabet, the common coinage of alien systems like Egyptian, Akkadian, and even Chinese, should have been the need to make a record of poetic expression. Bt rlly y dnt nd ll ths vlls, unless of course you are trying to record *MENIN AEIDE THEA PELEIDO AKHILEO*, "Sing, O goddess, of the wrath of Achilles, son of Peleus." The speakers of West Semitic had taken down oral texts by dictation for generations or from the beginning, but the concatenation of vowel sounds in Greek oral poetry needed to make the dactylic rhythm required an entirely different technology. By modern analysis, this complicated meter, called dactylic hexameter, consists of lines made up of six units, each of which can be a long and two shorts (— ∪ ∪ = *dactyl*, "fingerlike") or two longs (— — = *spondee*), except for the sixth and last foot, which only has two beats. The last syllable can be long or short, but was probably felt as a long because of the line ending; that is, the hexameter always ends with a spondee (— —). Need mothers invention.

Certainly we understand Mesopotamian writing, the oldest writing in the world, to have originated in the pressure-cooker of newfangled urban life of southern Mesopotamia in the late fourth millennium, where somebody had to keep track of all that grain and where it was coming from. We expect other systems of writing to serve similar functions, but we may be wrong. Such certainly was not true of the Greek alphabet, which on the evidence never served economic purposes of any kind for over two hundred years after it was invented. It did, however, preserve 28,000 lines of Homer's verse (and thousands of Hesiod's). Of course, the Greeks had no riverine redistributive economy or, in fact, wealth of any kind. In 800 BC their highest material artistic achievement was painted pottery.

The marginal and impoverished Greeks scarcely had an economy to serve and certainly no need of writing. Hesiod's detailed explanations of how to be successful as a small-holding farmer in his poem *Works and Days*, from the earliest days of Greek alphabetic literacy, never mention written accounts. Evidence is slim, and obviously we depend on the accidents of survival, but the earliest Egyptian writing, on commodity labels and commemorative slate pallets, memorialized the greatness of pharaoh and his achievements (unless we consider the labels from Abydos to be economic documents), and lexigraphic writing served a similar noneconomic purpose in Mesoamerica. There is no evidence whatever that early West Semitic writing was used for economic purposes. The earliest surviving lexigraphic writing from China was used only for divination. "Luvian hieroglyphs" are found only on monuments and seals.

By creating for the first time a graphic system with a rough correspondence in actual speech, the Greek alphabet, with its two kinds of signs and rigorous and inviolable spelling rules, destined the Greek language to become the dominant language of culture in the classical Mediterranean. The alphabetic systems of thought and values in poetry followed the conquests of Alexander into the ancient East, where the world had begun. How odd a tradition Greek poetry was! Beginning with Homer in the eighth century BC, Greek literature offered the aristocratic aspirant to literary achievement a poetic model in which poetic expression was far distant from vernacular speech, like the many archaic formations in Homer and words whose meaning was lost, that the alphabetic system preserved and made pronounceable. The so-called Homeric dialect is really an amalgam of two dialects, Ionic and Aeolic, with unique forms thrown in with extra syllables and an elaborate system of scarcely semantic particles to make the lines scan. No one ever spoke this "dialect," yet any Greek could understand most of it. That's the way all Greek poetry was, and its Latin imitations, distant from the vernacular but mostly intelligible to the poetry-loving crowd.

The alphabetic revolution was the third revolution in the history of writing, after the discovery of the phonetic principle itself through the rebus and the reduction of a signary to purely phonetic elements. The social consequences were gargantuan. In a stroke the need for a special class of men who mastered the system and served the state, and its religion, by the manipulation of graphically encoded information was disabled. Users of West Semitic writings had already extended beyond the narrow limits of the earlier logosyllabic elites, but nonetheless remained a special class: the "scribes and Pharisees" of the New Testament, the rabbis and mullahs of modern times.

In Greece there was no scribal class. Men of some means and better breeding placed their sons under a *paidagogos* to see they learned the abecedarium and the secrets of decoding poetic texts kept on papyrus and on folding wax tablets. Figure 18.1 shows an Athenian school from the fifth century BC. On each side of the vase are two pairs of teacher and student accompanied by a bearded, seated man, perhaps the pedagogue. In the scene shown at the top, the pair on the left are practicing the lyre. The teacher in the middle sits before a standing pupil and holds up a papyrus scroll with the hexameter ΜΟΙΣΑ ΜΟΙ/ΑΦΙ ΣΚΑΜΑΝΔΡΟΝ/ΕΥΡΩΝ ΑΡΧΟΜΑΙ/ΑΕΙΝΔΕΝ, "O Muse – help me – I begin to sing of wide-flowing Scamander," perhaps a line from the Sicilian poet Stesichorus (640–555 BC). Evidently the boy has just recited these lines and the teacher is correcting him. Two lyres, two drinking cups, a basket for papyrus, and a flute-case hang on the wall. On the other side of the cup, the two teachers are young and beardless. The teacher on the left plays a flute while his young pupil faces him. The teacher in the center holds a folding wooden writing tablet on his lap, his stylus poised above the wax coating to incise a character. Perhaps he is correcting the student's work. A roll of papyrus (?), an opened writing tablet, a lyre, a cross-shaped object hang on the wall. By memorizing such poetry, and above all the poetry of Homer, the basis of Greek and Roman education and still read today, the aspiring aristocrat could impress his colleagues in the all-male symposium where poetry, wine, conversation, and sex were in abundant supply.

Because the speech to which hexametric poetry was attached was highly unusual, thanks to the exigencies of the rhythm of oral song, the Greek

Figure 18.1   Athenian school. Red-figure Attic drinking cup, c.480 BC, found in Etruria. (Berlin, Antikenmuseen F 2285.)

aristocrat of the sixth century BC sought similar effects in new forms of poetic expression, but now created in the technology of alphabetic writing. The early users of the Greek alphabet realized that he (or she in the case of Sappho) could manufacture previously unknown words with subtle rhythms by which others could recreate their poetic song. For this reason all early Greek literature is poetry, much of it highly abstruse, arcane, rarefied, and distant from any vernacular.

Not until the fifth century BC did it occur to anyone to compose without the rhythmic and lexical embellishments of epic, lyric, and dramatic poetry. Herodotus (c.484–425 BC) invented prose as we think of it (though he had immediate predecessors), now meant to be read aloud from a papyrus, not memorized and reperformed like virtually all earlier Greek literature. Herodotus's style is rhetorical and expansive and reflects the oral world of antithesis, moral conflict, and composition in rings or spirals. His successor Thucydides (c.470–400 BC) preserved the earlier poetic obsession with novel expression, neologisms, and rarefied trains of thought in his highly wrought speeches, some nearly impossible to understand, which pepper the historical narrative as similarly highly wrought choral passages interfere with the narrative in a Greek tragedy. The power to make a word in writing that never existed in speech, that the reader could nonetheless understand, has characterized poetic style in Western literature ever since, and still does today.

The Egyptians covered the walls of their tombs with writing, but who was the writing for? Thanks to the labors of generations, we can ourselves read it, but must admit that the writing was never meant to be read by anyone, even (in some magical contexts) by the gods. Although the Egyptians lived long ago, they understood as well as ourselves that humans control their environment through the manipulation of symbols, and in Egyptian religion lexigraphic and semasiographic writing can guarantee the eternal fate of the dead. The writing lives and speaks by itself. Writing and art are magic, creating predictable effects when properly employed.

The Greeks and their heirs did not use writing like this. To them the alphabet was a tool that opened the rich flavor of Homer's song and all his moral pondering (useful also to inscribe curses on tablets of lead or to guide the dead on the paths of the other world). The genius of the Greek alphabet was its closeness to speech, although powerless to communicate prosody or tone or gesture or emphasis or the other factors inseparable from real speech. Its closeness to speech and the enormous resources of speech nonetheless allowed the Greek alphabetic writing to attain sublime heights of poetic expression, even to create what we think of as poetry. From this intimacy came the power to write down anything you can say in any language. Once this language was Greek, now it is English, understood over all the world.

The West is proud of its alphabetic culture, because the alphabet promoted the growth of science and democracy while the nonalphabetic cultures wallowed in ghost-fear, violence, and religious extremism (never found in the West!). Yet its appearance in history was accidental, never necessary. In some respects our taste for logography has turned us back to earlier habits. In history, systems of writing are sufficient unto themselves, they accomplish what is set out for them to do at that time and do not dream of greater glories. Greater glory might be the IPA, for those who wish accurately to preserve fine distinctions in speech, but in reality no one wants or needs that. The change from logosyllabaries to syllabaries and from syllabary to alphabet could only have taken place across linguistic and ethnic lines. Even so the motives of the inventors of the new technologies were always practical. They were not evolutionists, they were not scholars, they were not theorists, just practical men living in a harsh and unforgiving world.

As always with technologies, no matter how they come into being they take on a life of their own and go their own way, and there is nothing anybody can do about it. Native peoples are sentimental about native systems of writing, whether that is Devanagari or Japanese or Arabic, and they identify themselves with such systems, take pride in such systems, and even give their lives for the values they take to be encoded in such systems. Nonetheless, the Greek alphabet, backed by the political and economic power that the revolutionary technology made possible, is today found in virtually every corner of the world. It is unlikely ever to surrender its hegemony. The Chinese will learn to use the alphabet, but alphabet users will not learn to use Chinese. In this sense one can think of the alphabet as a superior system, because it is transcendent and because in its attachment to human speech it is a force for unifying the world. It is hard to believe that we owe so much to a single man interested in oral song, but evidently we do.

Glossary

abecedarium: An ordered list of the signs in a West Semitic or alphabetic system of writing; the ABCs.

acrophony, acrophonic principle: "Sound from the top," refers to a discredited theory of the origin of West Semitic signs by keeping the first sound of a word applied to an Egyptian "pictogram" and discarding the rest of the word, as if to represent the sound /s/ I chose the picture of a snake [S] because the word "snake" begins with an /s/. With small exceptions, acrophony appears to play no role in the formation of writing systems.

adfix: An element added to the beginning or end of a root to alter the meaning; for example [pre] in *pre*historic.

Afro-Asiatic: Referring to a large family of languages spoken in north Africa and in the Near East, including Akkadian, Babylonian, Arabic, Hebrew, Berber, Cushitic, and ancient Egyptian. Words in these languages are often built on a tripartite unchanging consonantal structure, around which vowels shift in order to create linguistic refinements.

agglutinative: "Glued together," a term coined by Wilhelm von Humboldt in 1836 to describe a language in which words are formed by joining together morphemes (the smallest semantically meaningful linguistic units). These morphemes indicate such features as "diminutive," "past tense," "plural," and so forth. Opposed to "fusional languages" like English, in which tense, mood, plurality and the like are indicated by changes of the root of the word, or changes in stress or tone.

Akkad: Capital of a Semitic group who, under Sargon, c.2330–2280 BC, established an empire in Mesopotamia; the site of ancient Akkad is unknown.

Akkadian: The Semitic dialects spoken in Mesopotamia, including "Assyrian" in the northeast and "Babylonian" near where the Tigris and Euphrates rivers converge.

allegory: "Saying something differently," a figurative method of representation when the meaning is different from the literal. For example, Dante's journey to paradise at a literal level is an allegory for the salvation open to all. Egyptian hieroglyphs were long held to be allegories for eternal truths.

alphabetic writing: Writing in which the signs represent elements of speech smaller than syllables, although such sounds do not exist in nature as separable elements of speech. In alphabetic writing *letters* predominate.

Amarna: A city in Middle Egypt built by the monotheist pharaoh Akhenaten, "servant of the Aten," c.1350 BC. A cache of 382 letters was found there recording in Akkadian cuneiform international diplomacy between pharaoh and mostly Levantine principalities; one of the most important sources for the history of the Late Bronze Age.

Amorites: An amorphous Semitic people living west of the Euphrates from the mid-third millennium, known mostly from names in cuneiform texts. Amorites came to power at various times in various places; they ruled the kingdom of Mari on the mid-Euphrates in the early second millennium.

Anatolian hieroglyphs: See Luvian hieroglyphs.

Aramaic language: A Semitic dialect spoken in Aram (= Damascus). During the Persian Empire (550–330 BC) Aramaic script and language served as a *lingua franca* all over the Near East.

Aramaic script: A form of West Semitic script internationalized by Aramaic scribes, ancestor to the modern "Hebrew" square script.

Assyrian cuneiform: A variety of Mesopotamian cuneiform used in Assyria.

Assyrian language: A Semitic dialect spoken in Northeast Mesopotamia until the destruction of Nineveh in 612 BC; a form of Akkadian.

Aten: An Egyptian name for the solar disk, used by Akhenaten to symbolize the one god who created and sustained the world.

auxiliary signs and devices: Marks and formatting that assist the reader's perception of the organization of thought, such as periods and white space between words; auxiliary to logography, syllabography, and alphabetic writing.

Babylonian cuneiform: A variety of Mesopotamian cuneiform used in Babylon.

Babylonian language: A Semitic dialect spoken in the city of Babylon on the Euphrates River, a form of Akkadian.

biliteral: An Egyptian sign that stands for two consonantal sounds plus unspecified vowels, or no vowels.

boustrophedon: "As the ox turns," referring to texts whose lines are written left to right, then right to left, in alternation.

Brahmi syllabic script: The ancestor of all modern "native" scripts in India, including Devanagari script ("sacred script of the city") in which today are written Hindi, Marathi, Pali, Sindhi and many other south Asian languages.

Calendar Round: A Mayan 52-year cycle reflecting the interacting of the 260-day and 365-day calendars.

Canaan: Ancient name for Palestine and the Lebanon coast; mentioned in the Amarna Letters from Egypt, c.1340 BC.

cartouche: French for "cartridge," from the shape of a ring drawn around the names of Egyptian kings and gods, symbolizing their power over the world.

consonant: "Something that sounds along with," refers to the obstructions and shapes made by lips, tongue, and throat to alter the sound of the vibrating vocal cords. One category of Greek alphabetic sign encoded these qualities. West Semitic and Egyptian hieroglyphic writing informs the reader about these qualities, but not about the associated vibration of the vocal cords.

consonantal syllabary: A phrase describing the West Semitic system of writings, which tells the reader the sound of the consonant but not the accompanying vowel, which the reader must supply from his own experience.

Coptic: From the Greek for "Egyptian," refers to the language of Egyptian Christians descended from that of the pharaonic Egyptians; also the slightly modified Greek alphabetic script in which this language was recorded since the third century AD. Knowledge of Coptic made possible Champollion's decipherment of Egyptian hieroglyphs.

Cretan hieroglyphs: An undeciphered iconic script used in the Middle Bronze Age in Crete, related to Linear A, found mostly on seals.

cuneiform syllabary: One of several cuneiform scripts, such as Hurrian, taken from Mesopotamian cuneiform but consisting mostly of phonetic syllabic signs.

cuneiform: "Wedge-shaped," referring to several writing systems of the ancient Near East whose forms were made by impressing a stylus into clay; generally, the oldest of these systems, invented in southern Mesopotamia and used c.3200 BC–AD 100 (Mesopotamian cuneiform).

Cypriote syllabary: A syllabic script probably based on the earlier Cypro-Minoan, but preserving the Greek language, eleventh–third centuries BC; deciphered in 1874.

Cypro-Minoan: An undeciphered Cypriote script based on Linear A, c.1500 BC.

demotic: An Egyptian script that appeared about 650 BC as a development of hieratic script, but containing many ligatures (two or more signs written as one) and cursive forms; also, the language encoded in this script, a form of late Egyptian, but capitalized as "Demotic."

Descriptive-representational device: I. J. Gelb's category for representations that communicate information by pictures of what is intended.

determinative: Older term for "semantic complement," a sign that places a word in a category – for example, "man" or "having to do with writing."

diacritical mark: Something added to a sign to alter its sound, as French [e] is /e/, but [é] is /ay/.

East Semitic writing: Mesopotamian cuneiform.

Elamite: The language and undeciphered script of Susa and the surrounding area in the Early Bronze Age, contemporary with protocuneiform; also, the unknown language and variety of Mesopotamian cuneiform script later used in the same area (one of the Behistun inscriptions, from the sixth century BC, is in the later cuneiform Elamite).

epigraphy: The study of written remains on such durable materials as stone, metal, or ceramic.

Fertile Crescent: A phrase coined by the University of Chicago Orientalist James Henry Breasted to describe the geographical area beginning in the Persian Gulf, arcing northwest along the Euphrates River, then west to the Levantine coast and south through Palestine to Egypt; the cradle of writing and of civilization.

forerunner of writing: A category coined by I. J. Gelb to describe representations that may communicate information, but without reference to elements of speech, including primitive art, the descriptive-representational device, and the identifying-mnemonic device.

grammatography: I. J. Gelb's term for "alphabetic writing."

Hatti: The name of the non Indo-European inhabitants of the area around Hattusas, named after them, in central Anatolia; the Indo-European Nesites took over this area in the Middle Bronze Age and hence were called Hittites in the Bible from "Hatti," whence the modern misnomer "Hittites" for what should be "Nesites."

Hebrew: A Canaanite Semitic dialect spoken in central Palestine. The language of the Jews.

hieratic: "Priestly" script, longhand Egyptian hieroglyphs.

hieroglyphs: "Sacred writing," referring to the iconic Egyptian script and, by extension, to other scripts with iconic features.

Hittite hieroglyphs: See Luvian hieroglyphs.

Hittites: The oldest attested speakers of an Indo-European language, their capital in the Bronze Age was at Hattusa in central Anatolia near modern Ankara. In the Iron Age they had powerful kingdoms in northern Syria.

homophones: Words with the same or similar sounds but different meanings, especially common in Chinese speech; also, signs in writing that look different, but have the same sound, a prominent feature in Mesopotamian cuneiform.

Hurrians: Called Mitanni by Egyptians, of unclear ethnic and linguistic affiliation, powerful in the Late Bronze Age in upper Syria; used a variety of Mesopotamian cuneiform writing reduced mostly to syllables.

iconic: Writing in which we can recognize things in the everyday world.

identifying-mnemonic device: I. J. Gelb's category for written signs that remind one of something through association.

ideogram: "Idea-writing," when a graphic sign stands for an idea, an eternal changeless Platonic reality, for example, unity, goodness. Probably ideograms do not exist. What scholars sometimes call ideograms are usually sematograms. The word is widely misused and should be avoided.

Karosthi script: Appeared in the third century BC in the Punjab under the influence of Persian bureaucratic use of the West Semitic Aramaic script and language.

language: Any system of symbols that serves the innate human faculty to communicate through symbols; a system of symbols that communicates through differences in form.

letter: A sign in alphabetic writing.

lexigraphy: Writing in which the signs are attached to necessary forms of speech.

linear: A noniconic script consisting of abstract lines.

Linear A: The undeciphered syllabic script of the Minoans.

Linear B: A syllabic script of around 87 phonetic signs, based on the earlier Linear A but encoding the Greek language. Numerous additional logograms or sematograms stand for commodities.

Linear Elamite: An undeciphered script used in and around Susa for a short period c.2150 BC, presumably a syllabary because it has around 80 signs; may be unrelated as a script and record a different language than the earlier undeciphered protoElamite.

logogram: "Word-sign," refers to a significant segment of speech but does not have phonetic value.

logography: Writing with logograms.

logosyllabary: A writing that consists of logograms, syllabograms, and semantic complements (determinatives), like Mesopotamian cuneiform and Egyptian hieroglyphs.

long count: In the Maya calendar, a day count from a fixed date in the fourth millennium BC, as recorded both in the Dresden codex and on many monuments.

Luvian hieroglyphs: A logosyllabary applied only to the Luvian language in Anatolia, a close relative of the Indo-European Hittite, c.1300–600 BC; probably based on Aegean writing, but with freely invented iconic forms; also called Hittite hieroglyphs or Anatolian hieroglyphs.

Luvian: An Indo-European language closely related to Hittite; the language underlying "Luvian hieroglyphs" and probably the ancestor to languages spoken in southern Anatolia (Lycia) and in western Anatolia (Lydia) in classical times.

matres lectionis: "Mothers of reading," when in West Semitic writing "consonantal" signs stand for vowels, but never in a systematic way.

Mesopotamian cuneiform: A general term including the various derivatives of the logosyllabic system created by the Sumerians in the late fourth millennium BC and refined by the Akkadian Semites c.2700 BC; later used by the Semitic Assyrians and Babylonians; the Indo-European Hittites; and the Hurrians, Urartians, and Elamites, whose languages we cannot categorize.

Minoans: The preGreek inhabitants of Crete, inventors of "Cretan hieroglyphs" and Linear A.

Moabite: A Semitic dialect spoken in Moab, the plateau east of the Dead Sea bounded on the north and east by Ammon (whose ancient capital is modern Aman, Jordan), and on the south by Edom.

morpheme: The smallest semantically meaningful unit of speech.

multiliteralism: When the scribe controls more than one script and more than one language, common in the ancient Near East.

Nesites: The name that the Indo-European Hittites applied to themselves, after *Kanesh* near modern Kayseri, their place of origin.

noniconic: Not looking like anything, abstract, referring to the appearance of characters in scripts.

Old Persian: The language and cuneiform script of the Achaemenid dynasty, c.600–330 BC; though made up of marks imitating a stylus pressed into clay, the syllabic script of 36 signs and some logograms is a free invention, probably inspired by Aramaic script, and not a derivative of Mesopotamian cuneiform. Old Persian was the first script deciphered in the Behistun inscription.

orthography: How things are spelled.

Palaic: "Of the people of Pala," a dialect probably spoken northwest of Hattusa.

petroglyph: primitive representations made by pecking or incising on rock faces.

pharyngeal: A consonant pronounced by constricting the throat, a sound absent from English but prominent in modern spoken Arabic.

Phoenician language: a Semitic dialect spoken on the coast of the Levant, in modern Lebanon and north Syria.

Phoenician syllabary: An early form of the West Semitic syllabary.

phoneme: A small particle of sound that makes a difference in meaning.

phonetic: In Chinese, the element in a complex character that contains a phonetic hint about the word intended; as an adjective, "referring to the sounds of speech."

phonetic complement: phonetic signs that reinforce value implicit in a preceding sign. For example, the st in 1st.

phoneticization: When signs become associated with sounds of speech.

phonogram: A sign to which a sound is attached.

phonography: Sound-writing, made up of phonograms, which have values but no significations.

phonology: Having to do with the systems of sounds attached to writing.

pictograms: Writing with pictures. The term is too cloudy to be meaningful and should be avoided.

pinyin: "Spell speak," a way of spelling Chinese speech in Roman characters, used to inform the reader of the correct Mandarin pronunciation for Chinese characters.

polyphony: When a sign has more than one sound, common in Mesopotamian cuneiform and in Mayan.

protoCanaanite: Refers to the many undeciphered experiments in writing that appear in Palestine in the Late Bronze Age. Their relation to the later West Semitic family of writing is unknown.

protocuneiform: The partly deciphered writing found on tablets from the late fourth millennium, especially in Uruk, antecedent to the later Mesopotamian cuneiform.

protoElamite: A writing used in the area of Susa and in far-removed territories from c.3050–2900 BC; consists of around a thousand mostly undeciphered markings related in unclear ways to protocuneiform.

protoSinaitic: Referring to undeciphered inscriptions found in the Sinai Desert at Serabit el-Khadim, consisting of 20–30 signs resembling Egyptian hieroglyphs, dated c.1500 BC; though claimed as an early stage of West Semitic writing, this cannot be proven.

radical: In Chinese writing, the element in a complex sign that places the meaning of the sign in a category; a semantic complement.

rebus: Latin "from the things," when the meaning of a sign is dropped and only the sound preserved.

semantic complement: A nonphonetic sign that places a word in a certain category.

semasiography: Writing in which the signs are not attached to necessary forms of speech.

sematograms: The elements of semasiography.

sign: something that stands for something else; same as *symbol* except a sign is part of a system. A collection of certain kinds of signs makes up a system of writing; loosely, any graphic character.

signary: The inventory of signs in any system of writing.

speech: Spoken language.

spelling rules: Define how signs work when taken together, often changing their values in certain combinations.

Sumerians: A people of unknown racial and linguistic affiliation who flourished in southern Iraq in the fourth millennium and invented the arts of civilization, including Mesopotamian cuneiform writing.

Sumerogram: When a word spelled in Sumerian is reduced to a logogram and associated with an Akkadian word of equivalent meaning.

syllabogram: A sign that has phonetic value but may or may not refer to significant segments of speech. The most common form is simple vowel (V) and consonant + vowel (CV), but other arrangements occur (VC, CVC).

syllabography: The signs represent syllables, the smallest apprehensible elements of speech. A syllabography is a system in which *syllabograms* predominate.

symbol: The same as *sign*, but not part of a system. Hence a star and crescent is a symbol of Islam; a cross is a symbol for Christianity. Often a symbol will be something concrete referring to something abstract, as a heart is a symbol for love.

Syriac: A late form of Aramaic used as the basis of Christian teachings between the second and eighth century AD across the Near East, written in a West Semitic script, originally the dialect of Edessa, a Hellenistic city in northern

Mesopotamia. Inscriptions in Syriac have been found in China, Central Asia, and southern India.

Thoth: The Egyptian god of magic and writing, represented as an ibis or a baboon; the inventor of hieroglyphs.

transcription: A redrawing of characters recorded somewhere.

transliteration: A notation of the sounds of an alien script in Roman characters.

triliteral: An Egyptian sign that stands for three consonants plus unspecified vowels or no vowel.

uniliterals: Egyptian signs that stand for a single consonant plus an unspecified vowel or no vowel.

Urartians: A people perhaps related to the Bronze Age Hurrians; in the first millennium BC they lived in the mountainous plateau of Armenia near Lake Van (Urartu) and used a simplified form of Akkadian cuneiform (the biblical Ararat is a variation of their name).

vowel: A sound made by vibrating the vocal cords.

West Semitic writing: A large family of scripts with from 22–30 characters that encode only consonantal values, requiring the reader to supply the correct vowels.

words: The things listed in a dictionary; a segment of speech taken to have meaning.

writing: A system of markings on a material substance with a conventional reference that communicates information.

Bibliography

Further Reading

General

In the present miraculous days of the Internet search, unprecedented opportunities exist for further research into almost any aspect of the theory and history of writing. Wikipedia has essays on every major script, and on many minor, with bibliography. Theoretically the essays can be naïve (with rumors of "abjads" and "abugidas" and "alphabetic syllabaries") but the facts are there, with good examples and the actual script in unicode. In hardcopy there are numerous general books on writing. P. L. Daniels and P. T. Bright, eds, *The World's Writing Systems* (Oxford, 1996) contains short essays on all the major systems by leading scholars. These are bare bones descriptions but include an actual specimen from each writing. Good bibliographies accompany each essay. Unfortunately the book introduces *abjad* and *abugida* for two different kinds of West Semitic syllabary, confusing an already muddied picture, and in general the book is weak on theory and on the historical forces behind change in writing. A similar, somewhat less technical reference is Florian Coulmas's *The Blackwell Encyclopedia of Writing Systems* (Oxford, 1999), with 80 contributors. *A History of Writing: From Hieroglyph to Multimedia*, edited by Anne-Marie Christin (Paris, 2002) has wonderful photographs and intelligent essays by French scholars. Badly outdated, but still rich in information, is David Diringer's *The Alphabet: A Key to the History of Mankind*, a general history of writing, in spite of the title; originally published in 1947, it was reissued in 1996 (New Delhi). A strong linguistic approach, which can be misleading, underlies books by Florian Coulmas, *The Writing Systems of the World*, (Oxford, 1989), Geoffrey Sampson, *Writing Systems: A Linguistic Introduction* (Stanford, 1990), and Henry Rogers *Writing Systems: A Linguistic Approach* (Oxford, 2004). The Rogers book, designed as a textbook, has an excellent bibliography. Good historical reviews of the major systems are found in *Reading the Past*, edited by J. T. Hooker (Berkeley, 1998). H. Jensen's *Sign, Symbol, Script* (New York, 1969, a version of *Die Schrift in Vergangenheit und Gegenwart*, 3rd edn., Hannover, 1969) is a superb historical study. An attractive and readable essay, with much fine sense, is R. Harris *Origin of Writing* (London, 1988). A fine popular study is *The Story of Writing: Alphabets, Hieroglyphs, and Pictograms* (2nd edn., London, 2007) by Andrew Robinson. Most of these books use inconsistent or contradictory terminology, call almost anything a pictogram, find ideograms everywhere, and confuse alphabets with syllabaries. Nonetheless they contain useful charts and other information. By far the best general book, and still basic after half a century, is I. J. Gelb's *A Study of Writing* (2nd edn., Chicago, 1963).

For an understanding of the complex history of the ancient Near East, background to developments in the history of writing, exemplary are Amelie Kuhrt's two-volume *The Ancient Near East, c.3000–330 BC* (London, 1995) and Marc van Mieroop, *A History of the Ancient Near East ca. 3000–323 BC* (2nd edn. Oxford, 2007). Also excellent is Michael Roaf's *Cultural Atlas of Mesopotamia and the Ancient Near East* (New York, 1990). For the general conditions of prehistory, Colin Renfrew's *Prehistory: The making of Mankind* (London, 2007) is inspiring.

For decipherments, Maurice Pope's *The Story of Decipherment: From Egyptian Hieroglyphs to Maya Script* (revised edition, New York, 1999) is outstanding. Andrew Robinson's *Lost Languages: The World's Undeciphered Scripts* (New York, 2002) has up-to-date information about Linear A, Etruscan, and other undeciphered scripts.

Origins of writing

Denise Schmandt-Besserat has nicely summarized her argument in *How Writing Came About* (Austin, 1996), an abridgment of the two-volume *Before Writing* (Austin, 1992). Early results from the Berlin team working on protocuneiform are published in H. J. Nissen, P. Damerow, and R. Englund, *Archaic Bookkeeping* (Chicago, 1993), one of the best books on the origins of lexigraphic writing. R. Englund has a thorough treatment of the origin and early phases of cuneiform in "Texts from the Late Uruk Period," in J. Bauer, R. Englund, M. Krebernik, eds, *Mesopotamien: Späturuk-Zeit and Frühdynastische Zeit*, Orbis Biblicus und Orientalia 160/1, Freiburg: Universitäts-Verlag (Göttingen, 1998), 15–233. Also excellent on the origins of cuneiform (though in French) is Jean-Jacques Glassner's *Ecrire à Sumer: Invention de cunéiform* (Paris, 2000). S. D. Houston's *The First Writing: Script Invention as History and Process* (Cambridge, UK, 2004) is up to date with fine or superb essays on the origins of writing by philologists deep in their disciplines, with discussion of the theory of how speech relates to written representation (though in its theoretical descriptions it is inconsistent and sometimes jargonistic). A superior web source for the study of the protocuneiform tablets is http://www.cdli.ucla.edu/index_html.

Cuneiform

All general studies of writing have chapters on cuneiform including C. B. F. Walker's excellent "Cuneiform," in the collection *Reading the Past: Ancient Writing from Cuneiform to the Alphabet*, J. T. Hooker, ed. (Berkeley, 1990). Jean Bottéro's *Mesopotamia: Writing, Reasoning, and the Gods*, tr. A. Bahrani and M. Van de Mieroop (Chicago, 1992), is a superior study of the role of writing in Mesopotamia by a leading Assyriologist. Also, Jean Bottéro, Clarisse Herrenschmidt, and Jean-Pierre Vernant, tr. T. L. Fagan, *Ancestor of the West: Writing, Reasoning, and Religion in Mesopotamia, Elam, and Greece* (Chicago, 2000). In a recent book, *When Writing Met Art* (Austin, 2007), Denise Schmandt-Besserat investigates the effect of literacy on visual art, explaining how conventions of writing inspired complex narrative in art (as on the Uruk Vase and the Narmer Palette); conversely, art influenced what writing wished to accomplish.

Egyptian hieroglyphs

For cultural background to Egypt, Barry Kemp's *Ancient Egypt: Anatomy of a Civilisation* is superlative (2nd edn., London, 2005). A recent translation of Horapollo's influential treatise is by G. Boas, *The Hieroglyphics of Horapollo*, with a foreword by Anthony T. Grafton (Princeton, 1993). The strange *Hypnerotomachia Poliphili: The Strife of Love in a Dream* has now been published for the first time in English translation (by J. Godwin, London, 1999). A compelling review of the Neoplatonic impediments to the decipherment is given in E. Iversen *The Myth of Egypt and Its Hieroglyphs in European Tradition* (Princeton, 1993; originally Copenhagen, 1961). W. V. Davies provides a good sketch of the Egyptian system in *Egyptian Hieroglyphs* (Berkeley, 1987), published separately and as one of the chapters in J. T. Hooker, ed., *Reading the Past*. Egyptian writing and its different forms and uses is also well described in R. B. Parkinson's *Cracking Codes: The Rosetta Stone and its Decipherment* (London, 1999). John Baines's "The Earliest Egyptian Writing" (in *The First Writing*) is the best summary of the topic. Egyptian may be more fun to read than cuneiform and M. Collier and Bill Manley have written the exemplary (and best selling) *How to Read Egyptian Hieroglyphs: A Step-By-Step Guide to Teach Yourself* (Berkeley, 1998) that teaches in a practical way how a logosyllabic writing works. James P. Allen's *Middle Egyptian : An Introduction to the Language and Culture of Hieroglyphs* (Cambridge, UK, 1999) gives a modern in-depth view, with excellent essays on individual topics. Antonio Loprieno's *Ancient Egyptian: A Linguistic Introduction* (Cambridge, UK, 1995) will interest those with a linguistic bent. Though outdated in various aspects, Sir Alan Gardiner's triumphant *Egyptian grammar* (3rd edn., Oxford, 1973), a monument of twentieth-century humanistic scholarship, is still a standard grammar of Egyptian.

Aegean writing

John Chadwick's *The Decipherment of Linear B* (2nd edn., Cambridge, UK, 1967) is fascinating. Chadwick worked with Ventris in the decipherment, giving him advice about the linguistic forms he might expect to find in the Bronze Age. Excellent, too, are Chadwick's concise introduction to Aegean writing in *Linear B and Related Scripts* (Berkeley, 1987, also included in Hooker's *Reading the Past*) and his description of *The Mycenaean World* (Cambridge, UK, 1976). In *The Man Who Deciphered Linear B: The Story of Michael Ventris* (London, 2002) Andrew Robinson gives a lucid picture of who he was and how he worked. For the role of scribes in Mycenaean society, and their power within the economy, see J. Bennet's essay *The Aegean Bronze Age* in W. Scheidel, I. Morris, R. Saller, eds, *The Cambridge Economic History of the Greco-Roman World* (Cambridge, UK, 2007).

West Semitic writing

West Semitic writing is a central topic in all handbooks, but always badly skewed by the word "alphabet" and the theory of the origin of West Semitic signs from "pictograms" via the acrophonic principle. Hence the rich and valuable, but old-fashioned, contributions of G. R. Driver, in *Semitic Writing from Pictograph to Alphabet* 3rd edn. (London, 1976, revised by S. A. Hopkins) need to be read with caution. The short summary in John Healey's *The Early Alphabet* (London, 1990, also in Hooker's *Reading the Past*) is short and sweet, as is F. M. Cross's essay "The Invention and Development of the Alphabet" in W. M. Senner, ed., *The Origins of Writing* (Lincoln, NE, 1989). The summaries of the varieties of West Semitic in Daniels and Bright (Oxford, 1996) are useful. The standard review of early remains of West Semitic is J. Naveh's *Early History of the Alphabet* (Leiden, 1982), that is, of West Semitic writing, an example of a leading epigrapher careless with history.

Chinese writing

There is a good background to the subject in S. Robert Ramsey, *The Languages of China* (Princeton, 1987) and Jerry Norman, *Chinese* (Cambridge, UK, 1987). Also, Chen Ping, *Modern Chinese: History and Sociolinguistics* (Cambridge, UK,

1999) and J. DeFrancis, *The Chinese Language: Fact and Fantasy* (Honolulu, 1984). R. Bagley's chapter on the origins of Chinese writing in S. D. Houston, ed., *The First Writing*, is fine on the oracle bones and other early inscriptions. For the disparity between Chinese and alphabetic poetic expression, see A. C. Graham's introduction to his *Poems of the Late T'ang* (New York, 1965).

Mesoamerican writing

A superior overview of the history of the question and recent progress on decipherment is given in Michael Coe's *Breaking the Maya Code* (New York, 1992). More than any single book, Linda Schele and Mary Ellen Miller's *The Blood of Kings: Dynasty and Ritual in Maya Art*, an exhibition catalogue from Fort Worth (1986), changed popular perceptions of the Maya from that of gentle forest dwellers to blood-addicted warlords. Linda Schele was one of the pioneers of the Maya decipherment and, like Champollion, Ventris, and Kober, died young (at age 56, of pancreatic cancer). Her *A Forest of Kings* (with David Freidel, New York, 1990) and *The Code of Kings: The Language of Seven Sacred Maya Temples and Tombs* (with Peter Matthews, New York, 1998) are also influential. For handbooks on Mayan writing, a superb product is available on the World Wide Web at http://www. mesoweb.com/resources/handbook/WH2005.pdf from a conference in 2005: Harri Kettunen and Christophe Helmke, *Introduction to Maya Hieroglyphs: Workshop Handbook*. 10th European Maya Conference, Leiden, December 5–10, 2005. Also helpful are: Stephen Houston's *Maya Glyphs* (Berkeley, 1989) and his essay in S. D. Houston, ed., *The First Writing* and *Reading the Maya Glyphs* by Michael Coe and Mark Van Stone (2nd edn., London, 2005); and Floyd Lounsbury's "The Ancient Writing of Mesoamerica" in the W. M. Senner, ed., *The Origins of Writing* (Lincoln, NE, 1989).

Greek alphabet

Many books purporting to be about the alphabet are really about West Semitic writing. An in-depth review of the formal and historical conditions surrounding the invention of the Greek alphabet is set forth in my own *Homer and the Origin of the Greek Alphabet* (Cambridge, 1991) and my *Writing and the Origins of Greek Literature* (Cambridge, 2002) follows out the consequences of the early use of the alphabet to create Greek literature. Of great value are the writings of L. H. Jeffery, especially *The Local Scripts of Archaic Greece* (Oxford, 1961; 2nd edn., 1990). Jeffery devoted her life to the study of archaic scripts and established the evidence on which all study of early Greek alphabetic literacy must be based. Ron Stroud's "The Art of Writing in Ancient Greece," in W. M. Senner, *The Origins of Writing* (Lincoln, NE, 1989), is good.

References

Albright, William Foxwell. 1966. *The Proto-Sinaitic Inscriptions and their Decipherment*. Cambridge, MA.

Allen, James, P. 1999. *Middle Egyptian: An Introduction to the Language and Culture of Hieroglyphs*. Cambridge, UK.

Bloomfield, L. 1933. *Language*. New York.

Chadwick, John. 1987. *Linear B and Related Scripts*. Berkeley.

Champollion, Jean François. [1824]. *Précis du système hiéroglyphique*. Paris.

Champollion, Jean François. [1824] 1984. *Lettre à M. Dacier relative à l'alphabet des hiéroglyphes*. Paris.

Coe, M. 1992. *Breaking the Maya Code*. New York.

Collier, M. and Bill Manley. 1998. *How to Read Egyptian Hieroglyphs: A Step-By-Step Guide to Teach Yourself*. Berkeley.

Daniels, P. L. and P. T. Bright, eds. 1996. *The World's Writing Systems*. Oxford.

Davies, W. V. 1990. *Egyptian Hieroglyphs*. Berkeley.

Englund, R. 2008. "Proto-Elamite History," http://www.cais-soas.com/CAIS/ History/Elamite/proto_elam_history.htm.

Gardiner, Alan. 1957. *Egyptian Grammar*, 3rd edn. Oxford.

Gelb, I. J. 1963. *A Study of Writing: The Foundations of Grammatology*, 2nd edn. Chicago.

Graham, A. C. 1965. *Poems of the Late T'ang*. New York.

Harris, R. 1988. *Origin of Writing*. London.

Healey, J. F. 1987. *Greek Inscriptions*. Berkeley.

Hooker, J. T., ed. 1990. *Reading the Past: Ancient Writing from Cuneiform to the Alphabet*. Berkeley.

Houston, S. D., ed. 2004. *The First Writing: Script Invention as History and Process*, Cambridge, UK.

Joyce, James. 1958. *Finnegans Wake*. New York.

Kettunen, Harri and Christophe Helmke. 2005. *Introduction to Maya Hieroglyphs. Workshop Handbook*. 10th European Maya Conference, Leiden, December 5–10. http://www.mesoweb.com/resources/handbook/WH2005.pdf.

Knorosov, Yuri. 1952. "Drevnyaya pis'mennost' Tsentral'noy Ameriki" ["Ancient Writings of Central America."] *Sovetskaya Etnografiya* 3 (2):100–18.

Kramer, S. N. 1981. *History Begins at Sumer: Thirty-Nine Firsts in Recorded History*. Philadelphia.

Lichtheim, M. 1973, 1976. *Ancient Egyptian Literature* vols. 1 and 2. Berkeley.

Li, Xueqin, Garman Harbottle, Juzhong Zhang, and Changsui Wang. 2003. "The Earliest Writing? Sign Use in the Seventh Millennium BC at Jiahu, Henan Province, China." *Antiquity* 77 (295): 31–45 (31 and 41).

Mallery, G. 1893. *Picture-Writing of the American Indians. Tenth Annual Report of the Bureau of Ethnology.* Washington, DC.

Naveh, J. 1982. *Early History of the Alphabet.* Jerusalem and Leiden.

Nissen, H. J., P. Damerow, R. Englund. 1993. *Archaic Bookkeeping.* Chicago.

Norman, Jerry. 1987. *Chinese.* Cambridge, UK.

Parpola, A. 1994. *Decipherment of the Indus Script.* Cambridge, UK.

Parrot, André. 1960. *Sumer.* Paris.

Pope, Maurice. 1999. *The Story of Decipherment: From Egyptian Hieroglyphs to Maya Script,* rev. edn. New York.

Powell, B. B. 1991. *Homer and the Origin of the Greek Alphabet.* Cambridge, UK.

Ramsey, S. Robert. 1987. *The Languages of China.* Princeton.

Ridgway, D. 1996. *Greek letters at Osteria dell'Osa.* Opuscula Romana 20.

Rogers, H. 2005. *Writing Systems: A Linguistic Approach.* Oxford.

Saussure, F. [1922] 1983. *Course in General Linguistics [Cours de linguistique generale],* ed. C. Bally and A. Sechehaye, trans. R. Harris. London.

Schaeffer, Claude F. A. 1939. *Cuneiform Texts of Ras Shamra-Ugarit.* Oxford.

Schele, L. and J. Miller. 1986. *The Blood of Kings: Dynasty and Ritual in Maya Art.* Fort Worth, TX.

Schmandt-Besserat, D. 1992. *Before Writing,* Vol.1. Austin.

Schmandt-Besserat, D. 1996. *How Writing Came About.* Austin.

Senner, W. M. 1991. *The Origins of Writing.* Lincoln, NE.

Steindorff, George, and Keith Seele. 1942. *When Egypt Ruled the East.* Chicago.

Thompson, J. Eric. 1950. *Maya Hieroglyphic Writing: An Introduction.* 1st edn., Washington, DC.

Walker, C. B. F. 1990. *Cuneiform.* Berkeley.

Index

CPSIA information can be obtained
at www.ICGtesting.com
Printed in the USA
JSHW012241301222
35592JS00006B/33